The Golden Age of British Hotels

Derek Taylor & David Bush

The Golden Age of British Hotels

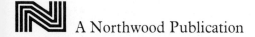

A Northwood Publication

Derek Taylor:
To Diane, Simon, Hugh, Timothy and Kate

David Bush:
To my Parents.

ISBN 7198 2593 8

© Northwood Publications Ltd, Derek Taylor and David Bush 1974

Book design by Philip Sharland

Published by Northwood Publications Ltd
(Trade and technical publishing subsidiary of the Thomson Organisation Ltd)
Northwood House, 93–99 Goswell Road, London EC1V 7QA

Printed in Great Britain by The Anchor Press Ltd, and bound by
Wm. Brendon & Son Ltd, both of Tiptree, Essex

Contents

Acknowledgements

We are grateful to the following for help with certain engravings, drawings
and photographs:
Athol Palace Hotel, Pitlochry; Barrow in Furness Public Library; Bath Public
Library; Brighton Public Library; British Temperance Society; British Transport
Hotels; Buxton Public Library; *Caterer and Hotelkeeper*; Thomas Cook & Sons Ltd.;
Derby Public Library; Dublin Public Library, Durrants Hotel, London; Eyre &
Spottiswoode, London; George Hotel, Stamford; Grand Metropolitan Hotels;
Grosvenor Estates; Guildhall Library; *Illustrated London News*; Manchester
Public Library; Maple & Co.; Matlock Public Library; Mr. Alex Newman;
Norfolk Capital Hotels; Queen's Hotel, Hastings; *Radio Times* Hulton Picture
Library; Railway Archives; Red Lion Hotel, Salisbury; Royal Institute of British
Architects; Royal Pavilion, Brighton; Southport Public Library; Trust Houses
Forte; Unilever Ltd.

Preface

Books about hotels are very often really books about the people who stay in hotels. *Imperial Palace, Grand Hotel*, and *Hotel* are the best fictional examples but a great deal of non-fiction has really covered the same type of ground. The stock hotel characters regularly appear; the temperamental chef, the aristocratic manager, the head porter with a heart of gold, the kindly old waiter, and the housekeeper with a 'past'. The background is equally familiar from the magnificent display of flowers in the Prince's suite to the delicate bouquet of a Château Beauregard '87. The immaculate dinner jacket of the tall, dark haired Restaurant Manager never creases as the guest ponders deeply before deciding between the Filet de Sole Emmanuel X and the Oreilles à la Rouennaise. The world has stopped in a fairyland where no-one grows older, accounts are settled discreetly, and the lowliest chambermaid knows exactly how much hot water Lord C. likes in his bottle.

This, however, is a book about the hotel business, not as it might have been, but as it was. The heroes and villains are the hotels themselves, and the people who succeeded or failed to make them profitable. For money was the name of the game; the opportunity to make a fortune, to climb out of the gutter, to keep the family from starving or just to keep a roof over your own head. The players are still famous like Cesar Ritz and Auguste Escoffier, or they are nearly forgotten like Frederick Gordon, Sir Polydore de Keyser, Sir William Towle and John Smedley. We think they deserve more than obscurity for they were seldom dull in their own lifetimes. They were pioneers, building and creating something quite new—a modern hotel. Very little has changed since the Golden Age; a soupçon of air conditioning, a few more floors in height, and some different building materials, but otherwise it is still the way the Victorians and Edwardians left it.

Who built all those hotels whose origins seem nearly as obscure as the statues on Aku Aku? Where did all the mystique come from, and the snobbery and the servility? Why did the business attract so many continentals and where did all the money come from?

A hotel is a factory producing goods as surely as tinned pears come off a conveyor belt, but it's a special sort of product, vanishing like the fairies when dawn breaks and the room was not let, the restaurant table empty, the bar stool unoccupied. As an industry the world of hotels is fascinating in its own right, and needs no carefully concocted literary plot to keep the reader's interest. If we fail to do so, the fault is in ourselves and not in the tale we have to tell.

Many kind friends have helped us with suggestions, encouragement and criticism and we should like to thank in particular Neil Benson, Evelyn Berckman, Eric Bernard, Norman Fowler, Donald Kamlish, Ian McGregor, Miles Quest, Alasdair Riley, Martin Stewart, John Tanfield, John Wharton and Geoffrey Wilson. We should like to gratefully acknowledge the generous cooperation of Bill Vine and the *Caterer & Hotelkeeper* Magazine for making a lot of valuable material available to us, and to particularly thank Peter Reed and Service Photography Ltd. for reviving old prints so expertly. Diane Taylor bore the brunt of our chaos and preoccupation, which went on for months, with patience and cheerfulness without which the task would have been far greater. We apologise for any names omitted, but all our friends know that we are in their debt.

Derek Taylor
David Bush

London 1974.

The story so far

I

"FORTY years ago" said the *Daily News* in 1887 "it was almost a sign of eccentricity to put up at a hotel. Where the hotel was not ultra fashionable it was suggestive of Leicester Square. Families came up every season for the sights, and took their lodgings in Norfolk Street. Many of the old fashioned houses still stand. The front room is a sitting room; the room behind it is a bedroom; the small enclosure behind that will hold trunks and with them at a pinch a son or daughter, or a maiden sister in the spare bed. The bill of fare was limited, and the cooking never professed to go beyond 'good plain'. It was roast and boiled and they were served at four. An odd man, not innocent of the odour of spirits, pervaded the street and was the herald of the modern commissionaire." In retrospect it certainly wasn't very attractive and the decor also received few plaudits, being labelled by another contemporary writer as dingy and fusty which the visitors "endured with a flickering belief that they were enjoying themselves, the appalling discomforts of the early Victorian furniture, grim in its ugliness, glistening malignly in its sticky beeswax and pricking maliciously through its horsehair seatings."

Of course there had been hotels for centuries; they may have been called inns but they provided a roof over the traveller's head and a certain amount of refreshment. Mind you, it was usually advisable to bring your own furniture; when Richard III was killed at Bosworth in 1485, the war chest of £300 remained hidden in the base of his bed at the Blue Boar at Leicester for very many years. The most famous inn was the Tabard at Southwark which was immortalised in Chaucer's *Canterbury Tales*, and indeed throughout the middle ages English inns had a good reputation. Because those which remain today are invariably public houses, we tend to think that they were always regarded in that light when in fact the best were amongst the most important commercial buildings of their time. In one inn on the Great West Road the Spanish Ambassador was invested with the Order of the Garter by Henry VI in 1445, and the King of Denmark was accommodated at the Ship Inn at Gravesend when he reviewed the Royal Navy as the guest of James I.

It was as well to plan your journey so that you *were* near a decent inn; when Queen Henrietta visited Tunbridge Wells to sample the waters in 1630 the Controller of her Household had to have timber cottages brought in on sleds and most of her entourage slept in tents. Charles II's wife, Catherine, found houses at Tunbridge in 1663 but still nothing like a decent hostelry, and when Bath was at its peak in the 18th century, the Saracen's Head which was built in 1713, could hardly have been expected to cope with the 8,000 visitors who flocked to the city a couple of years later. Instead the travellers took lodgings with families or rented houses for themselves.

In the 18th century there was a great increase in the number of stage coaches and their speed depended to a large extent on the inns that lined their routes. Within these substantial houses were stabled the fresh horses which could be harnessed up in under a minute, a necessity if you were trying to keep to a schedule of London to Holyhead in twenty-six hours or London to Exeter in seventeen. It was nothing unusual for the coaches to need twenty changes of horses for a long journey and the major coaching inns had far more room for the animals than they did for the people. A busy posting house could stable 600 horses and would expect to get its main additional revenue from selling food and drink rather than bedrooms. The coaching inns were a combination of hotel, stable and travel agent. It is still possible to see good examples like the Angel at Guildford with its double entrance, one for guests through the front door, and the other through the two tall wooden gates for the coaches. The gates led to a courtyard, on one side of which was the stabling and on the other the bedrooms and public rooms. Inside the hotel it would be possible to buy tickets for the other coach routes which stopped there, and at Cheltenham, for example, twenty-three passenger services ran regularly from the Royal. At the George Inn at Stamford there was an 18th century dining room where the doors which faced north and south were labelled Edinburgh and London respectively.

The Bull and Mouth was one of London's great staging posts. The coffee room was in fact a restaurant. Note the bedding hanging out to air.

In most of the inns the majority of the travellers had only a communal kitchen in which to eat, and dormitory accommodation if they stayed overnight. Only the wealthy were able to obtain private rooms where they could be served in any degree of comfort. Even if you could afford it, the rooms were often in short supply particularly in the more remote parts of the country. In Hawick in the only inn suitable for the stage you had to arrive early "lest other travellers should be there before you; there is but one sitting room at Hawick and only one tolerable bed-chamber with two beds". If the coach was carrying you further on your journey, there was very little time to eat in either room or kitchen, and landlords were accused of being in league with the driver who was bribed to call the passengers from their set meal before they had time to finish and get their money's worth. As a consequence the same cold joint could be offered to many different parties.

As the English road system improved in the latter half of the 18th century, so the number of inns proliferated, and by 1825 as many as 10,000 people a day were using the regular coach services. The development of roads was slower in Scotland which accounts both for the smaller number of staging inns and for the greater speed with

The George Inn at Stamford in Lincolnshire, on the Great North Road. In the days of the stage coaches, guests in the dining room could leave by the door marked Edinburgh or the one marked London.

which its hotel industry developed when the country became a popular destination for tourists. At that time the few existing inns were almost immediately unable to cope with the rush of visitors brought by the railways. Although it has been estimated that over 2,000,000 passengers a year were carried at the peak of the coaching days after the Napoleonic Wars, conditions were extremely rough. There were occasions when people actually froze to death in the coaches during the winter, and there was the very real danger of highwaymen holding up the stage and robbing the travellers. It was easy to catch cold at a time when influenza and pneumonia were deadly killers, and you were crowded together in a confined space with strangers who might have any one of a variety of contagious diseases, all of which only emphasises the primitive conditions of life in that era.

3

The origin of the word 'hotel' is French and it roughly equalled the English word 'mansion'. French innkeepers were permitted to use the diminutive 'hôtellerie' to describe their business but could not use 'hôtel' before the Revolution. During that period the aristocracy were hardly in a position to object, and in addition many of their best servants found themselves out of a job and became innkeepers. The former staff then used the word 'hôtel' frequently, as they felt themselves a cut above the rougher image of an inn. In Britain there is an early record of William Pitt writing to his mother in 1780 on the headed paper of Nerot's Hotel in London, so that we know the word had been copied by that time and was to become general. In the early part of the 19th century it had genteel connotations but this restriction did not last. The situation in London was somewhat different from the rest of the country in that the capital offered a wider choice of hotel, and if a visitor had his own coach, he would not stay at an inn which catered for the stage passengers. Of course, many wealthy people had their town houses as well as their country homes and did not need hotels at all, while many others received hospitality from their friends or stayed in lodgings. Nevertheless there were a number of fashionable hotels, many of them in the Mayfair area.

London at the beginning of the 19th century was a loosely connected series of towns and villages and it might well be necessary for instance, to take a bodyguard on a journey from Hyde Park Corner to Knightsbridge. The City was the business heart of London, but the entertainment centre was around the Strand with Mayfair the finest address in which to live. It was in Mayfair that the great houses of the aristocracy were to be found, and hotels like Pulteneys, the Clarendon and Longs. Pulteneys was at 105 Piccadilly and was built on the site of a house which had cost the Marquess of Queensberry (Old Q) 4350 guineas in 1792, but unfortunately burnt down soon after he purchased it. The new hotel was good enough to be patronised by the Emperor of Russia and his sister in 1814 and would have been conveniently close to St. James Palace. The Clarendon was at 169 New Bond Street and could count among its guests the Elder Pitt who lived there in 1741. It also housed a literary society founded by Sir Joshua Reynolds and Samuel Johnson. Even when the country was at war with Napoleon, the Clarendon had the reputation of being the only hotel in London where you could get a genuine French dinner even if it did cost £3 or £4 with a guinea for a bottle of champagne. Sir Walter Scott often stayed at Longs, which was also in New Bond Street, and the hotel was a great centre for dandies and country bachelors in the early 19th century. In Marylebone there was Durrants Hotel which still survives, a perfect example of a Georgian hotel, elegant in design, charming and gracious.

Then for the racing crowd there was Limmers which had a waiter called John Collins who created the famous long summer drink. There was a rhyme which went
"My name is John Collins, head waiter at Limmers
At the corner of Conduit Street, Hanover Square.
My chief occupation is filling up brimmers,
To solace young gentlemen laden with care."
Another solace for the patrons was a secret passage through the back of the hotel into Bond Street if the bailiffs were after them, a fate to be expected by unsuccessful gambling men. Officers on leave or business used Stephens Hotel in Bow Street, while Louis XVIII stayed at Grillions Hotel in Albemarle Street and, as was to be expected of a guest of this distinction, would have his own apartments in the hotel and use it in place of his own palace. He would expect the servants to be provided with liveries and indeed it was very unlikely that they would have been able to afford suitable clothes otherwise.

The owners of the hotels were often men with experience of service in aristocratic houses, and would acquire their first clients on the basis of this reputation, like William Claridge, who took over Mivarts at 49 Brook Street, Mayfair, in the middle of the century, changed its name to his own and died highly esteemed in 1882. George IV had wanted a hotel which he and his friends could use discreetly and set up Mivart in number 49 in 1813; it was from such questionable beginnings that the hotel became almost an annexe of the palace. Claridge was also very much a courtier; "Mr. Claridge's bows were celebrated; they were of a different depth according to the rank of the person to whom he bowed, and there was even the delicate difference in the salute that he gave to a Serene Highness to that with which he welcomed a Royal Highness."

La Belle Sauvage was the largest hostelry in London at the beginning of the 19th century. It not only boasted a French name but had adopted the French word, "Hotel".

As was to be expected, the coaching inns of London included some of the largest in the country like La Belle Sauvage in Ludgate Hill, the White Bear Inn which stood on the site of the present Criterion in Piccadilly, and the famous Golden Cross opposite today's Charing Cross Station; for many years the Golden Cross was known as Morleys Hotel. Put all the London hotels together though, and they were still a relatively unimportant section of the available accommodation, for most people still sought lodgings.

Trafalgar Square was created in the 1840s and this photograph is one of the earliest on record. Morleys Hotel had been known as the Golden Cross and was eventually demolished to be replaced by South Africa House.

The Golden Age of British Hotels

The Duke of Devonshire's answer to the Royal Crescent at Bath was the Crescent at Buxton in Derbyshire. There were three separate hotels in operation here with ample stabling for hundreds of horses immediately behind.

Even in the 18th century, however, there were a few exceptions to the plebeian coaching inns outside the capital. In Buxton for example the 5th Duke of Devonshire, copying the Royal Crescent in Bath, spent no less than £120,000 on building his own magnificent Crescent "a stately pillared stone building in the form of a segment of a circle with an arcade running the whole length of the segment." Over 100 yards long, the Crescent was used first for the Grand, the Centre and the St. Ann's Hotels, the ground floor fronts were occupied by shops, and nearby were the great stables which now house the Devonshire hospital. Such munificence in 1784 was only possible for someone like a Duke who had resources like his own copper mines. The Crescent is Doric and the guests in the hotels could well believe that their temporary home was superior to many a Manor House.

After Waterloo in the era of Nash many new hotels were built in the country towns and can often be seen to this day. They were usually three-storey buildings like the Bold Hotel in Southport whose "wooden portico with coupled Doric pillars underlies the Greek lineage of Regency architecture." One of the best known in its time was the

first Adelphi Hotel in Liverpool. This was built as part of a terrace in 1823 and by 1828 a London hotelier named James Radley had acquired the lease. As he was new to the city he decided to circularise his potential clientele and under a woodcut of the Adelphi and its address, he wrote

> "James Radley begs respectfully to inform the nobility, gentry and public in general that he has taken a lease of these premises and fitted them up at a considerable expense to form a complete hotel. The situation is central and good and the house combines the peculiar advantages of a private entrance for families, and an excellent coffee room contiguous to the general door in Ranelagh Place. The extent of accommodation is great including good sitting room, bedrooms, baths etc. etc. on each floor.
>
> Immediately behind the hotel are good lock-up coachhouses etc. J.R. has had much experience in this business in London and he begs to assure those families and gentlemen who may honour him with their patronage, that the most strict attention shall be paid to their comfort and convenience in every respect"

James Radley was an excellent hotelier and his advice was later sought by others in the profession. When Royalty needed accommodation in Liverpool they would choose the Adelphi and Charles Dickens was very fond of its cuisine. He stayed at the hotel in 1842 on his way to America and commented "I have not enquired among my medical acquaintances whether Turtle and Cold Punch, with Hock, Champagne and Claret and everything usually included in an unlimited order for a good dinner—especially when it is left to the liberal construction of my faultless friend, Mr. Radley, of the Adelphi Hotel—are peculiarly calculated to suffer a sea change; or whether a plain mutton chop and a glass or two of sherry would be less likely of conversion into foreign and disconcerting material. . . . I know that the dinner of that day was undeniably perfect."

The quality of hotel food might be good or bad, but it was better anyway to eat, drink, and be merry because tomorrow was very uncertain. The expectation of life was well under forty years and was one reason why there were only fourteen million people in the whole of England, Scotland and Wales in 1821. Smallpox, cholera, typhoid, tuberculosis, diphtheria and bronchitis all made it unlikely that you would grow old enough to die of a coronary or cancer. Life was still "nasty, brutish and short" and the search for better health was conducted with vigour and almost unquestioning faith. There were two main streams of thought which affected hotels. They both sprang from the continuing and growing belief in the good magic of water as against the bad magic of alcohol, and resulted in the temperance movement and the hydropathic institutes.

The beginnings of the temperance movement coincided with the passing of the 1830 Beer Act which was a measure of Lord Melbourne's Whig government and intended to

reduce the amount of spirit drinking by making it easier and cheaper to drink beer. The Act permitted anybody to open a beer shop on payment of a fee of two guineas and resulted in 20,000 new beer shops opening in the following decade. Far from reducing drunkenness, the Act ensured one of the greatest British binges of all time, and although the original temperance pioneers could not place the blame for this simply on a few hotels, they were in principle against anything which helped people to drink. There might be a tendency to regard the present day temperance movement as a little out of date, fighting battles which modern commonsense has already won, and a bit reactionary in our swinging permissive society. Irrespective of the truth or otherwise of such an assessment, the Victorian temperance movement was a powerful influence in a different world, just as Disraeli would probably consider the present Conservative Party to be Communist. To visit the past really is to be a stranger in a foreign land.

In the beginning the temperance advocates wanted to reduce the amount of drinking, not to abolish it. It was only when the hardliners took over the infant movement that the taking of the pledge of total prohibition became the sign of the true follower. Not to drink alcohol was initially regarded by the vast majority of the population as anti-social, foolhardy and unhealthy. It was anti-social because to offer a drink was the equivalent of offering a cigarette today. It was a sign of bonhomie, a touch of friendship and it was used to seal bargains, to mark the initiation of apprentices and in countless other aspects of business and social life. It was foolhardy not to drink because the water supply was so often polluted. Patients in hospital were always given mildly alcoholic drinks rather than plain water, and in private homes water would have to be brought up from the well if you had one, or carried from a public well. "Even in upper class households in the 1850's mains (water) supplies were intermittent" and in 1859 there was still a real need for the formation of the Metropolitan Free Drinking Fountain Association. It was during Victoria's reign that it was discovered that both cholera and typhoid could be traced to bad water and there was a good deal of commonsense in using alcohol to kill some of the bacteria in it.

Southport in Lancashire grew from a small fishing village. In the middle of the 19th century the principal buildings were:

A. Victoria Baths
B. Salt Water Reservoir for Baths
C. Mr. Salthouse's Victoria Hotel
D. Victoria Market in London Street
E. Mr. Waterhouse's Hoghton Arms
F. Christ Church
G. Claremont
H. Mr. Hunt's Scarisbrick Arms Hotel
I. The Independent Chapel in Chapel Street

The general population also considered it unhealthy not to drink because it believed that drinking gave you strength and did you good. Those modern day advertisements of musclebound giants drinking their 'beer for men' are first cousins to the popular Victorian image. As a consequence of these arguments and conditions the early temperance preachers often had a difficult time, and even had to flee the wrath of enraged mobs. The hard core of the pioneer temperance leaders were, however, made of stern stuff mentally even though a surprising number of them did suffer physical ill health through no fault of their own.

The health-improving properties of certain wells had been known for centuries and flourished in a series of spas from Bath, Sadlers Wells and Tunbridge Wells in the south to Buxton and Harrogate in the north. The waters often had iron in them and these are known scientifically today as Chalybeate springs. Some of the wells were credited to saints like St. Ann's at Buxton but from whatever foundation they attracted visitors with the freshness and purity of their surroundings, contrasting so vividly and favourably with the stench and dirt of the cities. The water was drunk and it was used for bathing.

In most circles of early Victorian society bathing was considered something of a fad, appropriate to the spas where drastic methods might be needed to restore one's health, but not all that necessary and sensible otherwise. It was not all that long before that Frederick the Great of Prussia, having failed to wash for thirty years, cut his leg and not unnaturally died of gangrene. Wealthy young men on the Grand Tour of Europe might visit Versailles and reflect that the palace of the Sun King had been built with one bathroom and two toilets. It wasn't surprising that hydropathists could believe that bathing in special water might have wonderful recuperative effects, and indeed there were and are ailments which respond to this treatment and tens of thousands of sufferers who have had their pains alleviated by visiting the spas.

The spas had also been an excuse for people to go on holiday, and for them the social round in a city like Bath could well be the highlight of the year. The spas were the 'seaside' before many people thought of going to the seaside. There was a more informal

J.   The Wesleyan Chapel in Eastbank Street
K.   The new gasworks
L.   The station of the Liverpool and Crosby Railway
M.   Mr. Mather's Union Hotel
N.   Mr. Whiteley's Promenade Lodge
O.   Lifeboat House
P.   Mr. Parkinson's original hotel
Q.   Belmont Castle
R.   Mr. Halfrey's Bold Arms
S.   Trinity Church in Hoghton Street
T.   St. Marie's Roman Catholic Church in Seabank Road.

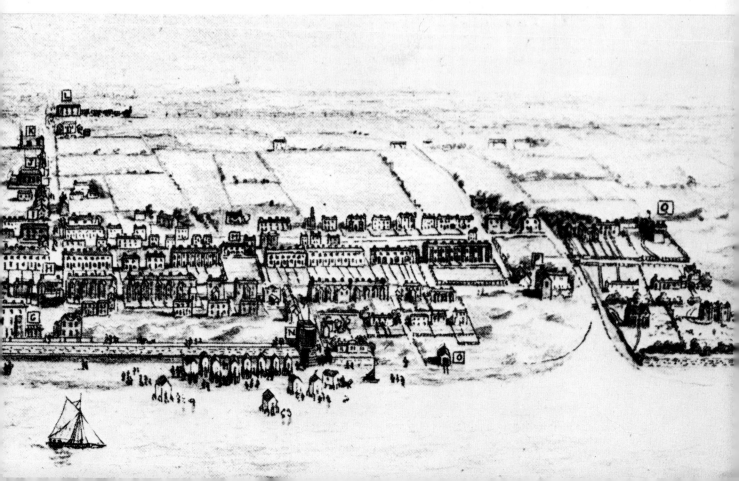

atmosphere about life at the spas and there were balls and concerts, lectures and recreational activities of all kinds. It was often a method of finding a suitable husband for a daughter, or a wealthy wife. Although the spas had never been part of a moral crusade as the temperance movement was now launching, they did have common ground in advocating the greater use of water.

Far away in Austria there lived a farmer's son called Vincent Preissnitz (1801–1851) who was claiming that the water on his land was exceptionally pure and capable of curing many diseases. By about 1830 he managed to receive very favourable publicity and became extremely fashionable. From Preissnitz came the hydropathists and the hydropathic institutions, which began in Britain soon after, and of which hotels like the Atholl Palace at Pitlochry, the Norbreck Hydro in Blackpool and the Peebles Hydro are surviving architectural examples. Vast sums of money would be spent on creating such establishments and they eventually became part of the hotel industry.

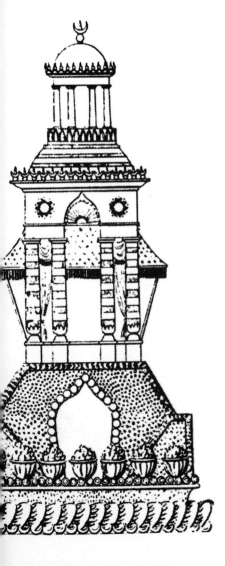

For such a craze to catch on there had to be powerful support. It came from eminent thinkers like Charles Darwin who wrote "I feel certain that the water cure is no quackery" and from public figures like Gladstone and Tennyson. It came from Sir Charles Scudamore who went to Graffenberg in 1843 to report on Preissnitz and came back convinced by his methods. As a doctor, Scudamore immediately fell foul of the College of Physicians who considered the idea nonsense and indeed "Homeopathists, Hydropathists and Morisonians were the dissenters in the Medical World threatening its established church—the College of Physicians". If you were very ill with tuberculosis, however, and Dr. John Balbirnie said that you could use water from the Highlands to treat the illness, then the gullible and desparate had little to lose. In defence of the water cure it would certainly have done little harm in the treatment of any illness, particularly by comparison with some of the hocus pocus practised.

It was also natural for the British to turn to the country spas because they had their roots deeply in the land and the village. The growth of the grim industrial towns and the movement of labour from the fields to the factories throughout the century only made the people more anxious to get away from the smoke and dirt when they could. Yet in the early days of the century the country was never all that far away; in 1840 the pigs for London hotel kitchens were raised in Notting Dale just up the road from Mayfair, and cows were kept in pastures off the Strand. The wealthy might flock to London for the season but they returned to their country homes for much of the year.

There were also a number of coastal resorts which had become fashionable and attracted a large number of visitors. Brighton was the most famous, but the pattern of accommodation was the familiar one of lodging houses and private homes with a small number of inns which could provide a bed. The attraction was not so much the sea bathing—indeed a number of the early lodging houses were built with their backs to the sea—as the many social events, and of course, the town was patronised by the Prince Regent who had first visited it in 1784. As late as 1853 Thackeray called it a city of lodging houses, for in common with all the smaller seaside towns almost any inhabitant would take in visitors. While a number of resorts had been favoured by visits from royalty —George III went to Weymouth for instance and the Princess of Wales to Worthing— the overall development was still slow. In Worthing in 1800 there was only sufficient room to feed forty-two guests in the two inns the town could boast, and if you were looking for good cooking, you were better advised to get invited to the home of an epicurean aristocrat. Even in those days it was accepted that the best chefs could be found in France and many were hired to lend lustre to a noble's hospitality. It was in this way that Marie-Antoine Carême came to Brighton after Waterloo to act as joint head chef to George IV, but he did not settle down, largely because he could not find any trained assistants. For the greatest chef in France, a man who had been chef de cuisine to Czar Alexander I, to have to rely on young kitchen maids if he did not do the work himself, was not only intolerable as far as he was concerned, but the clearest example of the paucity of experienced staff. If royalty couldn't get them, what chance did a humble hotel have?

Although there might not have been sufficient demand for resort hotels in the early part of the century, the seaside soon became very much a growth industry for trippers. In 1815 there were 21,000 visitors to Margate who came by sail from London, and this figure rose to over 40,000 in 1820 and 100,000 in 1830.

The reason for the lack of hotels both at the seaside and in other cities where the habit might have been created earlier, had much to do with the simple question of money. To build a large hotel was feasible for a Duke of Devonshire, but out of the question for lesser mortals. It was the sort of project which would require capital from the public and many difficulties were deliberately put in the way of raising it by such means. Of these the most awkward was the absence of limited liability. If you invested in a business as a shareholder and the business foundered with debts owing above and beyond the capital you had put in, then you were responsible for a proportion of those debts; you would not only lose all the money you had paid for the shares, but in addition you could be called upon for more money by the creditors. This legal condition had been devised as a consequence of the famous South Sea Bubble debacle in 1720 when thousands of investors in trade to the South Seas had been defrauded of their capital and the scandal had proved most embarrassing for the government of the day.

At the time of Waterloo it was fashionable for the best chefs to design extremely ornate dishes. Marvellous as these centrepieces of Marie Carême may appear, the food was often cold when the guest was finally able to eat it.

So, legislation was brought in to protect the public against directors of companies who might try to leave the shareholders and creditors holding the baby, and exceptions were only made when it was impossible to count on individual businessmen building an industry brick by brick. Normally an entrepreneur would be expected to start, say, with one spinning wheel and finish up after investing his profits steadily over the years with his own mill. This system was too slow, however, if you wanted as a government to create, for example, a national canal network, so canals were excluded by special Parliamentary Acts. So were a number of public utilities, but nobody would have been permitted to raise money for a limited liability company to build so speculative a venture as a hotel. This was the situation right through the early years of Victoria's reign, and it accounts in part for the small size of the vast majority of the hotels.

It was architecturally feasible to build a large hotel. The first was the Tremont Hotel in Boston, Massachusetts, which covered an entire city block and had nearly 200 bedrooms even though it was only three stories high. It was opened in October 1829 and could boast a main dining room with seats for 200 guests, carved walnut furniture and wall-to-wall carpeting in many of the apartments. Among the innovations which were not to be copied in Europe for a long time were free soap beside the bowl of water in the bedroom, an electro-magnetic buzzer which enabled the staff to see that you wanted service, and a special reading room. The Tremont, of course, did not have a lift and this restricted the hotel's tariff. If a guest paid a reasonable price he was not prepared to climb long flights of stairs every time he wanted to reach his bedroom, and indeed if he was elderly might not physically be able to do so. In British hotels as well, therefore, the top floor bedrooms had to be let more cheaply and were often used for the guests' personal servants. A Victorian hotel which was anxious to cater to the wealthy patron would have as many as half its total number of bedrooms set aside for the servants, and this explains the difference in height between the lower and upper floors, the difference in size and the small windows the higher up you went.

The United States was not only to be responsible for pioneering the large hotel, but also would produce the first lifts, electric light, and some of the most advanced building contractors for the hotel industry.

The catalyst which was eventually to transform the Cinderella of the accommodation market was the railway, and the British hotel industry owes George Stephenson a debt of gratitude for his enterprise. The railway had a shattering effect on the pattern of transportation, ruining the elaborate system of stage coaches and leaving almost derelict the coaching inns which had provided the horses and the refreshment for travellers. By the 1830s it was questionable whether you would get a worse reception in a coaching village as a railwayman or as a temperance preacher, but neither was at all popular. What the railways destroyed, however, was nothing to what they created, and we can look first at the point the railways had reached by 1837.

Although the first Parliamentary Act was passed in 1811 to permit the building of a railway line in South London, the railways didn't really get under way until the 1830s. They had from the beginning aroused great passions and great enthusiasms; passions from people who would suffer from their success, and enthusiasms from those who could see the fortunes to be made. As the growth of the railway hotels was a part of the development of the railways themselves, it is worth describing briefly how you had to go about getting permission to build a railway. It was first necessary to survey the route and

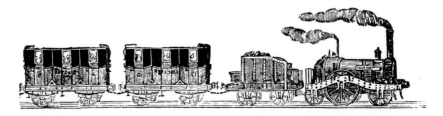

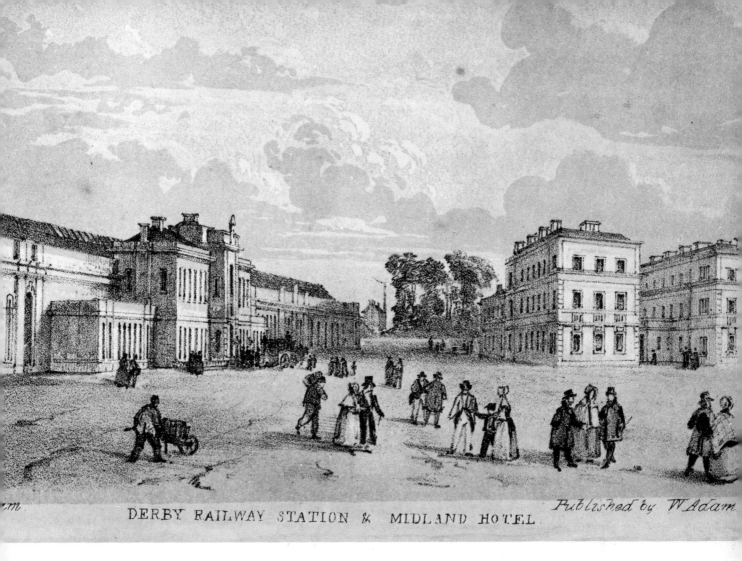

DERBY RAILWAY STATION & MIDLAND HOTEL

Published by W. Adam

The Midland Hotel at Derby was the first to be designed as an integral part of a railway station complex. Traffic jams and over-crowding were still far in the future.

to lodge the subsequent plans at the House of Commons. As the railway would cross the fields and property of many landowners, a Book of Reference to all the owners affected had to be compiled as well. This with ten per cent of the estimated cost of building the railway had then to be given to the Clerk of the Commons and only then could a Bill be introduced for permission to purchase the land compulsorily. If the Bill was approved, the price had to be agreed between the two parties, and if this was impossible, the local Justice of the Peace would arbitrate and as they were often part of the anti-railway lobby, there were many difficulties.

Railways brought noise, dirt, rough navvies and spoiled a lot of the scenery. They also brought industry, capital, work for the unemployed, and the possibility of substantial profits. Consequently two diametrically opposed schools of thought existed about the desirability of railways; opposition to the routes themselves came both from people who didn't want the line on their property, and from people who objected to the fact that it wasn't on theirs. The railways companies bought the land as cheaply as they could, and in the cities would endeavour to locate their main stations in a part of the town which was either completely undeveloped or run down. On such property most of the railway hotels in the provincial towns would be built.

The railway companies needed to build hotels for three main reasons. In the earliest stage of railway development, small hotels were put up at the country stations for the benefit of passengers who had to travel a long distance to reach the line. These hotels were invariably leased to other people and the railways did not run them. Many of the larger pubs in the countryside, still today called the 'Station Hotel', would have had their origins in this way. Because of the capital needed to build railways, the government

13

classed them with the canals and public utilities as an area where money could be raised from the public, but in order to offer the maximum protection, the money thus produced had to be used exclusively for the railway itself. When this was not done and senior railway executives used their finance for purposes like building steamers or even buying collieries to ensure the coal travelled on the right railway, any shareholder could object in court. The chairman of the West Hartlepool Harbour and Railway who had almost literally built the town by his own efforts was totally ruined in a long drawn out court battle in the 1850s over misuse of the funds of this nature.

A separate Bill had to be passed through Parliament to build a hotel or the money had to be raised through a separate company. There were a number of breaches of the law where hotels in the early years did benefit from the original shareholders' money, but fortunately for the directors concerned, any complaints failed to reach the courts. Many shareholders did object on moral grounds, insisting that they had been asked to invest in railways and not in establishments selling drink, but it was never suggested that the board were lining their own pockets in some way. The second reason for the railway's

The tariff of the Great Northern Hotel at Kings Cross. The cost of a room was more than doubled by the charges for service, candles and a hot bath.

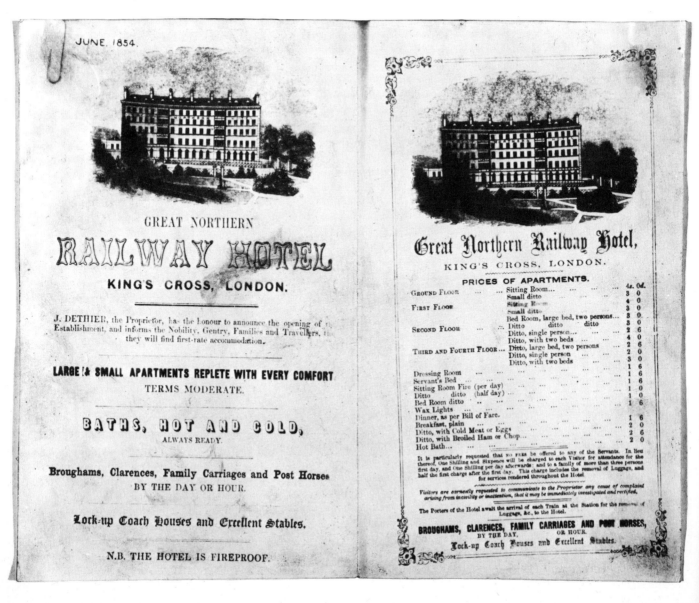

interest in hotels was that punctuality could not be guaranteed on the early trains and many would arrive late in the evening, stranding the passengers without anywhere suitable to sleep. Many trains also left on long journeys early in the morning and these created more hotel custom as travellers stayed the night before their journey. Some hoteliers were not above making the check out time an hour or two before the departure of popular trains so that the guests either had to vacate their rooms at an inconvenient point or pay extra for the privilege of staying until the train was ready to go.

The third reason was that the railways soon started to compete for traffic among themselves and some of them, like the Midland and the South Eastern, believed that putting up hotels would give them a competitive advantage. There were to be many railway lines to the different South Coast ports and resorts and many provincial cities were also served by more than one company. We can examine later the economics of this kind of travellers' perk, but the principle highlights the haphazard development of hotels, as of so much else, in Victorian England.

The Victorians were devoted to *laissez-faire*, to economic freedom to get rich or go bankrupt with the minimum amount of interference from the government. It was inconceivable in that climate, as indeed it is today, to gear the demand for hotels to the supply. Once it appeared that a hotel developer was on to a good thing, once a company thrived or an individual prospered, there was no lack of imitators. A decision to build the Zetland Hotel at Saltburn for the rich burghers of Middlesbrough who wanted to get away to the seaside from the town's grime, made admirable sense in isolation. What could not be foreseen was how long the people would be content to travel just a few miles to go on holiday, whether they would prefer another fashionable resort in time, and where the money was to come from to improve the buildings as new inventions were introduced. The small station hotels existed from the earliest railway age, but the larger ones like York, Derby and Paddington did not appear until after the railways could turn to the minutiae of their projects in the period from 1837 onwards.

Life in an early 19th century hotel depended on your purse. At the top end of the market the hotels had many amenities; there would be a lounge, and often a billiards

The Zetland Hotel in Saltburn-by-the-Sea, Yorkshire. The railway station platform was immediately outside the back door. Saltburn was the holiday resort for the richer inhabitants of Middlesbrough, and the sand beaches have few rivals in Britain even today.

ZETLAND HOTEL, SALTBURN-BY-THE-SEA

room. Billiards had been a popular British game for centuries; Mary, Queen of Scots, complained to Queen Elizabeth that her captors had taken her table away from her. Louis XIV played the game and it was popular with the aristocracy throughout the 18th century. White's standard book on billiards in 1807 describes the same game which is played today and apart from improvements in equipment such as the slate bed to ensure that the balls rolled truly, there has been very little change. At a time when people had to make their own amusements in the evening, the billiards room was very popular and often very lavish. If the hotel could boast its own dining room, all the guests who did not wish to take their meals in a private sitting room would be seated round one large table with the landlord or host presiding at the top. There would be a set menu, which is the origin of the term *table d'hôte*, and a choice of cold dishes.

At the other end of the scale, the common lodging house for the poorest travellers and the near destitute could hardly have been worse. The bedding was filthy, there were lice and rats, it was wise to sleep with your boots on for fear they would be stolen during the night, even if sleep was possible with the noise of the other members of the dormitory who could be drunk, half-mad, or using the place as a brothel. Lodging house guests would bring their own food or buy it raw, from the lodging house keeper and then cook it themselves in the large kitchen. It was very rough indeed, but there were thousands of itinerant workers who could afford nothing better.

It was a long way from a city common lodging house to an inn, deep in the country, but these might offer accommodation as well. Thomas De Quincey, the author and essayist, writing about his travels in Wales in 1802 speaks highly of the numerous inns which had been put up about fifteen miles from each other for the accommodation of tourists. A small English spa like Matlock could muster three hotels even if they did look exactly like large farmhouses.

Britain in 1837—for hotels a developing seaside, new hope for the spas, a wide network of doomed coaching inns and a small group of city centre hotels. Ready to change it all came the steady march of the railway navvies, building lines like the strings of a net which would finally gather up the diffuse communities throughout the country and make them accessible to each other.

The Pioneering years— 1837–1862

2

Hotel development during the twenty-five years between 1837 and 1862 was geared to the progress of the railways. Each new line opened up the area it covered, altering the existing communication industry, increasing or reducing traffic. Villages which had been staging posts on the main coach routes declined dramatically and large and prosperous coaching inns which had throbbed with the bustle of arrivals and departures soon took on the aspect of a foresaken stage set; the weeds spread through the derelict yards, the stables which had housed hundreds of horses echoed the footsteps of the few employees left; landlords were reduced to trying to sell the local butter and cheese as if they were running a roadside stall, or making ends meet by mending shoes or competing with the local blacksmith. The rare visitors remarked on the deserted corridors and the general air of decay and despondency. It was a very bad time for the districts affected, and with unemployment came a drop in land values, reduced turnover in the village shops and emigration from the area to the new industrial towns. There was nothing the villages could do, any more than a petrol station on a main road can replace the business when a new motorway diverts the traffic. All that was left was to sell drinks to the local inhabitants which was not sufficient to keep a considerable number of the inns solvent. All over the country they soldiered on as best they could and finally a lot of them closed.

Where the coaching inn was in a sizeable town, much depended on its position *vis à vis* the new station. Some inns in the early days were taken over by the railways to provide carriers' quarters or booking offices till more permanent arrangements could be made. If they were fortunate enough to be near a busy railway station, the change from coach passengers to railway passengers would be comparatively painless, but not many were so lucky. Some relics of the Elizabethan Castle and Falcon Inn remained at Aldersgate Station in the city as did parts of the 16th century Swan with Two Necks and Catherine Wheel in other parts of London. The Adelphi in Liverpool found itself very close to the new Lime Street terminal, and partly through this, and partly through James Radley's expertise, was able to expand by absorbing the other buildings in the terrace, but for the most part the inns were in the wrong place.

It is, of course, one of the major risks in building a hotel that the geographical and transportation patterns can change radically. If an area is fashionable when the hotel is built, the hotelier must still be able to attract visitors when the area has gone to seed even though the new conditions locally are no fault of his. There is an old saying in the business that the three most important factors in a hotel's success are "Location, location, and location" but the best location today can still be a backwater or a slum in a few years' time if the environment changes.

In 1833 the national total of coach and mail travellers had reached a peak at just over two-and-a-half million with about another twenty-five per cent arriving on post horses, canal boats, or in private carriages. By comparison in 1863 the total number of railway journeys was over 204 million so that this was a time of massive growth in travel rather than decline.

The railways produced hotels in two different ways: by creating the traffic for others to risk putting up new buildings or by building hotels themselves. But where there was competition in a town between two railway companies for permission to build a terminus, one of the common arguments used was the location of the existing hotels in relation to the proposed site for the station. In Manchester, the Liverpool and Manchester Railway wanted to put up a terminus at Store Street while the Manchester and Leeds wanted it sited at Hunts Bank and argued "The superior convenience of Hunts Bank as a central station is attested by the fact that of the 28 inns and hotels in Pigots Directory for 1841, 19 are nearer Hunts Bank, 2 are equidistant, 7 are nearer Store Street." New Street Station, Birmingham, situated 100 yards from the Royal Hotel, which was the best in the city, and the Oldham Road Station in Manchester in 1836 also near to the local hotel are further examples which obtained approval partly for that reason.

Money raised from the public to build railways could not be spent on building hotels. A new prospectus was therefore needed for the hotels at Euston Station in 1838.

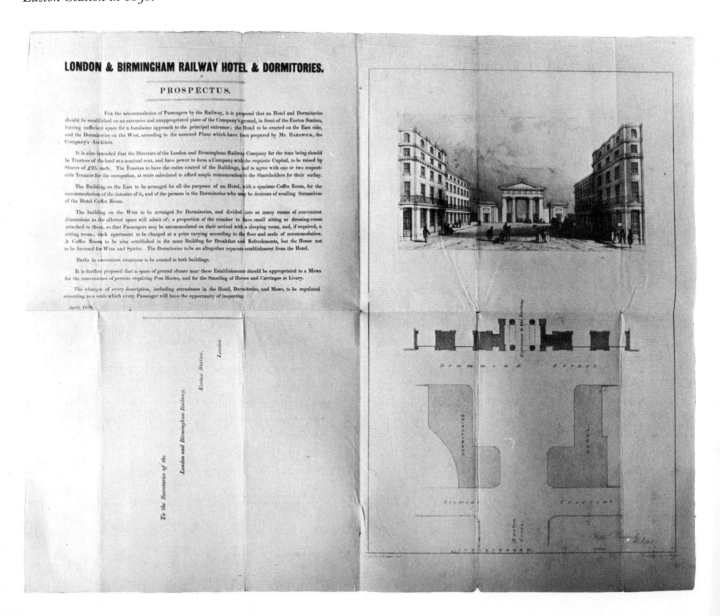

If the railways were competing with each other for permission to build a terminus, they might use the location of existing hotels to bolster the case for a central site, but ideally the railways wanted to buy the inexpensive land for terminii, and they preferred slum areas or positions on the outskirts wherever possible. When successful, there would not be sufficient suitable bedroom accommodation and then the railway would either hope that hotels would spring up without their assistance or alternatively they might invest themselves. The first railway hotel was in fact two hotels at Euston which were opened in 1839 by the London and Birmingham Railway. The prospectus for the raising of the capital was headed "London and Birmingham Railway Hotel and Dormitories" and here the money for the hotel was raised by the creation of a separate company in keeping with the laws on the use of railway funds. The idea was to build a hotel on the east side of the station and dormitories on the west. The railway directors would be trustees of the land on which the buildings would be erected and the money would be raised in £25 shares. Throughout the Victorian period the nominal value of shares was much higher than we normally find today; £5, £10 and £20 shares were the usual units and this, of course, restricted the share purchasing section of the population to a very small percentage.

Fifty years after the building of the Euston hotels, the manager of the Metropole Hotel in London, one of the finest and newest, would only earn £10 a week and to most people £20 was a small fortune. The new hotels at Euston were not licensed and were completely separate buildings. Although a number of the rooms in the dormitory building might have had several beds, the word 'dormitory' did not automatically imply this, but rather a place in which to sleep, and a proportion of the dormitories had small sitting or dressing rooms attached to them. The hotel was to have a splendid coffee room and there would be another in the dormitory building. The coffee room was open to the general public where the expression 'dining room' would indicate for some years that only hotel guests and their friends were admitted. Charges for sleeping depended on the floor occupied and "the scale of accommodation", and public bathrooms were placed in each building.

It was not until 1881 that the two hotels were joined together by a connecting block and altogether the original scheme was a limited effort. Even so it provided good accommodation for the time, and an improved setting for the railway directors themselves. These men were engaged in enterprises involving vast sums of money and they needed a 'prestige' building. The first attempt to raise over £1 million to create the Great Western Railway was at a meeting which had to be held in a Bristol inn and such arrangements simply were not good enough.

Euston Station had been opened in 1838 with the hotels as an afterthought, but at Derby the design for the station incorporated a hotel. It was opened in 1840 and was called the Midland although three railway companies used the station, the North Midland, the Midland Counties and the Birmingham and Derby. To modern eyes the whole development looks modest enough, but to an eye witness at the time "This is the most complete and magnificent Station yet erected. It has a frontage of 1,050 feet and the whole interior comprising sheds, workshops, engine houses and offices, is on the same stupendous scale". It looked so large because everything around it was so small. The buildings were detached with a wide street between station and hotel along which carriages and pedestrians alike would move without any danger of obstructing each other. Most people had no reason to take large buildings or big crowds for granted, and each new large hotel would have the impact of a Post Office Tower for years to come.

York and Hull soon had hotels as an integral part of the station design. Another early railway hotel was the Furness Abbey. This is a good example of a hotel built in an area made industrially attractive only by the invention of railways, and specifically needed to serve the buyers visiting the town. The 6th Duke of Devonshire was chairman of the Furness Railway Company and also the owner of the slate quarries and much of the other industry which was opening up the district around Barrow-in-Furness. A hotel was required to accommodate the merchants who came to negotiate for slate and the Duke

The Furness Abbey Hotel at Barrow-in-Furness, Lancashire, viewed from the tennis lawn. The first tennis club was formed at the Manor House Hotel, Leamington Spa, in 1872.

It is difficult to suggest any weapon in the modern travel agent's armoury that Thomas Cook did not invent, perfect, or utilise to its best advantage

is said to have paid for it and certainly took a great interest in its design for, like the 5th Duke at Buxton, he was an amateur architect. The hotel was built in a narrow, well wooded valley, and looked like an old fashioned country house; indeed, part of it had formed the home of the Abbot of the Abbey.

To a people who only knew travel in terms of walking, riding horses, or enduring a stage coach, the railways were an unparalleled marvel, but the early trains were hardly luxurious. For the poorer travellers the coaches were open and the speed must have seemed to many to be extremely dangerous, even though the *Rocket* averaged less than 30 mph when winning the competition for the most effective engine. Whatever the drawbacks, there was enormous excitement in taking a railway journey, and by the early 1840s the growth of excursion trains had started.

The first excursion train was run as a trip to see an execution and one of the earliest was Thomas Cook's famous arrangements for the supporters of his local temperance association, when a rally was held in Loughborough in 1841 and no less than 570 people paid one shilling each to travel from Leicester to the meeting in nine open coaches. Cook organised it as an enthusiastic temperance supporter but soon realised the opportunity which now existed to make a good profit, and went into the business as a sideline arranging similar outings. Very soon these began to cover longer distances, the railways themselves became interested, and many visits were organised to destinations as far afield as Scotland. There the growth of the tourist trade could be attributed to the popularity of the works of Sir Walter Scott and Robert Burns, and to a visit which Queen Victoria and Prince Albert paid to the country in 1842. With the trains making it possible to cover the miles in a reasonable time, Scotland found itself host to many more tourists and if they were led by a temperance man like Thomas Cook, the hoteliers could expect to take both money and advice. Reminiscing in 1886, Cook recalled "We had always a difficulty in Scotland in making hotel arrangements of a satisfactory character, and this was in great measure owing to the inveterate love of whisky which has been the drink and the curse of that country. . . . Nevertheless . . . the example I set before my travellers who accompanied me through these districts and the example others had upon Hotel Proprietors produced effects of a very beneficial character."

Cook also found that there was a lot of drinking in Ireland and when he addressed a meeting of Irish hoteliers on the principles of the temperance movement he was not amused that the owner of the hotel at which they gathered was very drunk indeed.

Ireland was a very poor part of the United Kingdom, but before the potato famine in 1846 with its resultant starvation and emigration, over one-third of the population lived there. Dublin itself had declined after the Act of Union which transferred the parliamentary business of the country together with a large number of the Irish aristocracy to London. The economy which had, among other products, supplied England with much of its corn during the Napoleonic Wars, was hit by inflation and the relaxation of import duties, and in that climate it was surprising that one Irishman, Martin Burke, had sufficient confidence in Dublin's future to invest heavily in the creation of the Shelbourne Hotel. In 1824 he opened it in the heart of fashionable St. Stephen's Square and even then could see the possibilities of the city as a tourist centre. The hotel offered private drawing-rooms for between three and four shillings [15p–20p], and Thackeray wrote later that a guest "is comfortably accommodated at the very moderate daily charge of six shillings and eightpence [33p]. For this charge a copious breakfast is provided for him in the coffee room, a perpetual luncheon is likewise there spread, a plentiful dinner is ready at 6 o'clock; after which, there is a drawing room and a rubber of whist, with tay [tea] and coffee and cakes in plenty to satisfy the largest appetite".

The luxury of the Shelbourne must have contrasted very strongly with the want and deprivation in the meaner streets of the capital.

The future German Chancellor, Bismarck, also remarked on the food in provincial British hotels when writing to his father during a visit in 1842, but in slightly less glowing terms. "It is the country for heavy eaters. The variety in the cuisine is small: roast beef, mutton, ham (boiled), bacon, roast lamb, veal, eggs, and potatoes are on the table at every breakfast, to which fish and a vile fruit tart are added at dinner. The soups are so strongly spiced with black and red pepper that few foreigners can eat them. The system of allotted portions is unknown; even at breakfast the most enormous pieces of each of these kinds of meat, such as we never see, stand before you, and you cut and eat as much or as little of them as you like, without any difference as regards payment. In the hotels when I have taken supper and breakfast . . . and spent the night there, I have always paid eight or nine shillings [40 or 45p]—that is with a tip."

The Shelbourne Hotel in Dublin was built almost as an act of faith in Dublin's future. From its appearance it could well have been a nobleman's town house.

Individual travellers were very welcome, but to the railways in England seeking traffic for their wildly expanding system, the excursion traffic was an additional boon, and its increasing popularity was one reason for the 'railway mania' which swept the country in the late 1840s. Hundreds of bills were passed by Parliament for new lines, and eventually and inevitably the stock market crashed, temporarily calling a halt amid the cries of the ruined investors.

The railways retrenched, amalgamated, and prepared for the Great Exhibition of 1851, when the total attendance of 6,009,948 visitors finally showed beyond doubt not only the new trend to mass travel, but also the ability to cater for it. Of course the attendance included vast numbers of Londoners but Thomas Cook brought up 165,000 people from the provinces himself, and such hotels as existed had their best year ever. The 1851 *Exhibition Guide* provided what advice it could, but there was little to choose from: West End hotels like the Clarendon, Fentons, Wrights, The Brook Street and Mivarts were booked completely. In the Covent Garden area the Bedford, Tavistock, Old Hummums and New Hummums were equally packed. In the city a room would cost six to seven shillings (30–35p) a day full *pension* but in the West End a sitting room and bedroom was anywhere between ten shillings and sixpence and a guinea (55p and £1.05) and the *Guide* recommended that you asked the price at the earliest opportunity as there was a tendency for hotelkeepers to name a figure the guest looked as if he could and would afford. In addition it would be expected that the waiter and chambermaid would receive the customary one shilling (5p) a day between them and the 'boots' sixpence ($2\frac{1}{2}$p) as well.

A minute proportion of the visitors to the Great Exhibition would have stayed in hotels but many an investor around the country saw the way the wind was blowing. One railway hotel was approved in the year of the Great Exhibition when in February 1851 a meeting of the GWR directors authorised "An hotel with Refreshment Rooms, Dormitories, Stables, and other conveniences for not more than £50,000" to be built at Paddington. The hotel was to be leased to a company directed by shareholders and officers of the GWR and the resulting Great Western Hotel was at its opening "the largest and most sumptuous hotel in England". Hardwick, its architect, persuaded the directors to accept a design which was in the style of the French Renaissance which was just beginning to be fashionable again, and this is one of the earliest examples of the close connection between hotels and the flights of Victorian architectural fancy.

Victorian architects had passed the period where stucco was used instead of brick to imitate the rustic stone, and retreated from the simplicity of Georgian and Regency design which they now condemned as monotonous. Professor Pevsner in his monumental *Buildings of England* explains the background very clearly. "Monotony had become the worst offence. It was detested as much by the advocates of the Italian as of the Gothic style. This high Victorian desire for richness, for rich relief, for ornate decoration also explains the next of the 19th century revivals, that of the French Renaissance."

For the directors of hotel companies in the luxury category, there was to be a continuous conflict of interest in the years to come as the architectural fashions grew steadily more lavish. On the one hand they wanted to have a new hotel which could be seen to be as stylish as possible, but they also wanted to keep the excessive expenditure which Victorian architecture could easily involve within reasonable bounds. At the Great Western Royal, John Thomas produced a splendid pediment on which carved figures illustrated the great Victorian virtues of peace, plenty, industry and science. It was stylish and artistic, but did it attract more customers to the hotel? It added nothing to their comfort, but it would be a talking point, and where did you draw the line anyway, for no hotel has an entirely utilitarian decor.

Time and again there were to be arguments along these lines, and many decisions were taken for reasons which had little to do with economics or marketing. The directors

Facing page:
Just before the full flowering of Victorian Gothic, the Great Northern Hotel, at King's Cross, was built in a more modest style.

Isambard Kingdom Brunel, chairman of the Great Western Hotel Company. Running hotels was a relaxation from his more arduous responsibilities. (Portrait by John Horsley, RA).

were often concerned with their own prestige and that of their company which the hotel was designed to enhance, and it must have been a great satisfaction to the board of the GWR that the hotel's success was immediate and "unheard of dividends were the result." Prince Albert, himself, made a tour of inspection before the hotel was opened for business on June 9th, 1854. Large hotels were very novel, and it was natural that royalty should visit them in the same way that they might look over a new space rocket today.

As the GWR had no professional hoteliers anywhere near board level, the chairman of the hotel company was the great engineer, Isambard Kingdom Brunel, who "found the supervising of the management a very agreeable relaxation from his other duties."

Although the "sad spectacle offers itself of England throwing away her heritage of originality and returning to a style of period imitation as barren in its neo-Wren as in its neo-Georgian form" and presumably neo-Gothic, neo-Italian Renaissance and neo everything else, it is also true that hotels provided the Victorian architect with the opportunity to create a new type of building or at least to push the frontiers for that type of building further forward. But Hardwick's Great Western was not typical of its day, and the Great Northern Hotel which was opened at King's Cross in 1854 was a far more modest and standard construction. There was another aspect of Victorian architecture which was strongly advocated by the influential theorist. A. W. N. Pugin, and he, in his pamphlets and buildings, endeavoured to make the neo-Gothic revival into an act of faith. It might seem a little far fetched today, but he wanted a Christian country to reject any form of architecture which was derived from pagan civilizations like the Greek or Roman, and this attitude was in keeping with his times. The Victorians could produce the weirdest extremes and extremists and when one remembers that the legs of a piano would be covered in many households as a seemly precaution against erotic thoughts, nothing is beyond belief.

VISITORS TO LONDON.

TRANTER'S

(Private, Family, & Commercial)

TEMPERANCE HOTEL

7, 8, 9, Bridgewater Sq., Barbican, London, E.C.

RECENTLY ENLARGED.

VISITORS to London will find many advantages by staying at this quiet, clean and home-like Hotel

MOST CENTRAL FOR BUSINESS OR PLEASURE.

Near St. Paul's Cathedral, G.P.O., and all places of interest; 3 minutes' walk from Aldersgate Street, and 5 from Moorgate Street Metropolitan Railway Stations; Termini of the Great Western, Great Northern, Great Eastern, Midland, L. and N.W., L. C. and Dover, and in connection with ALL Railways. 15 minutes walk to the Law Courts. Trains, Cars, Busses, every three minutes, to all parts of London and Suburbs. Highly recommended. Established 1859.

Write for "VISITORS' GUIDE," Showing "HOW TO SPEND A WEEK IN LONDON." (Regd.) With Tariff and Testimonials, post free on application to G. T. S. TRANTER, Proprietor.

⇥ TARIFF. ⇤

APARTMENTS, Etc.

Clean and Well Ventilated Bed-rooms.

Bed-room for one person .. .. 1/6, 2/-, 2/6 per night.

„ „ two persons .. .. 3/-, 3/6, 4/- „

According to the size and position of room taken.

The above charges include use of Spacious Coffee, Smoking, and Reading Rooms, Fire, Lavatories, &c., &c. Electric Light in Public Rooms.

PRIVATE SITTING ROOMS, from 4/- per day, including Gas and attendance.

BREAKFAST OR TEA.

Plain, with Preserves, &c., &c.	1/-	Plain, with 2 Eggs Poached on Toast 1/6
Ditto with Cake	1/3	Ditto with Rump Steak, Chop, Fish,
Ditto with 2 Eggs or Bacon ..	1/4	or Ham & 2 Eggs 1/9
Ditto with Cold Meat	1/6	*With choice of Tea Coffee or Cocoa.*

LUNCHEONS AND SUPPERS.

Chop, Steak, or Cold Meat, with Potatoes, Bread, Butter, and Cheese 1/6

Basin Bread and Milk, Gruel, or Oatmeal Porridge .. .. -/6

DINNERS.

Weekdays, as per arrangement. Sundays, at 1.30 consisting of

Soup, Joints, Vegetables, Sweets, and Cheese.. .. .. 2/-

Hot or Cold Baths, Hot 9d., Cold 6d.

SPECIAL INCLUSIVE TERMS TO AMERICANS AND OTHERS DESIRING IT.

Visitors are received at a fixed charge of 5/6 per day, to include first-class Bedroom, Boots, Breakfast and Tea with Chop, Rump Steak, Ham and Eggs, or Cold Meat at each Meal. (Special Reduced Weekly Terms during the Winter.)

PERFECT SANITARY ARRANGEMENTS. NO CHARGE FOR ATTENDANCE.

TELEGRAPHIC ADDRESS: "HEALTHIEST" LONDON.

It was also an act of faith for the temperance movement to go into the hotel business, for many of their leaders realised that the best way for temperance travellers to avoid the pitfalls of a licensed hotel, was for an alternative to be provided and "in 1836 the first Temperance boarding house . . . was opened in London, and the first Temperance hotel appeared in Aldersgate Street in the City, financed by William Janson who was also known as Barley-Water Billy". Unfortunately for guests who habitually used temperance hotels, a firm faith in prohibition did not automatically guarantee that the proprietor was also capable of running a hotel. Temperance hotels "were often opened by those who had failed at normal inn-keeping and by reformed drunkards who, with no aptitude for the job, were set-up in business by local sympathizers." The hotels were often very small indeed; like the one near Penzance which consisted of one room over a general store.

A temperance historian wrote in 1865, when there were nearly 200 temperance hotels in England, that "temperance hotels had in many cases, brought a reproach upon the movement because of their mean appearance and unsuitable management." It would be unfair, however, to tar all the temperance hotels with the same brush. Among many other dedicated proprietors, Mrs. Thomas Cook opened her own temperance hotel in Market Harborough in Leicestershire and the Cooks built a new temperance hotel in Leicester itself in 1853 for £3,500. The hotel was popular and well run, as one would expect from a man who always looked after the comfort of his tourists with such care.

While one temperance leader could complain of the management of temperance hotels and call them "Penal settlements of Teetotalism", the hotels did at least enable the temperance guest to carry out his pledge without enduring from servants or other guests the small slights which indicated that they thought his conduct mean, odd or unfriendly. Temperance hotels "were really attempts to enable teetotallers to survive in a drink-ridden society" though they were also used on occasions as fronts for less legal activities, as a funeral parlour in Chicago in the 1920's might conceal the entrance to a speakeasy. Gambling and disorderly conduct in certain so-called temperance hotels got them banned even by teetotal societies, and some brothels called themselves temperance hotels in order to allay suspicion. It was true that many of the hotels were drab and it would have been helpful if there had been some recognised standards of practice because the hotel keepers would probably have followed their society's instructions with care, but they did not develop in such an organised way.

There was one temperance enthusiast, however, who did make a fortune out of accommodating guests and he was John Smedley who started with the unlikely asset of a stocking mill in Matlock in Derbyshire. Smedley in his early years was a strong churchman who felt so deeply on the subject that he discouraged his workpeople from going to chapel, but he became converted in time into a dissenting preacher, and a very

Mrs. Thomas Cook was not just decorative. She ran the Temperance Hotel in Market Harborough in Leicestershire for her husband and took part in all his activities.

Facing page:
Temperance hotels competed with the licensed variety and very often with missionary zeal. The telegraphic address was probably inaccurate during the cholera epidemic in the 1860s.

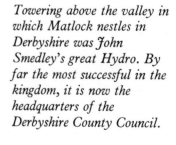

Towering above the valley in which Matlock nestles in Derbyshire was John Smedley's great Hydro. By far the most successful in the kingdom, it is now the headquarters of the Derbyshire County Council.

This photograph of John Smedley and his wife is at least 100 years old. Even at this distance in time, his determination and pugnacity are apparent in every inch of his bearing and expression.

powerful one at that. John Smedley was the epitome of the self-assured, enthusiastic, dynamic, God-fearing, Victorian entrepreneur and he had the useful capacity to persuade others to his way of thinking. At one stage, for example, he went overboard for a particular kind of quack pill and insisted on dosing his entire factory staff with it, and throughout his later years he waged guerilla warfare against the more conservative parsons and doctors.

The railway reached Matlock in 1849 and not long afterwards Smedley fell seriously ill with typhoid and was taken to Ben Rhydding, at Ilkley, to convalesce and to try the hydropathic water cure. This was a great success. He fully recovered his strength and in consequence the cause of hydropathy gained for its ranks a formidable advocate, as Smedley immediately started hydropathic techniques on his own long-suffering work force. To his delight the system seemed to work for them as well and in 1853 he bought a small existing hydro and started to run it himself.

When Smedley began to operate the hydro, the spa of Matlock had almost ceased to exist because it was no longer fashionable. Throughout the length and breadth of the country the spas had had a long run but they badly needed a new gimmick to correct their image as an old fashioned holiday. The social side had overtaken the medical to a great extent and the wealthy were seeking new and more modern methods of healing themselves, rather than being satisfied with the cures of their parents and grandparents. In 1818 the Old Bath Hotel at Matlock had accommodation for 100 visitors and there were smaller hotels like Saxtons and The Museum as well as a number of lodging houses, but for all that by Smedley's time it was a quiet village, slumbering in its beautiful countryside.

The hydro proved popular and Smedley put up a larger building on the site very quickly. The rumour was that he built it like a factory, so that if it proved a failure as a hydro, the money would not be wasted. Smedley had no need to worry, however, for his fame spread through the non-conformist world. He wrote a book with 512 pages entitled *Practical Hydropathy including plans of baths and remarks on diet, clothing and habits of life* which by 1872 reached its fourteenth edition, and you could not come in contact with him without imbibing at least some of his zeal and enthusiasm.

Matlock possesses tepid springs and the hydro did offer a formidable range of special baths and massage, but in addition much was achieved for the visitor by the regime he was expected to adopt. This consisted of plenty of exercise in the fresh air, going to bed early, and taking the pledge at least temporarily. The diet leaned towards vegetarianism and tobacco was frowned upon. It was an unusual kind of hotel where elderly gentlemen sometimes took offence at being fined for arriving late at the dining table and after the meal they had to lie down with a cushion on their stomachs to aid their digestions, but it would be wrong to think of the hydros simply in terms of hospitals. For nearly twenty years, Smedley had no qualified practitioner attached to the hydro. Treatment at first consisted simply of the application of water to the affected places, the use of wet sheets, douches, and baths, but even so there were many cures and the hydro was soon besieged with visitors.

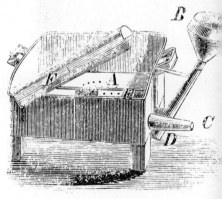

The hydro company which was created in 1875 after Smedley's death eventually paid twenty per cent dividends with great regularity, and it would have been surprising if this enviable combination of miraculous cures and a seemingly unlimited clientele had gone unnoticed or uncopied; "Smedley's success soon induced others to build similar establishments for the treatment of rheumatic and other complaints." The hydros were far more than this though, as they also looked after ladies who had more money than sense and a great deal of time to fill in finding imaginary ailments for the cures. The hydros helped reduce obesity in women after pregnancy, and dried out many a country gentleman who had imposed too great a strain on an elderly constitution. The fate of the hydros and how most of them eventually came to be purely hotels is part of the industry's story in later years.

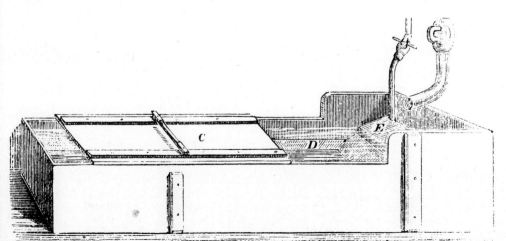

Hydropathy meant the treatment of disease with water, and bathing was a vital part of the cure. Baths came in all shapes and sizes of which these two illustrations are examples.

There was another haven for invalids and that was the seaside. Blackpool, for instance, was known for the therapeutic effects of drinking the sea water as early as 1784, and the custom continued until around 1850 in a number of other resorts as well. The seaside between 1837 and 1862 was also much affected by the development of the railways, and the best example of this is probably Bournemouth just because the railway did not reach there until 1870. The town had an early start thanks to the enterprise of the local landowner, Sir George Tapps Jervis, who realised the potential for the seaside earlier than most. He erected the first hotel in Bournemouth which was called the Bath, and opened on Coronation Day 1838, being described as a "very elegant, spacious and convenient structure under the careful management of the occupier, Miss Toomer."

Before John Smedley built his Hydro, Matlock was a quiet village and the first hotel was the Bath.

It is worth noting in passing that the cause of women's lib in the hotel industry at least, seems to have suffered a setback since the 19th century for on innumerable occasions there were women managers at that time, and far fewer are found today in such senior positions.

The railway was quickly built to nearby Poole, but the growth of seaside towns was initially due to day trippers and for them the journey from Poole to Bournemouth was far too long. The credit for the first railway excursion train belongs to Sir Rowland Hill who is, of course, better known for creating the Penny Post, but only three years after the first Penny Black he was chairman of the Brighton Railway Company. In the north a Lancashire manufacturer took his 650 workers to Fleetwood in 1844 and in the south by 1859 as many as 73,000 Londoners travelled to Brighton in a week, a figure which included almost no commuters and represented five per cent of the total London population.

Traffic in such volume justified the resident population of Brighton growing from 40,000 in 1831 to 90,000 only forty years later, but the influential citizens of Bournemouth did not want the excursion type of business. They believed that it was impossible to get wealthy invalids and lusty trippers to mix and the best way to avoid the problem was to stop the railway. Consequently the town stagnated and hotel development was slow. As, however, there was still a shortage of accommodation in hotels at certain times of the year, the existing hotels did quite well. The Belle Vue boarding house in 1840 flourished to such an extent that it was the Belle Vue Hotel in 1855 with the Union Jack flying from its new flagstaff, and a gazebo in the grounds. The ability to stop a railway was only one indication of the power wielded by a comparatively minute number of people in deciding the way a seaside town should develop.

In the early resort days there was much of the atmosphere of the original spas. Apart from the sea bathing the visitors would fill their time searching for interesting fossils, taking long walks, and visiting the Assembly Rooms. There was gaming with a faro bank at Scarborough in the 18th century and many guide books pointed out later the antiquarian appeal of the neighbourhood. At the libraries there were organized sweepstakes and raffles and auctions were conducted; greens were made available for archery and others for bowls. Into this calm and sedate society the masses of trippers arrived like a sudden high tide, and the middle classes who had formed the backbone of many of the resorts, took flight for new pastures. This is the reason for the development of those additional towns which are so often found cheek by jowl with the original watering places; St. Annes near Blackpool, Cliftonville near Margate and Westcliff near Southend.

The mere existence of such new resorts was a warning to far-sighted investors that the potential seaside clientele was fickle, but few entrepreneurs seeing the immediate prospects could be blamed for letting the long term future take care of itself. As John Maynard Keynes, himself, remarked many years later "In the long run we are all dead." The problems would come home to roost for succeeding generations. The older resorts had themselves grown from different foundations; Ramsgate, Torquay and Great Yarmouth had initially been fishing ports and Scarborough a spa. Some of the ports were to grow even more important because of the additional speed of railway connections, and here again there was severe competition between competing lines. The South Eastern Railway had built the line to Dover and, to stop travellers embarking from other south coast ports, were prepared to offer them every comfort and inducement. As many passengers who wished to take boats for France wanted to stay overnight at Dover, the railway decided to build the Lord Warden Hotel which was sumptuously opened with a grand public dinner on September 7th 1853. It was a Doric building named after the greatest and about the oldest, living hero, the Duke of Wellington, who was Lord Warden

The dining room of the Lord Warden Hotel in Dover about 1850. Although the guests might stay as individuals, they ate at one large horseshoe table. In a hotel of the quality of the Lord Warden, evening dress for dinner was de rigeur.

of the Cinque Ports and who took a keen interest in the original design of the one-hundred-and-eleven bedroom hotel.

Although the Lord Warden was erected and furnished by the SER the directors, unlike the directors of the GWR at Paddington, sought a tenant from the beginning rather than go into the hotel business. The hotel might have a "spacious *salle à manger* and a noble coffee room" but they decided it was a far cry from operating engines and carriages. Certainly a contemporary illustration of the dining room at the Lord Warden would have been enough to overawe all but the very sophisticated. It was a large room dominated by the one enormous horseshoe table, and amid the acres of snowy white tablecloth sat large fruit bowls on pedestals, each topped with an uncut pineapple. The table was so wide that it would have been quite impossible for a guest to speak comfortably to his neighbour on the other side even if etiquette had allowed. For those with a taste for display and formality, it was a rather splendid sight, but for the shy and retiring it was a sufficient explanation for the number of guests who chose to take all their meals in their own rooms. Authoress Lucas Malet wrote "Persons who in the security of their island home are well bred and really quite delightful, become as awkward as chased hens in an hotel." For the railways, however, there was soon to be precedent for both tenants and self-management to be the wrong decision.

In Swindon the GWR had opened both refreshment rooms and a hotel on the station platform in 1842. Originally all they had wanted was 300 workmen's cottages for the staff at their new engine factory, but in order not to pay for the houses, they had offered the builders both the rent from the workers and a peppercorn rent of one penny ($\frac{1}{2}$p) a year for ninety-nine years for the refreshment rooms. To ensure that the refreshment rooms were well patronised, an agreement was also reached that every train would stop for ten minutes at Swindon Station. The builders then sold the lease of the refreshment rooms to the Queen's Hotel, Cheltenham, for a premium of £6,000 and a rent of £1,100 a year, and later sold the whole lease for £20,000. After that every succeeding owner tried to make the maximum profit, but it all hinged on the trains stopping and that meant that the GWR could not run any through expresses. One owner lost £10,000 in five years and another sold out with a profit of £35,000 after only twelve months, while the GWR in desperation went to court in 1875 to get at least two mail trains through Swindon with only a five minute halt. That was the limit of their success, however, and in the end they had to buy the unexpired portion of the lease for £100,000 in 1895 to get out of the whole mess.

These were the pioneering years for the railways and the hotel industry often benefited almost by accident. There was no justification, for instance, for three different railway lines to be constructed to Harrogate. "The spa was not large enough to attract early railway promoters: the country was difficult for construction and seasonal passenger traffic alone would not justify the building of a line." There were only 3,500 inhabitants in 1851 and yet in the rush to build railways during the 'mania' three came to Harrogate. The York and North Midland Line terminated opposite the Brunswick Hotel (later the Prince of Wales) in 1848, and the existing hotels could smell the beautiful aroma of massively increased business in its smoky wake. The White Hart Hotel was rebuilt in 1846, the Crown in 1847, the George in 1850 and the Brunswick in 1860. The Leeds, Sheffield and Manchester merchants had already found the delights of Harrogate, and the hotels soon attracted specific clienteles. The Crown "was the choice of the aristocratic invalid who wished to be close to the waters. In contrast the Dragon and the Granby were sacred places. The Lords only graced the latter, while the wealthy commoner pleased himself in the former."

The first really large London hotels were built after the Great Exhibition of 1851. The Great Western led the way, and in 1858 the Grosvenor and West End Railway Terminus Hotel Company was formed. Known as the Grosvenor, which came off the tongue rather more easily than the G & WERTHC, the resulting hotel adjoining Victoria Station was not easy to build. The foundations had to be sunk through a series of quicksands, mudbanks, and old peat bogs and the architect J. T. Knowle had not chosen a

The magnificence of the structure of the Grosvenor Hotel at Victoria was visible from a long way off. Still the finest example of the Renaissance period in Victorian architecture, the Grosvenor was to have many changes of fortune.

simple structure; the Grosvenor today is the best example of the French Renaissance revival with its pavilion roofs and broken skyline. It has a massive appearance with a great many architectural frills and furbelows which do not detract from the overall impression of great solidity. There are touches of Italian Renaissance as well, and on the first and top floors of the hotel, in the spandrels of the arches, portrait busts of famous Victorians of the age can still be seen. The Queen, herself, is over the front door with Albert next to her and Palmerston, Derby and Lord John Russell represented among many others. For some reason Baron von Humboldt, a 90-year-old German explorer is also there. The canopy is much later, but otherwise the hotel exterior looks very similar today to the way it did when it opened, if rather more weatherbeaten.

As a contemporary account described the new wonder, "No object in the Metropolis strikes the provincial Englishman with more astonishment than the first sight of this huge building. From the dip of Piccadilly he sees it looming in the distance, far over the head of the royal palace, as he gets nearer it seems to grow into the air; and as he debouches full upon it from some side-street, it towers up like a mountain before him— a mountain chiselled from basement to garret with clustered fruit and flowers, all wrought in enduring stone."

Within a very few years of its launching, the hotel had new management, a new chairman, and a new secretary as expenses had got out of hand, but the company made sufficient progress in the next decade to pay reasonable dividends and was one of the success stories quoted when others considered building as well. The Grosvenor was one of the first hotels to have a lift, or a 'rising room' as it was known at the time. It was a hydraulic lift powered by water and worked with a rope which had to be pulled to get the contraption off the ground, but it made the upper floors as easy to reach as the lower and that could put up the tariff for the rooms at the top of the building.

At the other end of Victoria Street near Westminster Abbey, the *Illustrated London News* reported in 1860 on the progress of the Westminster Palace Hotel. "This monster hotel is in the course of being erected at the East End of Victoria Street by a company of noblemen and gentlemen, for affording hotel accommodation to members of Parliament

Your safety in the first lifts, or rising rooms, seemed doubtful and illustrations of this nature were designed both to explain and to guarantee the safety and solidity of the machinery. Ladies in crinolines tended to take up more than their fair share of the available space.

By knocking down slums in the vicinity of Westminster Abbey the ground was cleared for the Westminster Palace Hotel, which was also convenient for the Houses of Parliament.

WESTMINSTER PALACE HOTEL.—Messrs. W. and A. Mosley, Architects.

and to gentlemen frequenting the law courts, as well as to foreigners and the public at large. To make the hotel as perfect as possible the architects were directed to inspect various continental hotels and their investigations extended to upwards of 30 of the principal ones." Paris would have been one of their stops with the enormous Grand and Louvre Hotels. The Louvre could accommodate 500 guests and the Grand only a few less. The outside of the Westminster Palace is still standing at the corner of Tothill Street but the inspections did not produce a particularly inspiring looking edifice. Instead the coffee room was 98 feet long, 30 feet wide and 18 feet high and "the internal furnishings of all the principal parts will be on a scale of magnificence more generally to be found in palaces rather than in hotels." For once the architect was filling the area as economically as was reasonable and leaving the glamour to the rooms indoors. The shareholders, the noblemen and gentlemen, had chosen a fine location near the new House of Commons and nothing better than a very unpleasant selection of slum property had to be demolished to provide the site.

The restrictions on forming public companies were eased gradually during the late 1850s, but the pioneering years needed their nobles and gentlemen shareholders; their aristocrats to build hotels as a harmless peccadillo for some surplus funds or to further their immense interests, and the railways to bring the traffic or build their hotels, for these were the lines of development for the industry in those early days. Smedley was an exception because he would probably have flourished without the railway though not to such an extent.

As the Queen went into her long mourning for her beloved Albert, dead at forty-two after over twenty years of happy marriage, Britain entered into that dazzling period where she dominated the world, and the Liberals introduced a new Companies Act which was to revolutionize British business and with it the size of the hotel industry.

The ground floor plan of the Westminster Palace Hotel shows the division of the building into two main wings. This eliminated the need for a well but the rooms on the mews must have been starved of daylight.

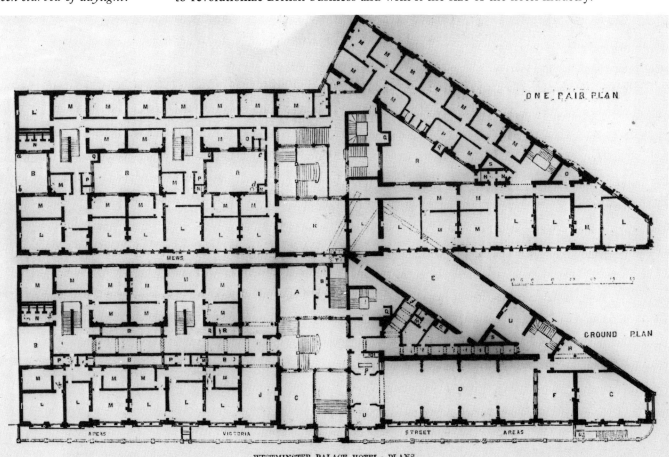

WESTMINSTER PALACE HOTEL: PLANS.

A Pause for Albert Smith— 3
the Critic

NOSTALGIA for the 'Good Old Days' is too often one of the great confidence tricks we play upon ourselves; the past is seen through rose coloured glasses, the rough edge of reality conveniently blurred in the mists of time. For a vocal section of Victorian opinion this was the way they looked at the inns of bygone centuries; a time when writers would have had you believe all English landlords waited upon their guests with unfailing concern, civility and charm compared to the disgraceful behaviour of continental inn keepers who were surly to a man, rude and uncooperative. Undoubtedly English inns did have a high reputation in the Middle Ages but the mid-Victorian dissatisfied with the existing hotels, would have found the inns of 200 years before a great deal rougher than he was led to expect and quite naturally so.

It was true that the reputation of continental hotels was growing steadily in the 19th century; this was due to the superiority of French cuisine, and the higher status of hoteliers in the European community. At the same time the development of the railways came later on the continent so that the downfall of the coaching inns in England after 1837 did not have a parallel in many countries abroad for some years.

While it is possible with hindsight to see this period as the start of a new hotel age, to the Victorians who had to put up with the hotels they had inherited until something better appeared, the choice looked grim. For five months in 1853–4 *The Times* included every day "a melancholy and monotonous array of hotel bills" as an avalanche of complaints grew out of the correspondence columns. In one period of three days more than 400 letters were received, all saying that hotel prices were too high. There was a famous jingle at the time about a small hotel near Newbury which summed up their feelings:
"The famous inn in Speenhamland
    That stands below the hill,
    May well be called the Pelican
    From its enormous bill."

The fact was that most hoteliers had lost their confidence; they would not take the risk of expensive refurbishing when they might find their business destroyed overnight by a newly constructed railway. Hoteliers who had happily put capital into booming stage-coach inns were now salting it away for a rainy day or waiting to see exactly what would happen. They could point to the unhappy condition of the hoteliers of Exeter who did wonderful business when the railway first reached their city; the passengers who wanted to travel further often had to wait for the coach and that usually meant staying at the hotels overnight. Everything seemed rosy until the line was extended to Plymouth and then to Barnstaple at which point the Exeter hotels barely managed to survive. It was not true that new hotels would automatically make money; a sizeable hotel was built at Cheltenham and proved a white elephant as did another large one at Sydenham in South London. Hoteliers had to be men of real vision to know whether they were at the nadir before eventual extinction or at the darkest point before the dawn.

The public were not concerned with the problems of the hotel keeper; the inn had been part of their landscape for so long that it was regarded more as an institution than a profit-making industry; poor inns were as much a national disgrace as scruffy seamanship or sloppy drilling by the Guards, and the public's complaints were crystalized in a little pamphlet produced in 1856 by an author and humorist named Albert Smith and entitled *The English Hotel Nuisance*. It was only twenty-eight small pages in size and yet it reverberated round the catering world for well over fifty years.

Albert had a number of complaints and a number of suggestions, the majority of which were, very surprisingly, later accepted by the hotels. Frankly there was very little that Albert actually liked about English hotels. He objected to the ambience of the average hotel, to "the chilling side-board with its formal array of glasses . . . the empty tea-caddy and imperfect backgammon board; the utter absence of anything to beguile even two minutes, beyond a local directory, a provincial journal of last Saturday, or Paterson's roads . . . in the majority of country places, the dreariness of the look-out; the clogged ink stand and stumped pens; the inability to protract a meal to six hours to get rid of the day; and above all, the anticipations of a strange bed, with curtains you cannot manage, and pillows you are not accustomed to, and sheets of unusual fabric." One suspects that Albert Smith would have welcomed a fly crawling up the wall.

It is in that mood, of course, that every little irritation gets out of proportion and he now took exception to the demand for a tip that seemed to follow the smallest service provided by the staff. The word 'tip' comes to us from the coffee houses in the city of London where merchants gathered to conduct their business. If they needed a note taken to a colleague or client, they could place it in a box provided for the purpose near the table, and then ring a bell which would attract the attention of a messenger. In the box they would place a coin as payment together with the note, and on the lid were the letters 'T.I.P.'—To Insure Promptitude. Albert Smith liked such organised arrangements and there is an impassioned plea for "all travellers, if the choice is offered, to patronize only those houses which advertise 'a fixed and moderate charge for attendance'. The practice is already extending, and as the railway scared away the tribe of

Mivarts was run by a former servant of George IV and eventually passed into the ownership of an equally well connected butler named Claridge. From such small beginnings came the great hotel which is still used by heads of state today.

hostlers, porters, coachmen, guards, postboys and other vultures, who fluttered about inn doors and yards, so we may be sure that the more we travel and insist on these changes the more rapidly will the old system blow up or decay."

As the years went by an attendance charge of about one shilling and sixpence ($7\frac{1}{2}$p) did become part of the bill, but as a later writer pointed out "the result of this change we all know. People began to pay twice for service instead of only once, as before, and consequently started that interminable growl against 'tips' which rises and falls as regularly as the tide." The extraction of tips in spite of a charge for service is still with us 120 years later, but at least the new hotels did try to do more to entertain their customers and fill those long hours of frequently rain swept day.

Albert Smith also objected strongly to the compulsory charge for wax candles which was invariably a stiff one shilling and sixpence ($7\frac{1}{2}$p), for "we are content with Price or Palmer or a moderator lamp, or gas." Until electricity it was common practice in hotels to have to guide the guest to his room at night by the light of a candle and to use candles for illumination in the rooms. Gas was available, but expensive and to the uninitiated potentially dangerous. Too many people at first blew out the lamp without turning off the gas and a number went out like the light. Most hotels preferred to charge for candles, and to play safe and cheap for as long as possible.

There was one case many years later in Switzerland when a guest decided that as he felt he had paid for the candles, he would pack them in his luggage when he left. The hotel keeper sued him for the return of the stumps, insisting that the guest had paid for light and not for candles, and the court found for the hotelier. But there seems to have been no British case of a similar nature.

In the better hotels it became the practice to include the cost of the candles in the charge for accommodation, though not until very late in the century was this a standard practice, as the poorer hotels took the opportunity to fatten their bills with this item among others; in 1884 for instance, the Waverley Temperance Hotels in Liverpool, Glasgow, and Edinburgh still charged one penny ($\frac{1}{2}$p) a night for them.

The condition of the stagecoach inns brought particular condemnation from Albert because of their outworn practices and shabby furnishings. "The rooms . . . have old forgotten names painted on them—The Chatham, the Portobello, the Ranelagh. The

At the Royal Pavilion, Brighton, in 1818, Carême would prepare anything up to 100 different dishes for the parties given by George IV.

The Yarborough was named after the local landowner whose other claim to fame is that he once held a hand at bridge without a single picture card, and named it a "Yarborough".

passages are dark and intricate, and on different levels, with obtrusive sills every now and then to trip you up; and the grand characteristics of the bedchambers are bad soap and four-post bedsteads, and inconvenient three-cornered washstands."

Four posters were particularly unfortunate because of their size. Originally they had been considered a luxury as the drapes which hung around the sides kept out the draughts at night. There was privacy in a four-poster, outside noises were muffled, and you were not awakened by the light in the summer streaming in at an early hour. Well kept up, the four-poster had all this to recommend it, but when neglected the drapes faded and gathered dust and the bed dominated the room. If the room was small, the other furnishings would so constrict the open space available that the guest would have to find somewhere else to use as a sitting room. There had to be a chest of drawers for the clothes when unpacked, a washhand stand for the jug of water, and a portmanteau stool to pile the luggage upon. Two chairs in the room took up space as well, and the bedchamber was therefore strictly an area for sleeping. "How great the contrast here presented to any foreign hotel you please to remember, with its airy comfortable simple bed—its half sitting-room bed-chamber, with tables, chairs, bright chimney ornaments, and convenient escritoire."

As Albert Smith had asked, the four-poster disappeared during the century and bedrooms became more like sitting rooms and this in its turn led to the vogue for the studio-type bedroom in our own time.

The variety of food in the hotels was limited too and Albert pleaded for "Something beyond 'Chop, sir, steak, boiled fowl'" to find its way onto the menu. Sure enough a wider selection did follow.

The English Hotel Nuisance became celebrated because it combined intelligent recommendations for improvements with a light though caustic touch. Few complaints about inattentive staff, for example, come home as well as Albert's meeting with the waiter in the coffee room. "I arrive in the coffee room about ten minutes before my time. A superb waiter—A Jeames in mufti—was reading *The Globe*; he scarcely raised his eyes as I entered, so I sat down, in awe and trembling, by the fire. No body was punctual that day, and when he had quite finished, in about a quarter of an hour, he brought the journal towards me—said 'evening paper' in the same tone that he croaked 'sherry' in my ear, at a later period; and then placing it on the table, walked away with the proud consciousness of having done a charitable action."

To his complaints about hotels one addition was made about the customs of the day, a plea for "the recognition of the presence of ladies in the coffee room, as in the *salle à manger*." The humour of all-male gatherings had palled on Albert after too many evenings of enforced attendance at such functions, and he felt that the presence of ladies would brighten up the surroundings as well as the conversation. He also objected to the fact that if a lady was not admitted, there was no alternative for her husband but to hire a private room in which to eat at considerable additional expense.

A few high-class hotels did introduce coffee rooms in succeeding years where families could sit and dine, and menus did improve considerably, though choice did not necessarily have anything to do with quality. The cost of hotel services had always been very difficult to ascertain before a guest received his final bill—which was another practice to which Albert took exception. This was eventually clarified by the production of printed hotel tariffs at which point the guest was reassured and prepared to stay longer. Until tariffs were printed, long-term visitors would usually only stay at hotels until they found suitable lodgings, and permanent residents were extremely unusual.

While the abuses and shortcomings continue in some areas to the present day *The English Hotel Nuisance* proved to be a remarkably effective piece of propaganda for hotel guests.

All aboard the band wagon—1862–1880

4

EIGHTEEN HUNDRED AND SIXTY-TWO was the year of the International Exhibition at Brompton in London, which was a little bigger than the Great Exhibition of 1851, but which has failed to live in our memories as vividly as the Crystal Palace and Prince Albert's patronage of the great spectacle in Hyde Park. Again, well over six million visitors poured into the capital, and again Thomas Cook worked day and night to transport his excursionists and look after their comfort. But this time Cook was offering a new idea; not just to take a day trip to London, but actually to stay in the capital overnight. There were to be two classes of accommodation and nothing illustrates more clearly the continuing lack of hotels in London than the fact that neither type involved a hotel. For the richer people Cook arranged lodgings in private homes while the artisans were housed in brand new blocks of flats, the Peabody Buildings.

Some rather harsh things have been said about Peabody Buildings in the 20th century but it is unfair to judge by the standards of later generations. In their time Peabody Buildings were a commendable effort to reduce the number of people living in London in dreadful slum conditions, and George Peabody sits in his large Victorian chair near the Bank of England looking as righteous as every statue to a Victorian humanitarian should. The flats that Cook used had just been completed and he took them for the Exhibition season.

Such hotels as London possessed had another field day and it was the last particle of encouragement the investors needed, for the Liberal government had that spring announced a new Companies Act which was to make limited liability companies much less difficult to float. For the next three years the number of new issues averaged a colossal £120 million annually. The country's wealth had increased dramatically because of its industrial lead over Europe which in turn was based on its manufacturing industries and huge Empire, and there was plenty of money to invest. Always a nation of punters, the British supported all kind of flotations, and a number of hotel companies were among them.

One of the fastest off the mark, and a hotel which had a famous name until it was bombed out of action in the Second World War, was the Langham. The building still stands at the top of Portland Place, which was the widest London street in its day and had been started by the Adam brothers in 1774. A large mansion called Mansfield House was demolished and the new hotel was constructed on the site of the house and its adjoining gardens. By any standards it was a major undertaking and the prospectus which was issued in June 1862 was for £150,000 in £10 shares. The Earl of Shrewsbury was the president of the company, and Lord Bury vice-president. Both men were in advance of their time for the aristocracy did not usually accept office in commercial ventures which could be described as 'trade'. It took three years from the prospectus to the open-

During the period of the Brompton Exhibition in 1862, Thomas Cook took blocks of Peabody Buildings like this to accommodate visitors.

Overleaf:
The Langham in Portland Place was an immense investment when it is remembered that no railway company was involved. Today it is a staff annexe of the BBC.

39

ing, and this is not surprising in view of the size of the hotel. It was half as big again as the Grosvenor at Victoria and could accommodate 500 guests. There were ten floors from the labyrinthine basements to the roof, and the directors took the precaution of sinking an artesian well so that the guests could have their own water supply. Cholera could break out in epidemic proportions at this time, and tens of thousands of Londoners died from it in the 1860s, even though the connection between the disease and water borne sewage had been discovered in 1854 by Dr. Snow. So although this was the first well under a London hotel, it was an eminently justifiable expense.

As the months went by, the original estimates could not be sustained and the company had to ask for a further £30,000. To obtain it, the investors were offered a preferential dividend of a handsome eight per cent on the new capital and even then there were protests from the existing shareholders. At a meeting held in November 1864 when the opening was still many months away, there was a call for a shareholders' committee to investigate the accounts, and it was only after a long discussion that the proposal was dropped. To investigate the accounts of a company headed by an Earl of the Realm was an extreme step for any shareholder to propose and it indicates the lack of confidence in the successful outcome of the venture which was echoed in many comment columns.

At last on June 10th 1865 the doors were opened and from noon till seven in the evening 2,000 visitors headed by the Prince of Wales inspected the new wonder. *The Times* reported with impeccable fairness that the hotel was smaller than the St. Nicholas in New York or the United States Hotel in Saratoga, but it found the Langham superior in decoration, planning and comfort. Taking the optimistic view, the correspondent remarked that new hotels had "when well conducted, proved as remunerative as successful mines" and complained that up to 1860 the available hotel accommodation had provided "at the best the comfort of a public house at the expense of a palace."

The language seems rather extreme and generalised for a newspaper of *The Times'* reputation but there was no doubting the writer's enthusiasm. He was enchanted by the hydraulic lift "which is little less than a well furnished room" and found the plumbing wholly exceptional. "Apart from the great saloons set aside for balls, wedding breakfasts etc. there are no less than three main dining rooms, fourteen lavatories and nearly 300 water closets." The significance of the last improvement can be seen from the advertisement of the Exeter Hotel in the Strand in 1856 announcing that there was a water closet on each floor!

There were three basements at the Langham where you could get lost among the bakehouses, laundries and packing offices. The 'servants' hall' could seat 260 and the kitchens were so large that fifty joints could easily be roasted at the same time. The ovens would hold between 1,000 and 2,000 plates and some years later communications were improved in the kitchens by installing a "quaint little tramway, which runs from one end to the other, with basket cars, that look quite unique when laden with dishes destined to be sent up to table." When the hotel was finally well established there was between two and three tons of meat maturing in the stores, 210,000 eggs to buy a year, and twenty-five women were needed to operate the laundry. Yet for all this expenditure, the beds on the upper floors fetched as little as one shilling and sixpence ($7\frac{1}{2}$p) a night.

The hotel was advertised as being ninety-five feet above the Thames high water mark, on a gravel soil in the healthiest part of London, presumably in contradistinction to the peat bogs of Belgravia. As you entered the Langham, you passed into a hall fifty feet square and "close at hand is a Trufitt's tonsorial establishment, then a newspaper and current literature stand, an office for railway tickets, then a ladies' drawing room prettily furnished, with a piano, elegant writing tables, shaded lamps, with flowers in vases dotted prettily about." The corridors in the hotel had gleaming white tile walls from floor to ceiling and £50,000 had been spent on furnishing the building. There were only 116 staff at the beginning, but as the hotel prospered, this number rose to 250.

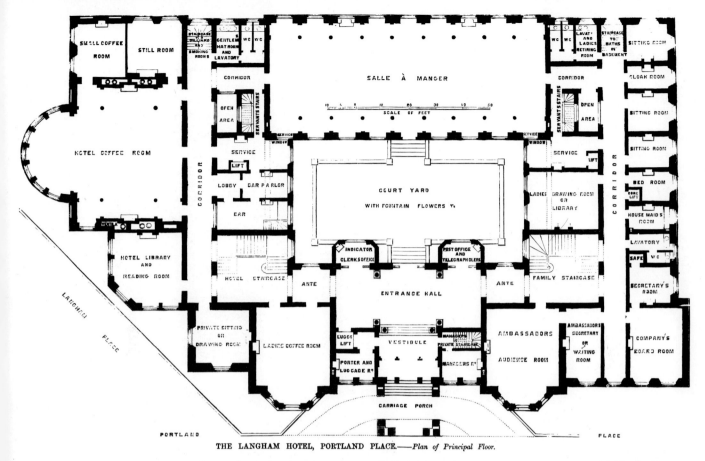

Image labels (from floor plan):

SMALL COFFEE ROOM · STILL ROOM · STAIRCASE TO BILLIARD AND SMOKING ROOMS · GENTLEMEN'S HAT ROOM AND LAVATORY · WC WC · WC WC · LAVATORY AND LADIES RETIRING ROOM · STAIRCASE TO BATHS IN BASEMENT · SITTING ROOM

HOTEL COFFEE ROOM · CORRIDOR · SALLE À MANGER · CORRIDOR · CLOAK ROOM

OPEN AREA · SERVANTS STAIRS · SERVICE WINDOW · SCALE OF FEET · SERVICE WINDOW · SERVANTS STAIRS · OPEN AREA · SITTING ROOM

SERVICE · SERVICE · SITTING ROOM

LIFT · COURT YARD WITH FOUNTAIN FLOWERS &c. · LIFT · BED ROOM

LOBBY · BAR PARLOR · LADIES DRAWING ROOM OR LIBRARY · BED LIFT · HOUSE MAIDS ROOM

BAR · LAVATORY

HOTEL LIBRARY AND READING ROOM · INDICATOR · CLERKS OFFICE · POST OFFICE AND TELEGRAPH CLERKS · SAFE · WC

HOTEL STAIRCASE · ANTE · ENTRANCE HALL · ANTE · FAMILY STAIRCASE · SECRETARY'S ROOM

PRIVATE SITTING OR DRAWING ROOM · LADIES COFFEE ROOM · LUGGAGE LIFT · VESTIBULE · MANAGERS PRIVATE STAIRCASE · AMBASSADORS AUDIENCE ROOM · AMBASSADORS SECRETARY OR WAITING ROOM · COMPANY'S BOARD ROOM

PORTER AND LUGGAGE R° · MANAGERS R° · LARCHER PLACE · PORTLAND · CARRIAGE PORCH · PLACE

THE LANGHAM HOTEL, PORTLAND PLACE.——*Plan of Principal Floor.*

The original manager was a Mr. Schumann but he was succeeded by an American, Mr. Sanderson, who had built up a considerable reputation in the United States. This was the beginning of that close association between the Langham and its American clientele which was to be its reputation until it closed. In its size, the Langham reminded Americans of similar hotels in their own country, and an American manager must have been a reassuring sight. As they all sat together round the large restaurant tables or took their ease in the hotel courtyard where the band played between six and eight-thirty in the summer evenings, it was the epitome of European civilization. As the band cost £1,200 a year, such an impression was dearly achieved.

This influx from the New World was to grow in importance, particularly when the end of the American Civil War enabled the United States to devote its attention to overseas trade rather than internal problems. Americans came on business as their exports, and in particular their cheap food grew in demand. They came also as tourists visiting a continent whose elegance and sophistication contrasted with their rather simpler ways and with the countries from which they or their parents had often sprung. Yet while American dress or theatre, society or cuisine might be less fashionable, their standards of hygiene and their expectations of technical efficiency were often in advance of their European contemporaries. When they came, they were likely to stay for a considerable time and the hotel which proved popular with them had a useful buffer against the harmful effects that an economic slump could have on the home market.

Once the Companies Act was passed—and indeed a few flotations like the Brighton Hotel Company (1859) and the Westminster Palace (1857) had taken place as soon as conditions were made less stringent—the Bristol City Company was launched in 1863 and the Bristol College Green Company in 1864, in the same year as the Adelphi in Liverpool, and the Great Western Hotel in Birmingham were floated. The Gresham Hotel, Dublin, was registered in 1865 and companies to build new hotels like the Alexandra Hotel in London were launched as fast as the prospectuses could be run off at the printers.

Every conceivable facility was planned for the Langham down to an Ambassador's audience room and at least two libraries. A band played in the courtyard. Tourists flocked to the hotel from all over the world.

43

A typical example, and one where fortunately the early records are more complete than most, was the Grand Pump Room Hotel Company of Bath. Originally the hotel was a small one, though very gracious and built adjoining the baths themselves. Bath had always been short of hotels during the season, and as Jerom Murch, the first chairman, told his shareholders in 1867 "What can be thought of more likely to restore Bath to the position it once held . . . " By comparison with the Langham, for example, the money involved seemed quite modest; a total investment of £20,000 and Mr. Murch made full

THE GRAND PUMP ROO[M]

Dr.   FOR THE YEAR [

CAPI[TAL]

To Cost of Land, Compensation to Tenants of Property and Legal Charges, as per last statement ...		....	£6,193 3
,, Cost of Building, including Architects and Surveyors, as per last statement	£15,856 12 8		
,, Paid since	1,653 3 11		
			17,509 16
,, Cost of Furniture, Plate, Linen and China, as per last statement	4,933 14 7		
,, Paid since	1,346 8 7		
			6,280 3
,, Interest paid to Shareholders, as per last statement ..	1,171 1 1		
,, Paid since	163 1 8		
			1,334 2
			£31,317 6
,, To Balance		....	£1,297 6

REVE[NUE]

To Cost of Wines, Spirits, and Provisions	....	....	....	£3,667	18
,, Ground-rent, Rates, Taxes, and Insurances	....	....	....	206	19
,, Stationery and Printing	....	....	....	116	0
,, Advertising	....	....	....	185	13
,, Coal and Gas	....	....	..	290	1
,, Salaries and Wages ...	....	....	....	895	13
,, General Charges	....	....	....	56	19
,, Carriage Hire	....	....	...	316	2
,, Washing	....	..	....	227	4
,, Interest on Mortgages	....	....	....	508	5
,, Repairs, alterations, &c.	....	....	...	94	15
,, Directors' Fees	..	....	....	200	0
,, Balance... ...	....	....	....	1,652	17
				£8,418	1
To Estimated Liabilities	...	....	....	£155	0

SUS[PENSE]

To Law Expenses in the action brought by Verrall against the Company £589 4

We hereby certify that we have

use of his highly reputable board, which included the Mayor of Bath, to advance the undertaking. The initial estimate had to be raised to £25,000 because "it had been ascertained that the total cost of the Building—including lifts, grates, chimney pieces, papering and Architect's commission—cannot be less than £13,000. This with £6,000 for the site, £4,000 for furniture, and £1,000 for extras, would require a capital of £24,000." The shareholders weren't quite so sure of the success of the venture by this time, and only stumped up another £1,000 towards the extra £5,000 needed, but the directors pressed on and opened the hotel two-and-a-half years after the original decision to form a company.

TEL COMPANY OF BATH,

D.

MARCH 25, 1871.   Cr.

UNT.

By 1907 Shares paid up in full	...	.... £19,070	0	0		
,, 18 ,, ,, part	....	.. 34	0	0		
,, 46 ,, forfeited	....	... 66	0	0		
					£19,170	0	0
,, Mortgages	..	....	....	...	10,850	0	0
,, Balance	..,	....	....	....	1,297	6	3
					£31,317	6	3

OUNT.

By Balance from last account	....		£715	4	10		
o dividend, paid to 25th March, 1870	....	£376 12 0					
, Directors' Fees, and Secretary	....	170 0 0					
			546	12	0		
					£168	12	10
By Gross Receipts	....	....				7,973	13	8
, Interest received on overdue calls	....	....				7	11	6
, Amount due from Visitors	....	... 107 14 9					
Less ,, ,, as per last account	....	83 15 5					
					23	19	4
, Stock of Wines, Spirits, and Provisions ...	....	866 2 11					
Less ,, ,, &c., as per last account	....	641 8 7					
					224	11	4
, Petty Cash in Manager's hands	....	....				20	0	0
					£8,418	11	8
By Balance	....	....	....	....	£1,652	17	7

OUNT.

ove Accounts with the Vouchers, and found them correct, 25th April, 1871.

JAMES BOURN, *Secretary*

J. QUIN, } *Auditors.*

Within 18 months of opening the Grand Pump Room Hotel in Bath, the directors were able to show a perfectly satisfactory profit on investment, but not the result of Mr. Verrell's law action.

At the initial meeting after the hotel was opened, the directors presented the accounts for the first nine months' trading and on a capital which had by then reached just over £29,000 the turnover was £4,408 which produced a profit of £715; £450 was then paid out as a dividend and a further £150 as director's fees. The idea of putting money away for a rainy day in any quantity was quite foreign to the early Victorian hotel companies. The investors took the attitude that they invested their money in order to get a decent return, and if profits were made, they expected to have the vast majority paid out straight away to the shareholders. It will be necessary to examine the effect of this in some detail at a later stage.

The Diamond Jubilee of Queen Victoria saw patriotic displays produced all over the country. The Grand Pump Room Hotel, Bath, was not going to be left behind.

For the first full year, which covered the period from March 1870 to March 1871, the turnover exceeded £7,500 at Bath and a profit of £1,652 was made. This represents a twenty per cent profit before tax and there wasn't much tax! As income tax was well under one shilling in the pound, the dividends were practically tax free as well, so that a company's profits could benefit the shareholders almost without deduction.

It had cost nearly £6,000 to run the hotel during the year and of this only £895 was paid out in salaries and wages. The percentage of wages to turnover was therefore about eleven per cent which would compare today to a figure of well over 20 per cent. The staff were not paid well, though the directors pocketed £200 for their trouble. The cost of wines, spirits and food was over £3,600, almost all of which was used during the year and therefore would account for well over half the turnover. Even so "not only are more and better rooms constantly required, but the working of the Hotel is less profitable in various ways than it might be". So said Mr. Murch as he endeavoured to raise still more money for an extension.

One of the items which do not appear today is the cost of carriage hire for the guests' enjoyment and to bring the visitors from the railway station; carriages cost £316 in all. A considerable proportion of that sum would have been recovered, however, as visitors would also hire the carriages in the same way as taxis or sightseeing buses might be used now. Washing for the hotel came to £227, but repairs and alterations were a minimal £95. Coal and gas were nearly £300 and nearly £200 was spent on advertising. The promotional cost is quite similar to the percentage approved nowadays by major British chain operations, but far in excess of the figure the average hotel would accept.

The directors' fees would appear very high now by comparison with both turnover and profit, but substantial bonuses for successful operations was the Victorian method of achieving the desired results.

Only one thundercloud had marred the sunshine of that first full year for the Grand Pump Room and this was the occasion when a visitor had reported that money had been stolen from his room. Although the hotel protested that he had been negligent in leaving a very large sum unattended, the case went to court and the hotel lost. The damages including costs were nearly £600, over a third of the profits for the entire year. Although we shall look at hotel law separately, in brief a hotel was classed as an inn under various Inn Keepers Acts and there was extensive liability for damages as this case indicates. To make matters worse, the judges differed in cases up and down the country so that the criteria for negligence did not have at this time nationally accepted precedents.

At the same time that the Grand Pump Room directors were wondering how to raise their £20,000, the directors of the Midland Railway Company were considering a far greater project, the construction of an enormous hotel at their London terminus, St. Pancras.

The railway hotels had continued to proliferate; the Charing Cross Hotel had been designed by E. M. Barry for the South Eastern Railway at its West End terminus and opened in May 1865. It was one of the first buildings in London to use extensively white glazed terracotta as a cladding material. The hotel was an achievement which gave Barry, who also designed the Royal Opera House, great pleasure with its mixture of Renaissance motifs and the same roof construction as graced the Louvre in Paris. The *Illustrated London News* pointed out that "the rising room is fitted with seats if visitors are indisposed to use the staircases" and noted with wonder that on the opening day it was "more than half occupied by the evening." Barry used the artificial stone again when he designed the Cannon Street Hotel for the S.E.R.s City terminus and the hotel was even more embellished, but neither could compare with Sir George Gilbert Scott's Midland Grand Hotel at St. Pancras.

Scott was a great architect, but a controversial one. He was an enthusiast, a devotee, even a fanatic for Gothic design and he was very fashionable. The directors of the Midland Railway had decided to hold a competition among architects for the prize of building the hotel, and eleven architects entered including Scott and Barry. While the winner would get his usual fees, there would also be three consolation prizes of £200, £100 and £50. The directors had specified the maximum number of floors they wanted and the maximum they wished to spend, but Scott gave them a design which added another two floors and an extra £50,000 to the cost. As you would expect, the result was a more imposing design and the directors couldn't resist it even though their decision

The architect responsible for the Midland Grand was Sir George Gilbert Scott who once said that his design was too good for the building.

One of the great Victorian architects was E. M. Barry who designed the Charing Cross Hotel

To survive in the rat race of railway competition, Sir James Allport believed it was necessary to give the passengers even better quality. That meant, among many other things, providing them with good hotels.

made nonsense of the competition, while the architect who came second complained bitterly and justifiably that Scott hadn't kept to the rules. Scott said later, with his usual modesty, that he thought his design was "possibly too good for the purpose it is to serve", but initially he set to work with enthusiasm to create what one modern writer has described as "to its admirers a place that restores romance to travel, to its detractors a wildly inappropriate Victorian extravagance."

That the building was extravagant can hardly be denied; high up on the facade, to take only one small example, Scott wanted carved figures; not just busts like Knowles at the Grosvenor, but full length statues which would have cost £100 each and could hardly have been seen. The Midland directors settled down to some sizeable rows with their architect. Yet they had deliberately agreed to a mammoth set-piece of a hotel, not only because Sir James Allport, their general manager, was determined to improve the amenities for passengers on the line, but also because "if the provincial Midland Company was to set up for itself in the capital, it must do so on the grand scale."

Nothing in Victorian commerce lent itself to the 'grand scale' as much as hotel design. The government of the day could put up their own splendid buildings, and the town councils could erect solid and substantial town halls, but hotels could be more impressive than either. To see a new hotel dominating the skyline and dwarfing the houses in its vicinity was far more imposing in Victorian times, as we have seen, than in our own days of tower blocks and skyscrapers. As the *Quarterly Review* said of the completed Midland Grand in 1872 "the building inside and out is covered with ornament, and there is polished marble enough to furnish a cathedral. The very parapet of the cab road is panelled and perforated, at a cost that would have supplied foot-warmers to all the trains for years to come".

Such exotica did not lack for critics and it was suggested that "to be consistent the directors should not confine their expression of artistic feeling to these great buildings alone. Their porters might be dressed as javelin men, their guards as beefeaters and their stationmasters don the picturesque attire of Garter-king-at-arms."

It is very hard to know whether to condemn the extravagance or cheer the courage of the men who created the Midland Grand. It was conceived at a most difficult time for the railways; the London, Chatham, and Dover Railway went bankrupt in 1866 and the Great Eastern in 1867. Investors were shaken when one of the biggest city discount houses, Overend and Gurney, closed its doors in 1866, a number of major railway contractors like Peto failed as well, and bank rate soared to ten per cent for three months. With the worst outbreak of cholera in London since 1854, the approval of a budget for the hotel of over £300,000 was as much a vote of confidence in the future as anything else. It must have influenced the Midland directors that their hotel would overshadow the neighbouring and competing hotels at Euston and King's Cross but even within the company there was opposition, for Edward Baines, M.P. was the chairman of the Shareholders Consultative Committee and against the hotel project, if for no other reason than because he was a prominent teetotaller.

The extra items of expense were certainly not confined to the outside fabric of the Midland Grand. Ten pianos were needed for the best sitting rooms, ranging from a grand piano in the finest suite to a cottage piano in the least expensive, but all in walnut cases. In the best suites the clocks cost the company £25 but in the poorer bedrooms only £8. The final cost of the Midland Grand was in the region of £450,000, but dinner, bed and breakfast was only fourteen shillings (70p) and there was accommodation for about 400 guests, though this figure included servants of the guests for whom the tariff would be lower. To bring costs to approximately modern levels, figures should be multiplied by somewhere between fifteen and twenty and this makes the Midland Grand a luxury hotel with a tariff to match, but expensively constructed. The passenger lifts, which could hold ten people, cost £710 each while the luggage lifts could carry eight hundredweight and cost £340.

One of Sir Gilbert Scott's original sketches for the great Gothic tower which flanked the Midland Grand at St. Pancras. The building is now the headquarters of British Transport Hotels.

To get some idea of just how massive the whole construction was, there is the statement of Lord Stamp, the chairman, in 1939, who said "it is impossible to put in a new piece of heating apparatus or anything of that kind without meeting with the same obstacles that would be encountered in modifying the Rock of Gibraltar." Yet even after the hotel was finally opened in 1873 there was still expense. The horses trotting over the cobblestones outside the building disturbed the guests and an arrangement had to be made with the local council to allow the Midland Grand to pay for the street to be covered with sound absorbing rubberised material.

The Manchester, Sheffield and Lincolnshire Railway had such terrible financial difficulties that it became known as the Money Sunk and Lost. In 1862, however, it helped raise the finance for the Sheffield Victoria Hotel.

Could such a hotel pay a fair return on capital? Although the Midland directors had remarked on the Grosvernor's eight per cent dividend to justify their decision to go ahead in the first place, they refused to divulge any of their own profit figures for many years after the Midland Grand opened. The excuse was that it might give useful information to their competitors, and although in the accounts they would use phrases like "a very handsome net revenue" (1878) a later chairman declared his own position categorically when he said in 1889 that he was not prepared to disclose any details of

the workings or management of the hotels other than to say that they made a profit. In 1895 the board relented and did announce that the hotels as a whole gave a return of five-and-a-quarter per cent on the capital invested, but they would go no further.

Outside London the provincial cities often possessed at least one new large hotel, so that Peterborough had its Great Northern, Hull its Royal Station, and York and Derby also had their railway hotels. In launching the project the individual efforts of local businessmen were more important than the sheer size of the town, as can be seen from the construction of the Victoria Hotel, Sheffield. The Tontine Hotel had been the most famous in Sheffield before the coming of the railway, but this had disappeared as the town had altered and grown, and it had not been replaced. The time came, however, when the Mayor of Sheffield was also the chairman of the directors of the Manchester, Sheffield and Lincolnshire Railway, a line which got into such financial difficulties eventually that it became known from its initials as the 'Money Sunk and Lost', and when combined with other railways into the Great Central as the 'Gone Completely'. During his term of office the Mayor was asked for his support for the construction of a hotel on part of the station site, and he was fortunately able to decide that his duty as Mayor and his duty as chairman of the railway's board were absolutely compatible. There had been previous sites suggested for a new hotel, but negotiations had always broken down over the price the landowners wanted for the ground, so that the station land was apparently a good offer.

There was, however, a good deal of opposition from the townsfolk, firstly because the situation was in a poor part of the town, and secondly because there were a number of small local hotel proprietors who did not want more competition. The promoters therefore appealed to the local Lord of the Manor who was the Duke of Norfolk, and His Grace announced that while he would not speculate by investing in the project, he would be 'honoured' if they would accept his donation of £1,000 and let him know if he could be of any further service!

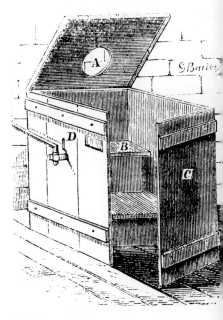

Baths at Hydropathic Institutes were not always designed for total immersion. This one was for the lower half of the body.

It was the sort of gesture which illuminates not only how the aristocracy retained their position as men of enormous influence, but also the gulf which existed between the few rich and the numerous poor; how many people could afford to make a grand gesture of the modern equivalent of £15,000 without even bothering to collect any dividends which might come due? After the Duke had donated, the majority of the money for the hotel was forthcoming, but it was still necessary to find someone with the necessary knowledge and capital to run the Victoria, and from a number of applicants the directors selected Mr. George Mayer. Mr. Mayer was not a Sheffield man but he brought with him "a large capital to the Victoria Hotel in order to fit it up in the first style of convenience."

At the opening banquet in the summer of 1862 one of the Sheffield aldermen agreed that Sheffield had needed a good hotel, but he suggested that they also needed a good town hall, a good main thoroughfare and a more complete system of drainage; so much for priorities and town planning. Mr. Mayer was obviously more of a shareholder in the enterprise than a tenant, and after his death the hotel continued in his family for a few years until arrangements were made for the railway management to take it over.

Many provincial cities had to wait until the late 1870s for their first 'grand' hotel, but a combination of the Companies Act and John Smedley's success with the pilgrims to Matlock made the development of the hydropathic institutes much more rapid. Smedley, himself, continued to be highly successful and became a very well known figure. On a hill outside the town he built himself one of those grotesque Victorian mansions which look like Ruritanian castles and are constructed, it appears, to enable the owner to resist a formidable siege. He called it Riber Castle, 850 feet above the sea and like the west wing of the hydro, it was battlemented "in accordance with Smedley's romantic notion of mediaeval splendour." Success never altered Smedley's non-conformist outlook, and he continued to preach regularly in All Saints Church, which sadly was used after his death as the engine house for the hydro, just as Riber Castle eventually became a zoo in the 20th century. Smedley also kept well within the bounds

51

of Victorian propriety at all times, providing for example "a shower bath for administering baptism to adults with proper decency" and when he died in 1874 the craze for hydros was in full swing.

Among the earliest imitators was the Rev. Shore whose chronic rheumatism was cured at Smedley's hydro and who, perhaps a trifle ungratefully, thereupon started his own in Matlock, as did a number of other people. The competition must have been fierce, however, for in 1866 Rev. Shore moved to Buxton and started a hydro there. He died in an accident soon after, but his heir, H. R. P. Lomas, built the business up well. Within twenty years there was accommodation for 200 guests and in the peak season of August and September the hydro would be completely full.

As Smedley had emphasised the importance of exercise and relaxation, the more secluded parts of the country seemed to many entrepreneurs to be particularly suited to the construction of hydros and in Scotland they started to mushroom. The hydro at Pitlochry cost £93,000, Callander £54,000 and Craiglockhart £60,000. There were hydros at the Bridge of Allan, Dunblane, Melrose, and Crieff. In the south of England at New Barnet, Torquay, Upper Norwood and on the Isle of Wight. With Scarborough, Ilkley Wells and Hexham among others in the north, an immense amount of money was poured in, but it was over-production on a vast scale.

Mrs. Baker Eddy, the founder of the Christian Science Movement, was obviously quite sincere when she said that the cure for cancer included a sip of pure water every half hour, but the sufferers still died. The famous Scottish doctor Jonah Horner insisted that patients in asylums should not have the water cure withheld from them, but it would have had little effect on their mental state. What is more there were only a limited number of patients who would suffer the rigours of the "medical head who used to keep patients in order like children and soldiers."

For a time a number of the hydros did make reasonable profits, but as a means of combating competition, many tried eventually to attract holidaymakers rather than just the unfortunate sick, and then it was said "the hydro is a high class hotel-*pension*, generally situated in some quiet, breezy place, surrounded by lovely scenery, which tempts the inmates to take solitary walks on hillsides and down valleys in pure air." Not only were they catering for invalids and people who needed a rest but they also tried to provide much more entertainment. While the Athol Hydro in Pitlochry was considered to have gone too far when it applied for a licence to sell drinks, the Callander Hydro offered its visitors fishing on Loch Vennacher, and the Coombe House Hydro at Kingston Hill staged out-of-doors theatrical performances. The Scottish hydros at Christmas would have fancy dress balls, reading and concerts, and there would be plenty of skating and curling. Lomas at Buxton staged informal dances, music in the drawing room, billiards and *tableaux vivants*. There were also concerts and theatrical performances in the hotel's 'recreation hall' and a little of the 'marriage market' crept in.

No matter how hard they tried, however, the hydros could not survive the glut of competition and they held an untenable position halfway between nursing home and hotel. Even as late as 1886 it was reported that "The Edinburgh Exhibition has taken away visitors from the Scottish Hydros." Yet while the holidaymakers preferred the exhibition "it appears that large numbers of tourists still believe that by staying at Hydropaths, they will have to submit themselves to a system of treatment." This was very often so in England, but had declined in Scotland, so that the hydro world had many heads but no instantly recognisable face.

Profits started to decline or disappear and a little price cutting appeared even on the published tariff. At the Bridge of Allan Hydro at Ochil Park there was a seven shilling (35p) a week reduction for the clergy, and a five per cent reduction if your bill was over £10. In many instances it was to no avail; the £60,000 Craiglockart was offered for sale by the Receiver at £28,300. Callander, from an initial cost of £54,000, failed to achieve its reserve at auction of £30,000, was offered again at £22,500 and was finally sold after

Facing page:
The brochure for Smedley's Hydropathic Establishment contained artist's impressions of its many attractions. Notice the head of the founder in the illustration top right. This is part of a stained glass window erected in his memory which can be seen in the illustration at the top left.

SMEDLEYS HYDROPATHIC
ESTABLISHMENT

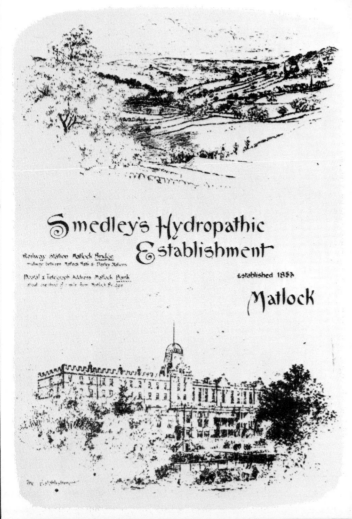

Smedley's Hydropathic
Establishment

Railway Station Matlock Bridge
midway between Matlock Bath & Darley Dales

Postal & Telegraph Address Matlock Bank
about one third of a mile from Matlock Bridge

Established 1853

Matlock

another four months on the market for £12,000. The gloomy news constantly re-occurred that "still another of the Scottish Hydros is in financial difficulties . . . having succumbed to what appears to be almost the universal fate." Dunblane, near Edinburgh, closed. The Mont Dore at Bournemouth, whose foundation stone was laid by the King of Sweden, and which was supposed to be the last word in hydros never made a profit and collapsed quickly.

The 1880s saw the bankruptcy of many hydros and at the same time more new ones being built or extended as the lesson failed to sink in. In Harrogate in 1884 a prospectus for a new hydro advised investors that "Experience shows that modern hotels combined with Hydropathic establishments, well placed, well built, and well conducted pay a very high rate of interest on the sums invested in them. The Queen's Hotel which immediately faces the proposed Lancaster Park Hotel pays ten per cent on the purchase of £58,000. The Swan Hydropathic is paying large dividends, and Smedley's last year showed a profit of upwards of twenty per cent and the undertakings in Southport, Tunbridge Wells and other places are also paying well . . . besides as more than ninety hotels in Harrogate are always full during the season and yield notoriously handsome profits, and as visitors increase in number every year, there is ample room for others without in the slightest degree militating against the existing ones."

Strangely enough, the authors of the prospectus did not feel the events at Craiglockart or Callander would be of interest to the prospective investor!

In 1891 it was the turn of the Scarborough Hydro, this time to be extended at a cost of a further £25,000 which provided another 120 bedrooms, a grand floral hall, and many other public rooms. But at Scarborough the establishment was at least under the care of Professor Wells, just as Dr. Gully and Dr. Wilson had made Malvern a Mecca for the sick without the trimmings of a gay social life. As some of the hydros failed to stay the pace, practical hoteliers moved in to pick up bargains, like Mr. MacDonald who got the Athol Hydro for £25,000.

Where the medical attention at the hydros meant something, they survived much better, particularly as more was being learnt all the time about the methods of treatment which were most effective. The massage could be very helpful, and inventors came up with a new type of bath almost as regularly as the annual Paris fashions. At the Imperial Hydro in Blackpool in 1885, there were ten different varieties: Turkish, Russian, Sitz, needle, spray, rain, plunge, warm, cold or sea water. The hydros were a world where there was room for the genuine healer and the quack, the professional and the amateur, but like a casino, the majority of the players lost.

Down at the seaside the twinkling star of fashion which was leaving the spas had apparently come to stay. At Bournemouth, for instance, the railway finally arrived in 1870 and the town mushroomed. Where before only the Exeter Park and the Lansdowne had made their debut since the Bellevue and the Bath, the next decade saw the emergence of the Criterion, Pembroke, Queens and High Cliff Mansions. Because Bournemouth had been exclusive, it attracted the rich clientele, and also one rich amateur hotelier, Merton R. Cotes, who purchased the Royal Bath—Royal after a visit by the Prince of Wales—and spent £100,000 on reconstruction in 1880. It was soon after Japan had emerged again from the seclusion of centuries, and Japanese decor was becoming all the rage. It is, of course, very dangerous for a hotel to go overboard on the fashionable decor of the day because once a style is *passé*, the hotel looks equally old fashioned. Mr. Cotes was, however, wealthy enough to be unconcerned, and apart from his private collection of Japanese curios in the Mikado Room, he turned the old smoking room into a Japanese drawing room; there were birds, hand painted on the soft yellow walls, peacocks, herons, flamingoes and storks with heraldry in between, and a dado of Japanese matting. Some of the furniture was imported from Japan but most was manufactured in the oriental style in England, including the piano. Branches were hand painted across doors, walls and windows, and bamboo light fittings were made to look like oil

lamps. Whether a visitor from Tokyo would have felt at home is doubtful, but the novelty certainly attracted the custom of such eminently desirable guests as the Queen of Sweden and the Empress Eugenie. Even so it seems very unlikely that Mr. Cotes ever saw a return on his investment which had any meaning except in terms of prestige.

Bournemouth did not have the racy reputation of Brighton or Margate, but its hotels attracted visitors who wanted a quieter setting, and in many seaside resorts a hotel's own reputation was more important than the town in which it was situated. A town could flourish and a prominent hotel decline, as with the Brighton Hotel Company, which was established as early as 1859, in a most popular town and yet the board ran into considerable debt and it took many years to put matters straight. Even when the dividend had reached a respectable six per cent the memory of those bad days kept the shares hovering at par, for there were high-flyers like the Queens at Hastings which had opened three years later in 1862 and managed fifteen per cent very regularly. The Queens had a highly successful management team in William Glade and his wife. Glade started as a waiter at the hotel, stayed over forty years and eventually finished up with a large slice of the equity. The Alexandra in Hastings was also paying more than ten per cent when the Brighton Company was struggling to reach its six per cent and, not unnaturally, the best hotel shares became difficult to buy with the lucky holders unwilling to sell and a restricted market emerging as a consequence.

Dominating the beach at Scarborough is Broderick's Grand Hotel. Even the ornamental domes are themselves ornamental.

55

For the seaside hotels which depended on a good summer season, the weather was important—a hotel like the Grand at Scarborough would only open for July and August. Admittedly there was effectively no continental alternative, for the numbers of people who were prepared to venture abroad on the International resort circuit was minute even if very high powered. Nevertheless, in a wet British summer profits would slump badly as visitors cut short holidays or simply stayed at home. In 1882 the manager of the Granville, St. Lawrence-by-Sea in Ramsgate, took one look at the hitherto elusive sunshine, and telegraphed the Royal Exchange in London "We have at last splendid summer weather. Come in your thousands and stop till Monday morning."

The seaside towns increased in size, importance and wealth as Britain itself grew greater during the '60s and '70s. The number of houses in Eastbourne more than tripled between 1861 and 1881 though as late as 1868 *Murray's Guide* tells prospective visitors that "for those who seek rational recreation and health-giving pleasures, East Bourne is altogether a very enjoyable place, but they who expect bustle and gaiety must go elsewhere." Yet within another fifteen years there were many thousands of visitors, a string

The Palace Hotel at Birkdale in Lancashire should have been built facing the beach, but it faced inland instead. With its vast grounds and handsome apartments, it was still too far out of Southport to survive economically.

of new hotels and boarding houses along the Marine and Grand Parades and a growing reputation as the "paradise of the lawntennysonians."

Where the original seaside clientele had been either the very wealthy or the day trippers, now the growing Victorian middle class came, and the hotels which were built for them were, at their most luxurious, modelled on the new city hotels and aped the continental fashions. Each seaside town wanted to have a showpiece in terms of a luxury hotel, and so Scarborough got the magnificent Grand in 1865, Southport the Palace in 1866 and Eastbourne the Cavendish in 1873. The Palace in Southport could advertise that it was only half-an-hour away from Liverpool by train, a boast which no longer holds true. The names were selected to give the hotels an often spurious connection with royalty so that Victoria Hotels abounded, as well as Imperials, Royals and the ubiquitous Prince of Wales. The local noblemen were represented by names like the Cavendish in Eastbourne and the Zetland in Saltburn, and famous royal residences were commemorated not only by simple plagiarism like the Palace, but also by use of the word 'Carlton' which derived from the old home of the Prince Regent, Carlton House.

Although the period after the Companies Act saw a massive expansion of hotel building, the idea that building a hotel was a licence to print money was very far from the truth. Hotel companies did crash, directors and managers were thrown out, debts were amassed and shareholders complained vociferously. In 1881 one chairman reminded his shareholders of the £40,000 worth of debts he had inherited from his predecessors; the Washington Hotel, Liverpool, failed to survive the competition of a larger reconstructed Adelphi and became Temperance; the Metropolitan Hotel, in the City of London, was offered for sale only months after opening; the Hotel Continental in the West End went bankrupt, and there were many other examples every year.

The penalties for poor planning and inefficiency were exacerbated by the bad slump which hit British industry in the latter half of the 1870s. For over twenty years there was deflation and rates of interest dwindled. Most commodity prices fell by a third due to cheap food imports from North America but in Europe there were a string of bad harvests and the French in particular suffered from a crippling outbreak of phylloxera which killed vast areas of the vineyards. Though cheap imports helped hotel expenses, the slump in the 70s affected the number of free spending visitors and British hotel profits and dividends slumped at the end of the decade. The Victoria Hotel, Bradford, sank from eight per cent in 1877 to four per cent in 1879, The Grosvenor, Victoria, paid no dividend from 1877 to 1880, the Grand, Scarborough, paid three-and-a-half per cent in 1877 but nothing in 1878, and only one per cent in 1879. Even the Langham sank from twenty per cent to ten per cent and the trade magazine, the *Caterer, Hotel Keeper, and Refreshment Contractors' Gazette* which had started publishing in 1878, prophesied at the beginning of 1879 a very gloomy commercial and industrial outlook. This was attributed partly to the alternate attraction of the Paris Exhibition to overseas visitors, but mostly to the stagnation of trade and a decreasing number of commercial travellers.

Few industries develop smoothly without setbacks and the overall picture for hotels in the '60s and '70s remains one of expansion on all sides. Sections of cities became known for their hotels, for just as the railways provided the communications to many seaside towns without building the hotels themselves, so whole districts round many of the major city terminii became centres for small hotels and boarding houses. "In London a small group of hotels grew up in Pimlico associated with Victoria Station. The same thing occurred, on a larger scale, in Paddington and Bayswater, near the main arrival point for travellers from the West Country. In Liverpool the hotel quarter also redistributed itself over the same period, from the old town to the neighbourhood of Lime Street, the main terminal for overnight passengers." There were occasions though when the ground landlords were not pleased to see the way their property was developing and "the functional influence of three large trunk railway termini was still reflected in the Bedford Office's losing battle to restrain the conversion of houses in the Bloomsbury Estate into private hotels and boarding houses during the late 19th century."

E. M. Barry designed the City Terminus Hotel at Cannon Street for the London and South Eastern Railway.

THE CITY TERMINUS HOTEL, CANNON STREET, LONDON.—Mr. E. M. Barry, A.R.A., Architect.

The Cannon Street Hotel had more banqueting rooms than the Charing Cross in view of its closer proximity to the City. Much of the ground floor was devoted to booking offices and waiting rooms for the railway passengers.

By the beginnings of the 1880s the slump had done its worst and economic conditions were once again improving. A new boom for hotels started, but the state of the economy was not the only condition which affected the health of the industry. As important in many cases was the effectiveness of the staff and so far they have remained in the background of the industry's development. By 1880 we have a reasonably full picture of what life was like behind the scenes of a new hotel.

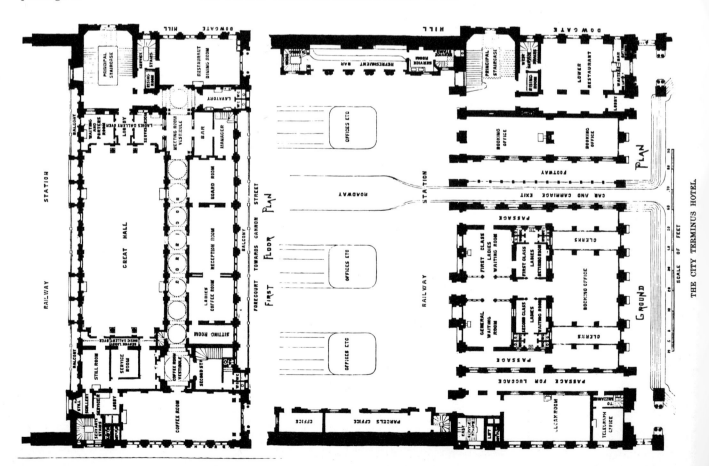

THE CITY TERMINUS HOTEL

A pause for the commercial traveller— the cornerstone

5

WHILE the hotels in the spas and seaside towns depended on the custom of the people with leisure and the money to spend enjoying it, the hotels in the commercial towns and cities were primarily supported by the salesmen who travelled all over the country on behalf of their firms. As the Penny Post only started in 1840 and the telephone and typewriter were invented towards the end of the century, business was conducted much more on a face-to-face basis than it is today. The commercial traveller with his samples not only called on wholesalers and retailers, but often took the place of the mail order catalogue as well. Before the railways he would load up his pony and trap and be sure of a warm welcome from the innkeepers he patronised, for part of the stock-in-trade of the commercial traveller was hospitality and the local hotel was convenient for showing his wares and for entertaining his prospective clients. For the small hotel the arrival of a high spending traveller was a great day, and the manager knew that he had to play his own part ensuring that the people who were to be entertained were suitably impressed.

The coming of the railways made it easier to move goods around the country, but the cost was high compared to the pony and trap, and in addition there were many small towns and villages which waited a number of years for the railway line to arrive. The traveller remained one of the lubricants of commerce and customers, though it could be a lonely life and the men relied to a great extent on the conviviality of their landlords and fellow guests to break the monotony, and, at least temporarily, to take the place of wife and family. A hotel which catered for commercial travellers kept this in mind and many made a considerable effort to offer the small services which were particularly needed by this type of visitor.

In many hotels the 'boots' would meet the train to help the traveller move his samples to the hotel, and, once installed, a room would be set aside for displaying them. When a retired commercial traveller, Mr. Wynn, took over the Dumfries Hotel in Cardiff and called it Wynn's he changed more than the name. He installed new writing desks as the travellers had to write out orders for head office and also reports on the progress they were making. Everything would have to be done by hand, nothing could be telephoned through, and in the evenings there would be the scratch of many pens as the last piece of drudgery was completed. Mr. Wynn produced a new stock room for the samples and a luggage room with a separate entrance from the street so that the goods did not have to be carried through the main lobby but could be out of sight as quickly as possible. The hotel manager might be stocking a warehouse but he didn't want to appear to be running one. There was also to be a new strong room with a "Hobbs patent fire and burglar proof door". This was a wise precaution as on the one hand the goods were often highly inflammable, and on the other the hotelier did not want to finish up in court trying to stave off a large demand for compensation if they were stolen.

Mr. Wynn was also aware of the importance of communications and advertised the fact that as the post was not delivered before the departure of some of the convenient trains from Cardiff, the hotel would pick up the mail for the visitors from the local Post Office very early in the morning and would distribute it before half-past-seven.

Although few hotels would have been as well geared to the needs of the travellers as Mr. Wynn's, all the hotels which hoped to attract this type of clientele had to make the attempt for there was a considerable grapevine, and no real shortage of alternatives in a reasonably-sized town. Each hotel would have a sort of working lounge called the commercial room, and one traveller who specified the ideal facilities listed, besides writing desks, the need for blotting paper pads, telegraph forms, pen racks, timetables for railway trains, a twine box and gum bottle, a post box, message slate and a morning call board. The inconvenience created by waking up late, failing to receive messages from office or client, missing connections, or ransacking the hotel for a piece of string must have produced a good deal of frustration for the methodical salesman.

Much as the hotel manager relied on his 'commercials', the travellers were likely to be tightfisted when their customers were not involved. Their expenses would be scrutinised when they reached home, and if they could pocket some of their allowance they were likely to do so. Money might be no object to the clientele at the Langham, but it meant a great deal to the commercial traveller and he expected the tariffs of the hotels in which he stayed to be formulated with this in mind. He did not expect his bedroom to cost him much and if he had to pay for his horse as well he would want this to be taken into account when settling the price for his own accommodation. A horse put up in a hotel stable in the latter part of the century cost sixpence ($2\frac{1}{2}$p) a feed and another sixpence if he stood on a pillar rein. One shilling and sixpence ($7\frac{1}{2}$p) a night was the average for stable room and while the horse was in his care, the hotel manager was responsible for any harm that befell it.

Consequently, the hotelier had to rely on the profits from food and drink in the bars and restaurant to see him through, and the mark-up for drinks was therefore high. A bottle of sherry which cost the hotelier three shillings (15p) would be sold for six shillings (30p) but a bottle of wine which cost one shilling (5p) would also be sold for six shillings, or very nearly. Many of the bigger hotels were associated with wine merchants as shareholders and this sometimes meant that the stock was not purchased at the most economic price, so that complaints about the cost of drinks was a continuing theme among the customers. Hotel managers would often bottle their own wines and indulge in every sort of malpractice, but then, there was also nothing to stop beer being adultererated for much of Victoria's reign and salt could be put into it as well to give the clients a still greater thirst. In view of the fact that the price of bedrooms had always been quite low, a custom had grown up, no doubt studiously fostered by the hoteliers, that guests should buy drinks "for the good of the house" and this only died out very slowly. Sheridan, the playwright, had summed up the situation succinctly a long time before when he announced "I call for a bottle of wine that my landlord may live, and I abstain from drinking it that I may live too."

When the commercial travellers assembled for dinner in their hotel, there would be one large table with the manager at the head, and during the meal the drink would flow freely. The only trouble for the abstemious was that there was another 'custom'—at the end of the evening the amount consumed would be totalled up and then divided equally between all present. Under these circumstances any manager anxious to improve his profits and careless of the condition of his liver was likely to be at the very least half-drunk by the time he got to bed every night. Apart from the fact that the system was unfair, it was also expensive and to counteract it many commercial travellers decided to 'Box Harry'.

Boxing Harry involved the traveller in returning to the hotel at teatime and consuming sufficient to last him for the rest of the evening so that as dinner-time approached he

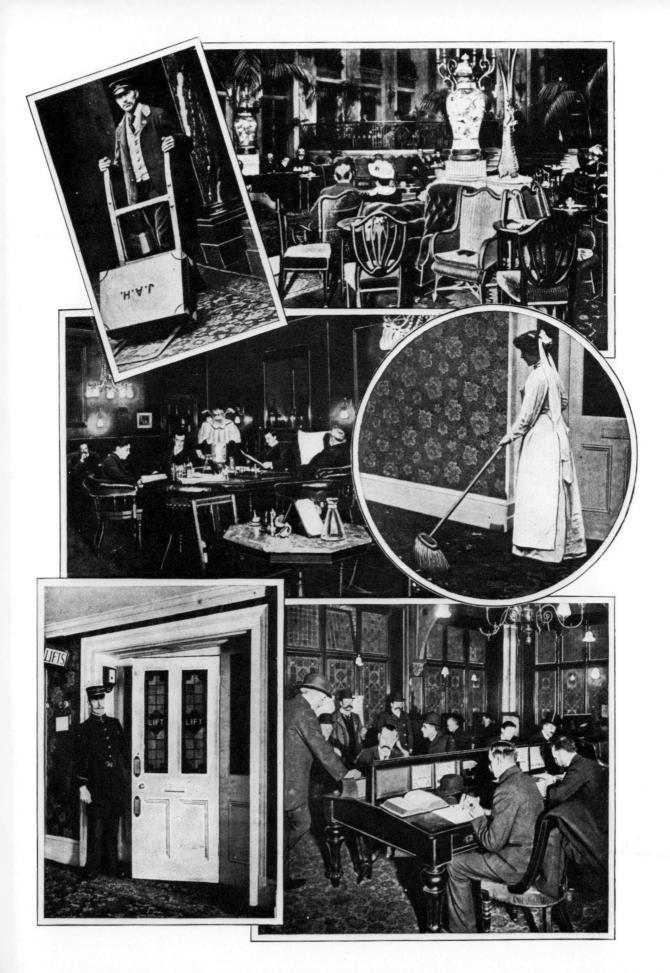

would sneak out of the hotel and thereby avoid paying for wine he hadn't drunk. The importance of eating sufficient tea is explained by the absence in most towns of any form of restaurant open in the evening, for although we now take it for granted that Indian, Chinese, Italian, and steak houses will flourish on every corner, only the major Victorian cities could offer any alternative to a hotel. Having 'Boxed Harry', the traveller, on his return, had to contrive a facile excuse for his landlord, who, deprived of his profit, would have to accept stories of relatives who had to be visited, a private assignation with a young lady, or a client who could only be seen in the evening.

Both hoteliers and commercial travellers were victims of the fact that the accepted tariffs were lopsided because providing a bed for the night had for so many years been the sign of Christian hospitality rather than a profitable occupation. Furthermore the cost to the hotel of a meal had to be measured by the quantities of food the Victorians expected, which made profits once again difficult to come by. In many cases the hotel manager was reduced to augmenting the meagre returns with comparatively extravagant charges for the morning newspaper, candles or a cup of coffee.

For the majority who remained for dinner, the event followed the well-trod paths of stag dinners throughout the centuries; the conversation would be boisterous, getting steadily more animated as the hours passed, and after dinner the old stories would be trundled out in an atmosphere growing steadily more blue with the smoke from the pipes and cigars as well as the subject matter. Here were manufactured, or, at least retailed, that legion of tales about the Englishman, the Irishman and the Scotsman which have tickled such assemblies ever since. Politics, religion and business were discouraged as topics, but there might be music at a piano, poems recited and lengthy discussions on sporting or domestic subjects while the drinks continued to be passed around, and this would be the fate of the traveller night after night as he moved from town to town.

The Grosvenor Hotel in Chester certainly seemed more in keeping with the local architecture than the neo-Gothic buildings. Notice the inn sign.

THE GROSVENOR HOTEL, CHESTER. — Messrs. Kyrke Penson, & Ritchie, Architects.

The temperance hotels like the Shaftesbury in Liverpool and the Trevelyan in Sunderland hoped to win the commercial travellers away from this type of atmosphere, but the number of men on the road could keep both types of hotel, licensed and temperance, reasonably full. One of the attractions of the travellers as a clientele, was that they were not confined to one season or one event; as regular business they were worth cultivating even though they might not mix too well with the upper crust. Even at many of the best hotels there was a commercial room with desks side-by-side and the travellers equally identical in their uniforms of sober suits and bowler hats which they seldom removed. This was hardly for security reasons though there were many court cases about lost umbrellas, hats and, more seriously, lost samples. On occasions the hotel would try to keep their two different clienteles apart so that when the Queens Hotel, Hanley in the Potteries, was redecorated, there was "a new smoking room, a bijou refreshment bar" and a new commercial room in one wing, but the coffee room was carefully situated on the other side of the house and reported as such. Miss Elliott, the manager, felt that this was more fitting for everyone concerned.

Little changed over the years in hotels catering primarily for commercial travellers; it was not here that the private bathrooms were installed, or the elaborate *à la carte*, but nevertheless it was just this type of traveller without whom the hotels would have been impoverished in many towns, and who furnished the first excuse when things were bad; "not as many commercials" was the cry, but thankfully they always came back with the return of better times.

Millions of girls went into service and the hotel industry depended on them. Before modern plumbing and electrical cleaning appliances, the chambermaids were indispensable. These women were employed by Frederick Gordon at the First Avenue Hotel in High Holborn circa 1900.

Behind the scenes

6

DURING the 19th century in Britain the hotel industry expanded out of all knowledge and as a result there was a great shortage of trained staff, though this was alleviated to some extent by continental labour coming to fill the gap. The welcome influx has continued to the present day and there are really two questions to answer: why were the continentals so much better at the hotel business than the native British, and why were they so keen to come to Britain?

There is no doubt that the training of hotel staff on the continent was at the time very much better. A senior chef was asked in 1893 to explain the difference between France and England in this respect; he pointed out that in France a father would pay a good head chef to teach his son, who would start at the very bottom and then having learnt one part of his profession, would be transferred to another specialist chef in the kitchen who would also expect to receive a fee. In this manner the boy would go right round the department over a period of years. As the chefs were being paid for their trouble, they were likely to teach the boy reasonably well and at the end of his apprenticeship the young man should have been thoroughly grounded. Even then it would only be the start of his career, but the foundations at least would have been well laid.

On the other hand in Britain where there was a shortage of labour in the kitchens, a boy would be paid to start work as a dishwasher. If he was enthusiastic and showed a modicum of intelligence he would be promoted to cook, but he would have little knowledge of the art of cooking except for what he had been able to pick up. There was no incentive for the head chef to train him or to get others to do so. The French chef also pointed out that there was a great deal of difference between an ordinary cook, a cuisinier, and a chef who was expected in France to be a leader of cooks. To be a chef on the continent was an honoured profession and there were whole families of them going through the generations from father to son. Eating was more a part of French culture and chefs could acquire more the status of artists than cooks. In England on the contrary, a chef would hope that his son would grow up to do something 'better' because of the relatively low social position awarded a man who made his living in a kitchen.

The great French chefs would teach many young men during the course of their careers and these pupils would always be proud to be able to say that they had received their original training from one of the masters. When Adolphe Dugleré died at 79 in 1884, he was still described in his obituary as a pupil of Carême, and Herbodeau remained till the end the man who had been taught by Escoffier. Moreover he was proud of it and did all he could to perpetuate the memory of his boyhood hero. None of this really applied to the English chefs, though many were excellent and ran great kitchens, like Thomas Jordan who was head chef of the Langham for many years. More than any other nation it was the French who dominated *haute cuisine*, made their language its own, and their employers proud to have a French chef working for them; men like Pierre Lecomte who controlled a staff of fifty at the Grand Hotel, Trafalgar Square, in 1881 and who had been *chef de cuisine* to Napoleon III, a Russian ambassador, Baron Rothschild and the 1st Life Guards.

Many of the chefs have been immortalised by the dishes and culinary expressions which still bear their names; Brillat-Savarin invented the mould which is used for making savarins; Dugleré created the sauce which garnishes fillet de sole Dugleré and Bechamel the basic white sauce.

The great reputation of French cooking is attributed to the influence of Katherine de Medici in the 16th century. This Italian born Queen of France brought in her retinue Italian chefs who were greatly superior to their French counterparts. French cuisine had been as unimaginative as English up to that time but the Italian Renaissance had fostered many skills and the French developed the culinary art from then on. Even so the development of the cuisine was a spasmodic process and in the 19th century the reputation stemmed more from the general French predominance in so many cultural and aesthetic areas since the time of Louis XIV. French was the language of diplomacy and what the French did fashionably today, the English were likely to do tomorrow. In the 18th century the French nobility entertained lavishly and employed chefs who were expected to live up to their masters' pretensions. Some of these chefs found their way to the homes of the English aristocracy, particularly after the French revolution had decimated the number of potential French employers.

After the Napoleonic wars the political conditions in France were stable for a time, but the 1830 revolution had some French chefs on the move again, notably Alexis Soyer who had a couple of his staff murdered before his eyes, and decided that the Duke of Cambridge's home was likely to be more conducive to the undisturbed preparation of *haute cuisine*. Soyer was only twenty-one-years-old when he came to England to work for the Duke, an indication of the high esteem in which French chefs were held, and he became the greatest name in British cooking before Escoffier, writing many books, working to relieve the famine in Ireland when the potato crop failed, and helping to feed the troops in the Crimea. Soyer achieved his fame without ever working in a British hotel but instead spent thirteen years as *chef de cuisine* at the Reform Club.

Alexis Soyer was the greatest chef and the greatest influence on the cuisine of his day, yet he never worked in a hotel.

When it came to hotel managers, the British held their own with their continental colleagues a good deal better than in the world of the top chefs. Even so there were a considerable number of foreign managers, and the attraction of Britain lay partly in exactly those circumstances which had driven Soyer to this country. Europe was often not a very safe place to be in the 19th century; wars and revolutions were commonplace as the 'haves' fought to keep the 'have nots' out of power. The purges of the enemies of the state were inclined to be indiscriminate, and many foreign workers came to Britain to escape political or religious persecution. The British attitude to Europe for much of the century was summed up in the famous headline "Thick fog in channel. Continent isolated", and to emigrate to Britain from the middle of the century onwards was to live in the richest, most politically stable, most powerful and most inventive country in the world. It was peaceful and while it is true that two demonstrators were killed in disturbances in Trafalgar Square in 1887, this was so exceptional that it was solemnly recorded in the history books. In Central and Southern Europe it would not have been noticed, but in England the vast majority of the nation considered itself above political violence, the police were unarmed, and the troops were very seldom needed for other than ceremonial purposes, except overseas. There was no conscription unlike the continent where many an intelligent man fled the country rather than serve in the army of a man he considered a despot.

There was also the simple fact that you had a good chance of getting a job in England in the catering trade. Mario Gallati, who opened the Caprice Restaurant in the West End of London after the Second World War, recalled in his autobiography his own reasons for coming to Britain at the turn of the century. "At this time there was considerable unemployment in Italy and many other Italians had left their home country to work in England. I wanted to learn English . . . and I also wanted to widen my experience in every possible way. One advantage of being a waiter was that you could, with luck, travel the world, working in any country in which you happened to find yourself. A smattering of French and English was enough to get by in most restaurants, French being the international language of the cuisine and English the language spoken by most of the diners and tourists". The Italy that Mario Gallati left he remembered with little affection. "My memories of Milan in the 1900s are mostly of the tremendous political and industrial strife, with long hours and poor wages driving the people into making continual demonstrations". He was working as a commis at the age of ten and was lucky to have a job at all.

Whether it was Italy in the 1900s, Hungary after 1848, France in the days of the Commune or Russia at almost any time, there were good reasons for emigrating. Coincidentally while the continental hotel staff came to Britain, the British were emigrating as well. There were 6.8 million people living in Ireland in 1820 but only 4.4 million in 1900, and between 1880 and 1910 over $8\frac{1}{2}$ million people emigrated from Britain in all. In spite of the fact that real wages rose fifty-seven per cent over a twenty-five year span, life was hard in the industrial towns and unemployment stalked the declining countryside. But hotels were not 'dark satanic mills' and for hotel workers there were no industrial diseases to be caught from the dust under the beds.

In 1899 when the Boer War broke out, a high proportion of the volunteers for the army were rejected on medical grounds, and the ensuing scandal was further fanned to a blaze when Seebohm Rowntree in 1901 "concluded that twenty-eight per cent of the inhabitants of York could not afford a diet adequate to sustain a normal day's work." Charles Booth, another famous reformer "found that over thirty per cent of the population of London was living at a level below that necessary to maintain mere physical efficiency."

By comparison, the servants' hall of a good hotel served breakfast at 8 or 8.30, dinner at 12, tea at 4.30 and supper at around 8 in the evening. In a large hotel there would be cold meat for breakfast, though only bread and butter in small ones; hot meat and potatoes would be served every day for dinner, green vegetables twice a week, and pudding on Sundays. There would be a plain tea but cold meat and cheese for supper. The smaller hotels would be likely to give meat for supper only on alternative days and cheese otherwise. Beer would be either provided at a low price or an allowance would be made of about two-and-a-half pints a day for men and one-and-a-half pints for women. For the staff in the kitchens and restaurant who had access to leftovers there was even more to eat, and while the idea of people keeping up their strength on scraps from a rich man's table is anathema to us today, it was obviously preferable for the Victorian and Edwardian hotel worker to going hungry.

While the staff wages appear low, they did not compare badly with other industries. Typical salaries in 1883 were about £5 a month for a cook, £4 for a head waiter, £3 for a cellarman, 2 guineas (£2.10p) for a head porter or head laundress, £2 for a head chambermaid and £1 10s. (£1.50p) for a still room maid.

The attendance charge which Albert Smith had made seldom went to the staff but guests soon got used to paying twice for service. If they did not, the *Daily Telegraph* in 1882 warned them of their fate when they left "passing through scowling faces to an unhonoured exit". Charles Dickens' *Dictionary of London* in 1880 offered one solution "Attendance is now usually included in the bill. When this is the case, the servants invariably expect very much the same gratuity as when it is not included. But unless you propose making a long stay, or a very speedy return, it is by no means necessary to meet their views in this respect." Of course a lot of guests did, and if they were unaware of the destination of the charge for attendance, there were doubtless many staff to fill the gap in their knowledge. Asking for tips was, however, frowned upon and when a waiter at the Royal Forest Hotel, Chingford did so in the '80s he was dismissed on the spot. He promptly took his employer to court for a day's pay but he lost the case.

Some of the staff who were in contact with the guests regularly might not receive wages at all. Many waiters in restaurants worked for tips alone, and in some restaurants they even paid the proprietor a levy in order to keep the job. Commissionaires often had to pay for the privilege of donning the hotel's livery as well. We have seen that in the early years of the Grand Pump Room Hotel, Bath, the wages were about ten per cent of turnover and the same was roughly true throughout the better hotels. The Langham in 1889 paid out about £8,000 from a turnover of £80,000 and the Prince of Wales Hotel, Southport £1,877 out of about £18,500. In Switzerland in 1884 a national survey produced figures of 16,000 employees in the industry costing £200,000 out of a gross revenue of £2,112,000, a very similar percentage.

The size of Victorian wine cellars illustrated clearly the dangers of drinking water. Shown here is only a portion of the cellars at the Grand Hotel. The advertisement appeared in an early edition of the "Caterer, Hotel Keeper, and Refreshment Contractors' Gazette."

The above Illustration represents a portion of the Cellars at

THE GRAND HOTEL, TRAFALGAR SQUARE,

the whole of which were completely fitted with Wrought-Iron Bins, &c., by

W. & J. BURROW,

Iron Wine Bin Manufacturers and Wine Merchants' Engineers,

62 & 63 GREAT TOWER STREET, E.C.

Estimates for Wine Bins and all Cellar Fittings Free on Application. — Illustrated Catalogues

Staff turnover depended on the reason for working in the hotel in the first place. Not only could a skilled craftsman travel if he wished, but many continentals came to Britain in order to learn the language and then return home. British visitors were an important part of the tourist market in many European countries, but they seldom had mastered a foreign tongue and expected the senior staff of the hotels they patronised to cope with English, while the linguistic deficiencies of the American clientele were even greater.

The English supported the Swiss economy as Professor Hunziker gladly acknowledged in his official history of 100 years of Swiss tourism, calling Thomas Cook's tours in the 1860s "The foundation of the Swiss tourist industry." They had also been among the first to popularise the French Riviera, as the Nicoise charmingly conceded by calling their main beach road the Promenade des Anglais, and their hotels by such names as the Westminster, the Royal and the Cecil.

So the continental staff with ambition obligingly came to Britain to learn the language and as they came from countries which regarded hotel work as an honourable occupation, they were able to raise the craft standards of the hotels, and they were acknowledged as superior by the British themselves. The palatial Highland hotels upheld their status by employing continentals "typically a French chef, German waiters, and an Italian or Swiss manager." The *Globe* in 1880 commenting on the improvement in British hotels said that the guests' "Comfort [is] enhanced by service in public rooms being performed in great measure by foreigners. English staff are not as good."

Continental staff were to be found all over the country, but they were still far outnumbered by British employees, and in a good successful hotel the staff were likely to stay on year after year. At Buxton Hydropathic in 1888 about half the staff of thirty to fifty had worked for Mr. Lomas for between twelve and twenty years, and in 1879 the night porter at Hummums in Covent Garden had been receiving 15 shillings (75p) a week for the past fourteen years.

While the continental men travelled and worked, the women seldom did and the female staff in hotels were usually English or Irish. The private houses of the well-to-do, hotels and boarding houses would all have been in chaos without the dogged efforts of the enormous numbers of young women who went into 'service'. Between 1890 and 1910 one-in-three of the girls between fifteen and eighteen in the country were employed in this way. It was the largest single occupation open to them and over a million girls accepted it. While other areas of an hotel might become the province of the continental worker, the housekeeping department was dominated by the British, unless the head housekeeper was the wife of a continental manager, as one of the chains of promotion to management lay through chambermaids promoted to housekeeper and eventually to manager. It was often the case that a husband and wife would be taken on as a team and while the husband looked after the accounting, the reception department and the restaurant, the wife undertook the housekeeping responsibilities.

Competition was fierce for the better jobs as can be seen from the response to the advertisement for a manager for the Marine Hotel, in North Berwick in 1890. No less than 400 applications were received, and the position was finally given to Mr. and Mrs. Niebecker, thus providing another of the superior Scottish hotels with continental experience. In 1890 too when Mr. Meyer of the Victoria Hotel, Sheffield, had died and the railway took the hotel over from his widow, the new appointment was of Mr. and Mrs. Ranhart, with Mrs. Ranhart specifically designated as manageress and housekeeper. The Ranharts came from the Palace Hotel, Hastings. It was accepted by the owners of hotels that good managers would have had varied experience rather than produce for a new employer evidence of their ability to settle down for many years in one job. Joseph Gams, the manager of the plush Alexandra Hotel in Hyde Park in 1883 was Viennese, had worked, for Delmonicos in New York, then returned to manage the Imperial Hotel in Vienna, gone on to control his own hotel in the spa town of Marienbad, given that up and become a wine salesman, and eventually settled down at the Alexandra.

In a Britain starved of top hotel management, the successful Europeans could often take a tough line with the owners. When Robert Etzensberger, who had been manager of the Victoria Hotel in Venice and in charge of the commissariat for Thomas Cook's excursions by steamer up the Nile, was offered the job of manager of the Midland Grand at St. Pancras, he said that he would only take the position if the hotel were completed according to Sir Gilbert Scott's original plans. The Midland directors, who had been hoping to economise in some additional directions, eventually agreed to this and Etzensberger stayed thirteen years until he drowned on holiday in Switzerland.

He was succeeded by a man who was to be the most prominent British hotel manager of his age. This was William Towle, later knighted, who had started his career at the age of fifteen at the Midland Hotel in Derby and by the time he was twenty-two had been made the manager. During his time in Derby he pleased his directors by introducing the concept of luncheon baskets for train travellers. There were no dining cars at the time, and the luncheon baskets were good profit makers, besides providing the passengers with an additional service.

The general manager of the Midland Railway, Sir James Allport, having decided that the best way to overcome competition from other lines was by improving the service on the Midland, was prepared to consider any ideas to these ends with enthusiasm. He introduced more comfortable carriages and pioneered the abolition of the second class so that its rolling stock could be used for third class passengers. He also introduced the American Pullman service with its even greater standard of comfort. Better hotel facilities fitted in well with his planning. The combination of Allport and Towle created the conditions for a group of railway hotels which became prominent in the '80s and '90s and which by the 1920s was the largest chain in Europe. Both William Towle and his two sons, Frank and Arthur, occupy an important position in the later years of the industry.

Left:
The general manager of all the Midland Railway Hotels was William Towle who was knighted a year after his son, Frank.

Sir Francis Towle served a long apprenticeship with his father, and in 1920 became managing director of Gordon Hotels at a salary of £7,000 a year.

Arthur Towle took over from his father, Sir William Towle, and was in charge of all LMS hotels after the Great War.

Sir Polydore de Keyser, the first Catholic Lord Mayor of London since the Reformation was born in Belgium and built the de Keyser Royal Hotel at Blackfriars, which at the time was the largest in London.

As hotels grew in importance, a number of hoteliers achieved prominence in civic affairs, particularly in towns where hotels were an essential part of the prosperity of the community. Merton Cotes, for instance, became Mayor of Bournemouth more than once, and in the cities there was Philip Matthews who ran Harkers and the North Eastern Hotel in York and who achieved the highest civic office; unfortunately Matthews failed to last the course, dying of typhoid soon after his election. Members of Parliament included Jabez Balfour, the owner of the Victoria Hotel near Trafalgar Square for some years, James Bailey, the proprietor of Baileys in Kensington, and Sir Blundell Maple who created Frederick Hotels.

Pride of place, however, goes to Sir Polydore de Keyser who overcame many of the prejudices of his time to become Lord Mayor of London in 1887. Sir Polydore was born in Belgium and although he was educated in Fulham, he never lost his continental accent. His father ran the Royal Hotel at Blackfriars which prospered sufficiently for the family to build a new hotel at Blackfriars Bridge on a site which is now Unilever House. This was the de Keyser Royal Hotel which was opened in 1874 by the King of the Belgians. Polydore was naturalised in 1862 and elected to the Court of Common Council in 1872 without much trouble. In 1882 he was elected an Alderman for the ward of Farringdon Without, defeating an ex-Sheriff named Waterlow, and it was at this point that he had to face some very dirty political skullduggery. Waterlow tried to overturn the result by digging up an ancient ordinance which said that no tavern licence holder could become an Alderman, a rule that went back to Richard II and Henry V. As Polydore was not only a licence holder—though to call the de Keyser Royal a tavern was *lèse majesté* with a vengeance—but also a Catholic and foreign born, there was plenty of fuel for prejudice to feed upon, and Waterlow must have felt reasonably certain that he would be upheld by the city fathers.

When the election was discussed, it could not be denied that the ordinance was still in existence, but while it was confirmed that it would not be altered, a decision was also reached that an exception could be made in de Keyser's case and the election result should stand. British history in the 19th century is notable for the number of victories for the forces of tolerance and humanity, and by 1882 a great many of the discriminatory laws against minorities had been rescinded. This was another good day for the men of good-will and when de Keyser was eventually elected Lord Mayor he became the first Catholic to hold the office since the Reformation. He certainly justified the confidence reposed in him; he was an indefatigable worker for the Guildhall School of Music, a governor of a number of hospitals, and very charitable. His charity took the practical form of clothing the poor children at the parish schools in his district, entertaining them at Christmas and generally alleviating distress whenever he could. He was rewarded not only with his knighthood, but with a Fellowship of the Society of Arts, of the Royal Geographical and Statistical Societies, and membership of six guilds.

It was, of course, more likely that an owner manager would be elected to office by his fellow citizens than an employee manager, but there were at least useful financial rewards for success for the latter. A top position like Mr. Devine's at the Metropole in London in 1886 brought him £500 a year, and many managers had a bonus written into their contracts payable if their hotel made sufficient profits. At the Victoria Hotel, Southport for instance, the accounts for 1885 were sufficiently good for the directors to declare a four per cent dividend free of tax and the manager received £96 as his bonus.

In a first-class hotel the manager would have a large staff. His main assistants would be his sub-manager, head day porter, head night porter, head chef and head housekeeper. All the female staff would be under the head housekeeper except the book-keepers, the barmaids and the kitchen maids who would be responsible to their respective heads of department. There would be a superintendent for the public rooms of the hotel such as the lounge and billiards room, and four separate head waiters; one for the coffee room where the general public would be welcome, one for the *table d'hote* room, one for the ladies room where families could eat together, and one for the private banqueting rooms. There would be an engineer, a head cellarman, and a head plateman; the cellarman to look after the stocks of wine and spirits and the head plateman to look after the crockery and cutlery. The size of these latter tasks can be visualized by the racks of wine at the Metropole, Brighton, which accommodated "a duty paid stock of over 185,000 bottles." When the Grand Hotel in London reordered plates in 1889 they bought another 12,000! Then there would be an usher for the servant's hall, a timekeeper, linen room, still room, and laundry staff as well as a large contingent of chamber maids.

In the kitchen the head chef would be equally well supported. His second in command would be the kitchen clerk, so that while the chef drew up all the menus and examined each dish before it went to the client, the kitchen clerk would take the orders from all over the hotel and check everything to see that it was correct. The second chef would look after the ovens and then there would be a roast chef, sauce chef, pastry chef, cold larder chef and a number of apprentices. In luxury hotels today the kitchen work is usually done entirely by men, but in Victorian times there would be a head kitchenmaid, a fish maid, a head and under vegetable maid and a couple of 'scrubber maids'. The

The full kitchen brigade at the Piccadilly Hotel just before the Great War. After a disastrous start under Sir Polydore de Keyser's nephew, the hotel flourished as part of the R. E. Jones company.

kitchen porters and washers-up would be men, and, when the hotel was particularly busy, the manager would hire extra chefs "of which there are always plenty seeking employment and who are paid by the day." Quantity of course did not necessarily equate with quality and when the porters, page boys, lift men and receptionists were included in the complement, it can be seen that labour had to be cheap to keep the wage costs as low as they invariably were.

There were three types of people to be fed in a hotel; the staff themselves, the servants of the guests and the guests. The servants of the guests were looked after in the stewards' room which was also usually 'below stairs' and they were looked after well. It was generally agreed that a servant who was dissatisfied would very soon ensure that his employer was equally unhappy with the hotel. It was therefore prudent for the hotelier to see to it that, though the tariff for servants was below that of other guests, the quality was very similar. The second housekeeper or the linen keeper would be present at all meals to keep an eye open for any problems, and one of the head waiters would carve. A few of the senior staff in the hotel would also eat in the stewards' room and it is a telling comment on the position of children in Victorian society that they would often

eat there with the nanny, who was herself usually not allowed in any public room if she was in uniform. There always had to be one milk sweet on the menu for the children, but such light eating did not apply to anyone else. For breakfast the menu would include fish and meat, and for lunch it would be soup or fish on alternate days, followed by a choice of joints with two vegetables and then a dessert and cheese. There would be tea, jam, and toast for tea and cold joints and cheese at supper, together, perhaps, with something which had proved unpopular on the *table d'hôte*. Some hotels gave a pint of beer to the guests' male servants and half-a-pint to the female, but others charged extra.

The Victorians travelled with a considerable retinue, and, as we have seen already, a large number of the bedrooms at the best hotels were designed to be used by the servants. Indeed, before the invention of lifts, the rooms at the top of the hotels would be most easily sold to them, and, of course, there was a good deal of residential accommodation for the hotel's own staff as well. Both sexes might be provided with living-in accommodation and the *Engineer* journal reported approvingly about the Midland Grand in 1867 "male and female departments having no communication with each other and approached by different staircases."

Though Jabez Balfour had departed the scene, his Cecil Hotel was completed with its 1,000 rooms and its spacious courtyard. It became a very popular rendezvous.

Hotels were an ideal stage on which to display the elaborate etiquette of staff seniority, and woe betide any hotel which failed to give the visiting nanny her last jot and tittle of status, or any junior staff member who didn't 'know his place.' Retribution would be severe and it must never be forgotten that to lose your job could be an unmitigated disaster, far more terrible than today. There was no social security to draw if you were unemployed, nothing to do except pawn your last belongings and then go to the workhouse or starve to death. If you had a wife and children to support or if your relatives were as poor as you, the threat of unemployment and the fear of being unable to work through sickness was a constant worry, even if it could be pushed away for a time into the back of the mind.

When Mario Gallati was accused unjustly of stealing a piece of steak, he was fined two-shillings and sixpence ($12\frac{1}{2}$p) and when he refused to pay it, he was dismissed. The famous restaurateur recalled many years later "This was a mistake due to pride; in 1905, to be out of work in October meant you would be out of work all the winter." Only another waiter falling sick after Christmas produced a job for Mario Gallati after he had looked fruitlessly for a post for three months and, not surprisingly, he stayed with his new employer for years.

It is with this background in mind that the absence of a trade union for hotel staff becomes understandable. The people who worked in hotels were able to keep body and soul together and there was always the possibility of a fat gratuity on which to pin your hopes. Rosa Lewis was tipped £100 when she cooked a dinner for a private hostess who was entertaining the Kaiser, and although this was exceptional, it was the stuff of which dreams were made if you were earning a couple of pounds a month. The hours were very long and when eventually the Shop Act was introduced just after the turn of the century, it created great indignation among hoteliers. Youngsters under eighteen could then only be worked a maximum of twelve house a day on five days a week and fourteen hours on the sixth!

So seventy four hours a week was the total permitted and hotels started to fall foul of the law, protesting that anything up to a hundred hours a week was perfectly reasonable. Before the Shop Act these hours were common, but the conditions weren't so bad that your friends died of them as they might in a match factory, building a railway, or in the mines. The incentive to join together to form a union was missing, and it was particularly difficult when the prospective members often didn't speak English well, didn't stay long in one place, and when many of the foreign workers equated union membership with revolution. To be a member of a union in many European countries could lead you into direct conflict with the state, and most immigrant workers were concerned only to earn a living and enjoy what they knew to be the more enlightened attitude of the British government. The fact that they would not have had to face deportation if they had formed or joined a union was beside the point; the scars of their experiences in their home countries led them to leave well alone.

While there was no move to form a union, there were a number of hotel societies; in 1877 the Hotel Employee's Society was founded and in its first seven years it paid out over £1,000 to sick members. There were branches of the society all over Europe, and during the same period employment was found for over 4,000 people. This combination of assistance against the twin evils of sickness and unemployment could be supported by both staff and management, and the annual functions of the Society were always supported by managers from the best hotels. The Hotel and Tavern Keepers' Provident Association was also a charitable institution, looking after a number of old and infirm members who in 1885 shared £215 among twenty-four applicants. It was a small gesture, as was the £133 given from the Sick and Pension Fund of the City Waiters Provident and Pension Society in 1883. At the annual dinner that year a whip-round produced £180, but anybody contemplating his own future would have been well advised to adopt the Victorian ideal of self help rather than depend on the slim handouts available from such organizations.

Frank Bourne Newton took over the editorship of the Caterer and Hotel Keeper very soon after it began in 1878 and remained connected with it until his death during the Second World War when he was over 90.

The drawing room at the Welbeck Palace Hotel, complete with piano, aspidistras, coal fire and radiators.

If employees made only relatively puny efforts to band together, the same was also true of management. Attempts to form an English Hotel Association fell on stony ground as soon as the question of money came up. An attempt to form an Association and Defence League in 1886 got no further than a meeting at the Westminster Palace, and five years later a movement sponsored enthusiastically by the *Caterer & Hotel Keeper* did little better. It was to be a Hotel and Caterers Union this time, to be formed either as a limited company or a club with a five guinea (£5.25) membership. Editorial support was given in the form of articles and lists of prominent hotel managers who had pledged their support, but after meetings at which people were solemnly elected to the chair, the minutiae of minutes and procedure carefully thrashed out and endless talking, there was no money to speak of actually forthcoming, and the idea faded away for another decade. The editor and owner of the *Caterer*, Frank Bourne Newton, was not discouraged however, and lived to fight successfully another day. In fact he lived till 1943 and died a nonagenarian, no doubt reflecting that the journal had come a long way since it first appeared carrying an advertisement for a sure-fire hair restorer.

While this situation existed in England, there were better results in other parts of Britain; a Hotel and Restaurant Proprietors' Association of Ireland was created and also a Scottish Hotel Proprietors' Association. In Scotland the basic reason was the one which would eventually bring into being the Incorporated Association of Hotels and Restaurants which became the British Hotels, Restaurants and Caterers' Association; legislation was hurting the Scottish hoteliers. It was in 1881 that the first meeting was held at the Waterloo Hotel, Edinburgh, and the grievances aired, which were afterwards placed before the Lord Advocate of Scotland by a deputation. The hoteliers started by objecting to paying house duty on their entire premises when the guests occupied a good part of it. House duty was paid by every home owner and the hoteliers held that as visitors had paid their own where they lived, the tax was being paid twice if the hotel paid as well. Stores were exempt so why not hotels?

The amount involved was five per cent on the rental for the hotel and, not for the first time, the hotel industry was trying to find out where it belonged; there surely had to be a difference between a private house and a business where the product was bedrooms for sale. Many hoteliers also took strong exception to paying the licence to run a carriage for the whole year when Highland Hotels only needed the licence for the few months of the season; the same applied to the bar licence in a seasonal hotel. Finally the hoteliers wanted to know why so much competition was allowed. Clubs, they felt, should not open at hours when hotels had to be shut, and railway companies should stick to running trains rather than venture into the hotel business. If only hostelries were legally allowed to receive travellers, the Scots held that hydropathic and temperance institutions were illegal. The Lord Advocate said that he would look into all these complaints, but the whole exercise did very little good, except that an association came into existence, which was more than resulted from the efforts of the Sassenachs.

As hotels became more complex structures, larger and better, the tasks and skills of the manager became greater as well. The host of the Staging Inn was a long way removed from the controller of the 'giant caravanserai' as the big hotels were lovingly labelled. To start with, the managers had to tackle the large numbers of new inventions which were often of fundamental importance; gas cooking apparatus was produced by E. D. Owen in 1849, lifts were coming in by the late '50s, Edison perfected the incandescent lamp in 1879 and there were major improvements in drainage and water supplies and refrigeration. Ice had been imported from the United States at first, but by 1880 the main supplier was Norway, which shipped 30,000–50,000 tons a year. Boats carrying 500 tons or more would unload at Surrey Docks and although half the original weight would melt in transit, at two shillings and sixpence (12½p) a hundredweight, there was still a fair profit to make.

While today we would pick up a telephone—they too were invented during the period —and get a plumber, engineer, or electrician to solve the problem, the good manager in those early days would want to understand the technicalities involved to a much greater

The Welbeck Palace Hotel in London's medical district possessed a dining room which epitomised the solid well-being of the middle class. It is now the Londoner Hotel.

extent. While the *Caterer* would still be running a series of articles in 1891 on the correct way to look after stables, there were also cheek by jowl complicated expositions on laying drains and installing electric bell systems. Managers faced a long list of problems which seldom worry them today.

The new inventions were costly. It was easy enough to carry out the necessary work for a hotel in the course of construction, but exceptionally difficult when you had an existing hotel with the solidity of construction which has been seen already. Although the courtyard at the Langham was lit by electricity in 1879, the directors did not readily provide the money to fit up the whole hotel as ten years later the bill for this was £5,000, or about three months profit. Sometimes the costs of the invention itself were unnecessarily expensive; the Electric Light Act of 1881 made it very difficult to get a supply for private houses into which category the hotels were put again, and consequently many hotels had to install their own dynamos. As a result the effects of a power strike today are not felt by the Victorian hotels who invested in this way and simply use their own supply. Although the cost of electricity could eventually be a half-penny (about $\frac{1}{5}$p) a unit, the right to sell it was originally vested in private companies who charged extortionate rates, but "through wells and dynamos, hotels can be independent of water and electricity companies with their exacting arbitrary conditions."

Of course, the public's only concern was to obtain these wonderful new facilities and if a new hotel could provide them where an old one could not afford the expense, then the guests' loyalty was likely to switch quickly. Decisions on heavy capital expenditure must have given many managers sleepless nights as they contemplated the technologically advanced newcomers. When the Metropole in Brighton opened, the Grand suffered badly, and eventually a shareholders' committee investigated the management, but it found nothing to complain about except the existence of the Metropole! As building programmes grew, more and more managers had to fight new competitors for the business they had carefully nurtured over the years.

It was also true that the new inventions themselves could get old-fashioned, as hydraulic lifts, for instance, were overtaken by electrically operated ones. The guests preferred the smoother ride and with lifts there was originally some of the fear among the public that characterised the first passenger rides in an aeroplane years later; were they safe, would they crash, wasn't it more sensible to take the stairs rather than tempt providence? Gas could be lethal as we have seen, and there were a number of fatalities with gas water heaters, which were introduced around 1880; Thomas Cook's only daughter was tragically one of the victims.

A death in a hotel has always been one of the nightmares that haunts a manager, but fire is even worse, and many hotels had their own fire fighting teams; there were two resident firemen at the de Keyser Royal who did nothing else but wait for a blaze. There were day and night firemen at the Langham and there would be regular fire practice at new hotels like the Cecil. As late as 1960 there was a night fireman employed at the Piccadilly Hotel though actually he never had to put anything out. In the country areas, of course, the problems were even worse; the Railway Hotel, Sandown, was burnt to the ground in 1879 because the fire engines at Sandown were out of order, the Marine in North Berwick had to be rebuilt after a fire in 1883; with only horses to pull the machines, the fire brigade could easily arrive too late or have insufficient water power to stem the conflagration.

When fire broke out at the George Hotel, Axminster, in 1881, the local fire engines were not enough and two extra appliances had to be sent by rail from Exeter, a distance of 27 miles. Not unnaturally by the time they got to the blaze it had a good hold, burnt for ten hours, and did £10,000 worth of damage. The hydros were particularly vulnerable as many were situated high on hills because of the panoramic views. The luckless Callander Hydro was practically destroyed in 1893 and the Cairn Hydro was completely burnt out. The fire engines could not get up the hills or provide the necessary water pressure.

Hotel managers, like airlines in the future, did not know whether to talk of their safety record in terms of fire precautions and the fireproof construction of the house or to keep quiet about the whole thing. No doubt the manager of the Wheatsheaf Hotel in Manchester, which was said to be Britain's oldest, gave the matter careful thought as well, but in the summer of 1882 his hotel was destroyed anyway—struck by lightning—and it was to be some years before the solution to that hazard also emerged.

By the beginning of the 1880s the pattern of management was becoming clearer; with the growth of large hotels it was more difficult for a hotelier to own his business and the divide widened between the board of directors and the manager they employed. There would still be men who would successfully jump the gap, but the manager as just another employee was a growing trend, and the cause of much friction and bad feeling. There was no prejudice though against employing women in the position; the names of able Victorian ladies adorn the letterheads of countless hotels of the time and in addition the manager's wife was very often the real power in the house. If none of these mana-geresses has achieved a place in the industry's Hall of Fame, they nevertheless stood comparison with their male colleagues in every respect. Rosa Lewis ran the Cavendish in Jermyn Street, Marie Ritz served on the board of Ritz Hotels in an active capacity after her husband's death, and Lady Towle played an important role in the running of Midland Railway hotels.

Life behind the scenes in a hotel towards the end of the century involved long hours, only moderate wages, and demanded the capacity to accept a degree of servility, but it was also a warm roof over thousands of grateful heads.

Rosa Lewis ran her Cavendish Hotel in London both autocratically and efficiently.

"The Napoleon of the hotel world" was the title bestowed on Frederick Gordon, the founder and chairman of Gordon Hotels, the best brain the industry produced in the 19th century.

MR. FREDERICK GORDON.

A pause for Frederick Gordon—the winner

7

UNFORTUNATELY for the researcher, Victorian hoteliers were not public figures in the sense that their lives and actions were faithfully recorded for posterity in immaculate detail. On the contrary their origins were often in doubt, their private life a mystery, and they were forgotten almost as soon as the obsequies were over. They would have had hundreds or, indeed, thousands of acquaintances during their lifetime as they welcomed guests, paused in a lounge to enquire whether all was well, or settled minor disputes in the sanctity of their offices, but what they were really like behind the face the public saw, or behind the beard and moustache which so often hid even the surface of the Victorian hotelkeeper, remained to all, but their most intimate friends and relatives almost totally obscure. This was even true of the greatest of the Victorian hoteliers, the head of by far the largest company the hotel world had ever seen, for in his own time "there are few persons who know what manner of man the head and forefront of the business is." His name was Frederick Gordon.

The founder of The Gordon Hotels Company is too important as an influence and a prototype to be allowed to remain merely a footnote on the Register of Companies, the name of an Avenue in Stanmore, Middlesex, or the occupant of a massive but overgrown grave in the same parish. Consequently, although it is not possible or even desirable to study a large number of the Victorian hoteliers in depth, we can examine the life of this one extraordinary individual, a man who started with practically nothing and in the best traditions of all Cinderella stories finished up with a Royal, not to mention the Grand, and the Metropole and many more.

Frederick Gordon was born in Ross-on-Wye, Herefordshire, a small West Midlands market town, his father, Charles Gordon, having gone there in the early 1830s from London in order to take a job with a local house decorator. The Gordons were a large family and Charles Gordon's wife was the daughter of a well-known local man, Thomas Minett. Her brother, Henry, was a solicitor and when Frederick grew up, he was articled to his uncle. In 1843 Gordon had a brother, Alexander, and in 1846 a younger sister, Lizzie. Father Gordon did not remain in Ross. It is quite possible that the agricultural community may have fallen on harder times, and Charles Gordon returned to London, where he carried on his trade as a decorator, but began to specialise in 'principal dining rooms'.

These dining rooms we would call restaurants today, and they were springing up to cater for the vastly increased business community which London was spawning as the city grew ever greater in importance and magnitude. The prosperous new middle classes needed somewhere to eat, somewhere respectable, and father Gordon was kept busy. Decorating dining rooms was not, however, as lucrative or as physically untaxing as managing them, and father Gordon decided to obtain a position as manager of some dining rooms, with daughter Lizzie as cashier.

83

It was about this time that Frederick qualified as a solicitor and started up in business in Holborn, and in the summer of 1864 he married twenty-one-year-old Emily Warman in Chigwell, Essex, where they set up home. Frederick had not entirely lost touch with Ross, and after his first son was born, Emily had their first daughter, Ellen, at the family home in Herefordshire, in the spring of 1866. There is no evidence that Frederick, a short, cheerful man, was a very successful solicitor, but he managed to garner a living from his practice in Holborn, and made a good friend out of his new brother-in-law, a twenty-five-year-old engraver called Horatio Davies who had married Lizzie in 1867.

How long Frederick would have struggled on with his business is academic, for his life changed course completely when he was thirty-four-years-old with a wife and two small children and making little headway. At that point he suffered a blow which would have been the last straw for many men; two days before Christmas Emily died of pneumonia only twenty six years old.

For Frederick it was a watershed, and his phenomenal rise to fame and affluence dates from this time. To start with, he decided to submerge himself in city politics and managed to get proposed and seconded for the Bishopsgate Ward of the City of London Common Council. Sometimes these elections are uncontested, but in 1870 there were fifteen candidates for fourteen places so that a ward mote was necessary, and on a show of hands Frederick came last. A few years before he might have accepted the defeat, but he was tougher now, he had the two motherless children to fight for, and so he demanded a poll, and in the short time at his disposal lobbied furiously for support. When the count ended and the result was announced on the first anniversary of Emily's death, Frederick had come top.

It was just the beginning and Gordon knew it. In the charmed world of the city magnates, a small solicitor from an artisan background with little money and few contacts, had a long way to go. For the rest of his life Frederick kept his origins deliberately hidden; he never gave an interview to the Press, and even his grandchildren were to have no knowledge of the identity of his first wife, for Frederick did marry again, a lady called Harriet Philips who was eleven years his junior, and might well have been a widow herself. She bore him eight sons and a daughter and surprisingly for the age, they all lived.

How Frederick came to go into the catering business we do not really know. His father was in it, and his brother-in-law, Horatio Davies, gave up engraving some years later to take over a restaurant in Poultry, in the City of London, called the London Tavern. In time Davies bought other restaurants, like Pimms, and, of course, made a fortune from the spirit-based drinks named after the restaurant. We have only two clues to Frederick's first steps in catering; there is a story in the family that one day when the legal practice was getting started, he was looking for a cheap lunch, and couldn't find anywhere for a snack. He decided to start a restaurant to fill this gap in the City for people like himself. The other clue comes in his obituary in the *Financial News* many years later where we read "many will remember the buffet in Milk Street which he founded." Milk Street is at the back of the Bank of England and it seems likely that his modest start took place there.

Business must have been brisk for soon Frederick took a lease on a famous city landmark, a former home of Richard III called Crosby Hall. Since 1466 it had been known as a place for eating and reference can be found to it in Shakespeare. By the time Frederick started to restore it, all that remained of the original palace was the great banqueting hall, the council room and the associated chambers. It was very dilapidated, but Sir Thomas More had lived there, as had Erasmus, and every caterer knows the value of a large slice of history if you want atmosphere. Frederick decided that he would try to suit all pockets, and by the time he had finished, you could have a stand-up snack at the counter for fivepence (2p), or a "recherché dinner in the Throne Room" for two guineas (£2.10). The latter was "a place set apart for higher priced dinners than those served in the Banqueting Hall and specially intended for the benefit of ladies." Crosby Hall was restored with stained glass windows and historical wallpapers and Gordon obviously backed his judgement with all the finances he could muster.

Frederick Gordon was at best an innovator, but if inspiration failed him he was always an excellent plagiarist. He was a stickler for cleanliness and a feature of Crosby Hall was the "40 neat and civil waitresses . . . The crowd between 12 and 3 seem to fill the building, ample and commodious as it is." There was, surprisingly, no smell of cooking, and the dining tables were supplied with 'pure filtered water' as Frederick characteristically cashed in on the publicity attendant on the cholera deaths.

The restaurant was a tremendous success and the city fathers and sons flocked to it. Soon he was able to open a second restaurant in a building which had been known as the Holborn Casino. Casino was a word for music and dancing and the new venture was simply called the Holborn Restaurant.

The origins of the word 'restaurant' are complicated; it starts with a particular recipe for a fine chicken soup in 18th century France which was nicknamed the 'divine restorer'. The ingredients were, however, too expensive for the poor people and so a bright chef created an imitation and sold it in shops. The 'restorer' could be sold by people who were unable to offer set meals, for to do that a licensed victualler needed a charter from the Society of Rotisseurs. Those who possessed such charters were called Traiteurs. Eventually the 'restorers' got together with the 'traiteurs' and became restaurateurs.

The Holborn opened in 1874 and this time Frederick was able to take advantage of the burgeoning banqueting trade. The Holborn had its own Masonic Temples, which were well patronised as the craft expanded, but there were also many other social functions like the Oxford and Cambridge Boat Race dinner, and regimental gatherings. The latter had been confined to a few cavalry regiments up to 1860, with the dinners held in June and concentrated on Derby Week, but now they were becoming more and more popular. Again Gordon provided a new facility for a growing demand and flourished.

Just as Frederick built his catering expertise, so he also constructed a following in the City. The papers wrote "he had the great quality of inspiring liking in all whom he met. Nothing escaped him and he left nothing to chance. He was an indomitable worker." "Always of a cheerful disposition, Frederick Gordon went through life in an atmosphere of contagious optimism." "Few men have had a wider circle of personal friends and still fewer are in his position of having no enemies." Even on his tomb there is a deep cut inscription "till we meet again." The optimism reminds one of John Smedley and, if Gordon was no teetotaller, he was, like Smedley, properly prepared to turn down business he considered of a dubious and perhaps immoral nature.

Brighton.   Metropole and Grand Hotels

A hotel was grand until something grander was built. The creation of the Metropole in Brighton was ruinous for the neighbouring Grand.

Throughout the 1870s he worked on the Common Council on the Committee for Markets, for Orphan Schools, Coal, Corn and Finance, Law and City Courts, sat as a Commissioner for Sewers, and was on a number of other committees as well. He met and worked with important figures in the powerful city guilds, and by 1877 he was ready to rely on the support of his twin pillars of a city reputation and a successful catering business, to enter into a new and potentially dangerous venture; to build a new hotel in Trafalgar Square, at a cost of £85,000, to appeal to the middle classes, and led not by the aristocracy, but by other businessmen like himself. The site was excellent as Trafalgar Square was relatively new and a great attraction for visitors, while neighbouring Charing Cross was both central for entertainment and for government offices and transport.

What was potentially dangerous was the state of the country's economy as once again the Victorian world dipped from boom to slump. Cheap food was pouring in from America and ruining large numbers of British farmers, while the competition of newly emergent nations like Germany was threatening British exports. In 1876 the slump which had been confined to relatively small areas of the country up to that time, started to become general. In 1877 unemployment reached nearly five per cent, nearly seven per cent in 1878 and over eleven per cent in 1879. This had its effect on commercial companies because of the resultant drop in demand and there were many bankruptcies including, most seriously, the City of Glasgow Bank in 1878. In spite of so many flotations, the bank was still not a limited liability company and the debts had to be settled by the shareholders.

The first large London hotel built specifically with the middle classes in mind was the Grand in Trafalgar Square. Frederick Gordon's brainchild, it opened in 1881 and was an instant success.

An optimist always, Frederick probably felt that the economic ills would right themselves in good time, and things would get back to the normal boom conditions quickly. But it was still 300 rooms, £85,000 and a tremendous undertaking for a man who was in hotel terms a complete novice.

16

CHARGES FOR CARRIAGE, ONE HORSE, AND COACHMAN.

	£	s.	d.
Two hours in Town	o	7	6
Two and a half hours in Town	o	9	o
Three hours in Town	o	10	6
Three and a half hours in Town	o	12	6
Four hours in Town	o	14	o
Four and a half hours in Town	o	16	o
Five hours in Town	o	17	6
Five and a half hours in Town	o	19	6
Six hours in Town	1	1	o
Day in Town, or to Kew or Richmond	1	4	o
Theatre or Dinner, short distance	o	9	6
Kensington	o	12	6
Ball, short distance	o	13	6
Kensington, etc.	o	15	6

Baits extra.

COACHING.

The Proprietors are prepared to arrange for Four-horse Coaches to the Races ; also for long or short Excursions. During the Season some of the regular Coaches out of London start daily from the Hotel. Seats may be engaged at the Secretary's office.

BREAKFAST.

The ordinary Breakfast-table of the Métropole allows of considerable choice in the matter of the

first daily meal, in proof of which the following Ménu du Dejeuner may be cited :—

FISH.
Finnon Haddocks.
Fried Soles.
Grilled Mackerel.

ENTRÉES.
Beefsteak au Beurre d'Anchois.
Grilled Ham or Bacon, and Eggs.
Grilled Devilled Legs of Chicken.
Omelette aux Fines Herbes.
Pommes de Terre Sautées.

SUNDRIES.
Oatmeal Porridge.
Cold Meats.

This Breakfast, including Tea, Coffee, Cocoa, or Chocolate, costs 3s. 6d.

Building started in 1879 on the site of Northumberland House, the old ducal mansion of the Percy family, and a board was created for Gordon's Grand Hotel with a membership designed to appeal to the widest possible section of the investing public. The City was represented by John Pound, a highly respected name and a future Lord Mayor. The brewing industry was taken care of by Alexander Johnstone on behalf of Bass, Ratcliff, some of whose directors had large shareholdings, and the men-about-town investors by Francis Cowley Burnand, probably the most famous editor that *Punch* has ever had. Flair, probity, proven success, and the strength of the brewers were all there, and Frederick also invited Horatio Davies on to the board to see that the family were well represented. It was a young group with Pound the oldest at forty-nine and Davies only thirty-six.

On May 29th 1881, the Lord Mayor of London opened the hotel which was reported as "providing luxury and comfort to which the travelling public had hitherto been little accustomed." Architecturally speaking the building was a mess, built on an irregular, semi-circular, half-triangular site. 'A shapeless pile' it was called "But one is amazed at the richness and magnificence of its interior. All that marble, mosaic, meralis, alabaster and gilding can do has been done. Reds, greys, whites and golds are admirably harmonized and blended. There is no barbaric profusion of gilding. The typical gloom and mustiness of English hotels is dispelled. The arched roof of stained glass over the dining room gives a flood of daylight. The fittings of the dining room are gorgeous. A spectacle almost distressing in its magnificence. There is soft and diffused electricity. A smaller dining room, and a general Reception Room which is a sumptuously fitted, lofty, spacious apartment with marble pillars and with walls and chimneys of carved walnut."

The Metropole in London's Northumberland Avenue was Frederick Gordon's third opening in five years. It was very convenient for the Palace at the top of the Mall and Edward VII, when Prince of Wales, used it on many occasions.

Not only was the hotel successful, "contrary to many predictions" said *The Times*, but the efforts of the nearby Charing Cross Hotel to hold back the tide and its clientele by cutting prices were of little avail. A new hotel was too great an attraction unless a management had earned exceptional loyalty. It was difficult to compete, for instance, for feminine custom when the ladies' drawing room at the Grand was so exotic: "the walls above the dado of black and gold are covered with green silk damask, the ceiling is full of gold stars, and the fireplace is adorned with enamelled plaques by Elkington."

Frederick also had an idea to obtain a strong male clientele. It so happened that the Conservative party had at last recovered, thanks to the efforts of Disraeli, who had led the first major Conservative administration for thirty years. The two principal Conservative clubs, the Carlton and the Junior Carlton were packed to capacity and there was no hope of becoming a member except through dead men's shoes. Tired of waiting, a group of 100 men under the Marquis of Abergavenny got together to create a new club, the Constitutional, and one of them was Frederick. Having formed it with the Marquis of Salisbury as president, the list of members swiftly grew to no less than 5,000 and Frederick was elected to the committee. When the question arose of where to build the new club premises, he was able to persuade his colleagues that 28, Northumberland Avenue would be ideal, right next door to the Grand! With his brother, Alexander, a member of the club and manager of the Grand, the country members of the Constitutional were unlikely to look further; it was a great coup, and well justified the decision to extend the Grand by a further seventy rooms.

Though the hotels grew larger, the charges remained very much the same. The extras were still going to be a lot more than the cost of the bedroom.

Gordon was forty-five when the Grand opened and he immediately set to work to raise the capital for another new hotel, the First Avenue in Holborn, so named because Frederick approved of a movement which wanted the streets of London to be numbered like New York for the sake of simplicity. When the First Avenue opened in 1883 Gordon started yet another new one down the road from the Grand at the corner of Northumberland Avenue and called it the Metropole. Throughout the '80s he was expanding and

---

BREAKFASTS.

AS SERVED FROM 8 TO 11 A.M.

TABLE D'HOTE BREAKFAST, with Tea, Coffee, Cocoa, Chocolate, and a variety of Hot and Cold Dishes	3s. 6d.
Plain Breakfast with Eggs, Swiss Honey, Toast, &c.	2s. 0d.

LUNCHEONS.

FROM 12.30 TO 3 P.M.

TABLE D'HOTE LUNCHEON, consisting of Soup, Fish, and a variety of dishes according to daily Ménu	3s. 6d.
Hot Joint or Cold Collation, with plain Vegetables, Cheese, Salad, &c.	2s. 6d.
Soup with Bread	1s. 6d.

DINNERS.

THE GRAND TABLE D'HOTE DINNER.

FROM 6 TO 8.30 P.M.

Is served at separate tables in the Grand Salle and the Secondary Salle, HORS D'ŒUVRES; Soups, Fish, Entrées, Releves, Roti, Entremets, Ices, Dessert, &c.	5s. 0d.

TEAS.

Tea and Coffee with Hot or Cold Meats or Fish	3s. 6d.
Plain Tea with EGGS, BREAD AND BUTTER OR TOAST	2s. 0d.

Extra charges will be made for all meals served in sleeping apartments or sitting rooms.

APARTMENTS.

BED-ROOMS per day from 4s. to 10s.
BED-ROOM AND SITTING-ROOM en suite 15s. to 30s.
PRIVATE SUITES OF APARTMENTS including Dining or Drawing-Room, with three Bed-Rooms, Bath Room, &c., 3 Guineas to 4 Guineas.

BATHS.

Sponge or Hip Bath in Bed-Room, 6d.
Cold Bath in Bath Room, 1s. 6d. | Hot Bath in Bath Room, 2s.

FIRES & LIGHTS.

Fire in Sitting-Room per day, 2s.6d.; Fire in Bed-Room, evening only, 1s.
Ordinary lights are included in the several charges.

SERVANTS.

Servants' Apartments charged according to selection.
Servants' Board, each, per day, 5s.

ATTENDANCE.

A charge of 1s. 6d. per day for each Visitor is made in lieu of gratuities to Attendants.

An extra charge for Apartments is made to all Visitors who do not Board at the Hotel.

Visitors are requested not to pay any money without receiving a bill.

Visitors leaving the Hotel must give notice of their intention before 3 o'clock or the apartments will be charged for.

In addition to the Ladies' Drawing Room, and the pleasant Reading and Writing Room on the first corridor, there is a spacious and sumptuously furnished Reading and *Reception* Room on the right of the Grand Vestibule.

A comfortable and quiet Smoking-Room appropriately appointed is reached by a special staircase from the Hall.

for the year ending November 1888, the three hotels showed a profit of over £210,000. This was the rock-solid foundation on which he intended to base the biggest flotation the hotel industry had ever seen.

The aim was to raise no less than £2,201,000, and the package the shareholders were to purchase included all the most fashionable investments in hotel terms; in addition to the famous London hotels, there were some good seaside names; the Burlington in Eastbourne and the Metropole in Brighton were very fashionable resort hotels, and the Royal Pier Hotel in the Isle of Wight was on the island most beloved of Queen Victoria. To add the last touch of glamour the company was also to own the newly built Metropole Hotel in Cannes, and the Metropole Hotel in Monte Carlo.

Gordon was one of the few English hoteliers to invest in the Riviera which was then in the middle of a get-rich-quick boom similar to that experienced in the 1960s by the West Indies. It was a fabulous world of almost unlimited tourist wealth, attracting crowned heads and millionaires during the season, the mecca of the aristocracy and the *nouveau riche*. For a few people it was an immense goldmine; men like Camille Blanc who had the concession for the Casino at Monte Carlo, and a handful of really expert hoteliers.

It was a four months' season from December to April and, like London, the stories of boom business attracted so many new hotels that the market was soon flooded. There were fifty first-class hotels in Monte Carlo at the turn of the century, and as a consequence the available business was spread too thinly for more than a few to be successful in the long term. It was also a totally international clientele, and consequently affected by the vagaries of European politics to a considerable degree; a royal assassination or *coup d'etat* would keep the aristocracy affected at home awaiting developments; a diplomatic row between France and another nation would cause a temporary boycott; the area was primitive in many ways, and outbreaks of cholera or smallpox would frighten off the visitors and could ruin a season. The whole operation was as risky as the roulette tables which provided one of the main attractions. The casinos operated in Germany during the summer, like the one at Baden-Baden at which the Blanc family had flourished originally, and the balmy winter weather on the Riviera complemented the German social round.

Frederick had two splendid locations for his Riviera hotels; the Metropole at Monte Carlo still stands in its sub-tropical grounds adjoining the Casino while the Metropole at Cannes had a magnificent panoramic view over the bay high above the little town. As it was a winter season, the attractions of sea bathing did not interest the visitors, and the remoteness from the town made the hotel equally distant, hopefully, from any plebeian epidemics.

By 1890 Trafalgar Square was becoming the hub of hotel London, with Morleys, the Charing Cross, the Victoria, Metropole and, here, the Grand all competing for business. Bomb explosions in the square in 1887 were not good for business.

89

As Cannes changed its character between the two World Wars, the position of the Metropole became a disadvantage and it was sold in the thirties to the Bishop of Nice as a seminary. Walking round its overgrown but still impressive gardens today with the cactus plants and palm trees, its tennis courts flanking the hotel on both sides, and wide sweeping paths to the great ornamental gates at the front, one cannot fault Gordon's planning. He could hardly be blamed for failing to see the way habits would change forty years hence, and if he had satisfied those future generations, he would have done little business in 1890. It was the everlasting dilemma of the resort hotelier.

With his successful record, his London, seaside and Riviera hotels, and his own persuasive charm, even the immense issue of over £2 million was a success, and in 1890 Frederick Gordon, the house painter's son, found himself the chairman of an enormous hotel company, happily selling beds to his clients, and retiring in the evening to his country mansion, Bentley Priory at Stanmore. For it was Frederick Gordon who stated most clearly the core of hotel profits: "we think it is very nice, of course, to get visitors into our *Table d'hôte*, but we do not go in, as some of the other large hotels in London do, for making—I will not say the chief business, but at any rate a very considerable proportion of it, restaurant business. We prefer if we can to let our apartments, and you may rely on it that the backbone of hotel business is the letting of apartments." From a man who made all his early money in restaurants, this was a very clear-sighted viewpoint.

The progress of Gordon Hotels after 1890 cannot be seen separately from the development of the whole industry, which we left as the slump of the 1870s was coming to an end, but whatever the future might bring, Gordon epitomised the Victorian ideal of self-help, courage and determination leading on to fame and fortune.

Frederick Gordon originally thought of Bentley Priory at Stanmore as an opportunity for his guests in town to visit country. This was not very successful in spite of the fact that he built a railway line to it from Harrow. Undismayed he moved into the house himself.

Above:
Bond Street was equally as
fashionable in the 18th
century as it is today. This
scene outside Long's Hotel
proves the point.

Durrant's Hotel, London,
a perfect example of
Georgian hotel architecture
and still family operated.

The Red Lion Hotel in
Salisbury is a near perfect
example of an 18th century
coaching inn. The large
entrance led to the
courtyard for coaches and
horses.

THE HOTEL. COLLEGE·GREEN. BRISTOL.

*Facing page, top:
The de Keyser Royal Hotel
at Blackfriars in London,
where now stands Unilever
House. The goods came in
direct from the river; the
entrance for coaches is
clearly visible.
Facing page: bottom:
The pediment of the Great
Western Royal Hotel at
Paddington Station,
London. The carved figures
depict peace, plenty,
industry and science—
a Victorian conversation
piece if nothing else.*

*Originally "The Hotel" on
Bristol's College Green
alongside the Cathedral.
The facade is little changed,
but the hotel is now called
The Royal.*

*A gimmick is always good
for business—The Grand
at Brighton had a splendid
one for it was probably
the first seaside hotel to
have a lift or "rising room"
as it was then known.
Its profits went up and
down as well.*

Facing page, top:
The Queen's Hotel,
Hastings—financially, one
of the most successful hotels
of the last century.
Facing page, bottom:
Sir George Gilbert Scott's
extraordinary Midland
Grand Hotel in London,
more commonly known as
the St. Pancras Hotel.
"The very parapet of the
cab-road is panelled and
perforated, at a cost that
would have supplied foot-
warmers to all the trains
for many years to come."

Left:
Scotland has many thriving
examples of the "Golden
Age". These three are
among the finest.
Top: The North British
Hotel, Edinburgh, alongside
Waverley Station.

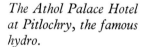

The Athol Palace Hotel
at Pitlochry, the famous
hydro.

The George Hotel, Edin-
burgh, was a worthy
addition to the acclaimed
George Street architecture.

Afternoon Tea

The Louis XI Lounge

Far left:
The Connaught Hotel just off London's Grosvenor Square was called The Coburg until German names became unpopular during the First World War.

Immediate left:
The Piccadilly Hotel was built with the American tourist market very much in mind. These elegant illustrations of the Edwardian "jet-set" appeared in United States magazines of the day.

Overleaf:
The Australian oak panelling at the Piccadilly Hotel in London. One of the few pieces of "Golden Age" decor that is still in mint condition.

ILLUSTRATED BOOKLET AND TARIFF SENT POST FREE ON APPLICATION TO TOWN & COUNTRY OFFICES 89 FIFTH AVENUE NEW YORK.

THE GRILL ROOM LOUNGE

The pleasure of your company—1880–1889

VISITORS to London in 1880 could obtain the advice of the greatest living British novelist on all their problems by purchasing Charles Dickens' *Dictionary of London*. On the subject of hotels he wrote "One of the latest changes in London, during the last score or so years is in the matter of hotels. In proportion to its size, London is still worse provided in this respect than most of the great Continental or American towns. Almost every great railway, however, with the exception of the South Western has now a handsome hotel in connection with its terminus . . . None of these hotels are at all cheap for people who do not understand hotel life, but they are very convenient for the new arrival, especially at night, and will probably prove quite as economical in the end as hunting about in a cab for a cheaper lodging. Indeed we may go further, and say that it is possible, with judicious management, to live almost as cheaply at one of the large hotels as at any of the ambitious second-class houses."

Dickens lists the well-known hotels like the Langham, Westminster Palace and the "Buckingham Palace Hotel just opposite the great ballroom window of Buckingham Palace" but also discusses the cheaper ones. "There is also a large class of comfortable and more old fashioned hotels, such as the Bedford, Covent Garden, for families and gentlemen; the Tavistock also in Covent Garden for bachelors where bed, breakfast and attendance costs seven shillings and sixpence [$37\frac{1}{2}$p], and which has one of the best smoking rooms in London. Among the cheap hotels, special reference should be made to the Arundel on the Embankment . . . but it is of very little use to look for rooms there, unless bespoken beforehand. Nearly all the streets from the south side of the Strand are full of small private hotels, a sort of compromise between hotels and lodging houses, where the casual visitor will find himself comfortably, if perhaps a little roughly quartered, and where he will be in a thoroughly central position, even for business or pleasure. Hotels on the 'temperance' principle will be found at Shirleys', 37, Queen Street, Bloomsbury; Fithians, 17, Great Coram Street . . . Foreign visitors will do well to bear in mind that the continental custom of taking all, or the great majority of meals out of the hotel does not obtain in England, and that a London hotel-keeper under such circumstances will consider himself ill-used."

Dickens was a good judge of hotel life and had travelled widely. London was *still* under-hotelled, particularly as the capital was becoming more and more the centre of the world's business and the core of a great Empire. By 1880 the railway network was all but completed though there were still additions to be made in some remote areas. The development of rail travel with its side benefits of additional customers for hotels was also being augmented by the increasing number of passengers on liners.

The first steam-propelled passenger ship to cross the Atlantic was the *Savannah* in 1819 though nobody would actually pay for the journey and she therefore arrived in

Liverpool with her new cabins still unused. The second steam ship was the *Royal William* in 1833 which did little better and only managed to attract seven paying customers on her inaugural voyage, and, for many years after, the growth in transatlantic travel by steam was very slow. The sailing boats were well established but they were at the mercy of the winds and could lie becalmed for days or even weeks. Travel by sea was dangerous, and until the middle of the century it was quite usual to hold religious services and take leave of your friend as he prepared to board a ship, very much as if he was on his death bed.

There were also some very costly failures like Brunel's *Great Eastern*, a mammoth ship which bankrupted the company originally set up to build her, and lost her reputation in a disastrous voyage in 1861 when a violent storm left her drifting helplessly for days. "For a few short unprofitable years . . . the *Great Eastern* was a *bona fide* transatlantic liner carrying thin lists of hundreds, in space prepared for thousands of passengers." But from the hotel industry's point of view there *were* hundreds, where there had been scores on smaller boats, and some lines were expanding successfully. There were more people travelling on the ships operated by Samuel Cunard, for instance, a Canadian whose vessels could proudly boast that they had never lost a passenger.

In the effort to make transatlantic ships pay, there were three main sources of business: freight, immigrants and travellers, and it was a long time before the travellers became more than the icing on the cake. Much depended on new inventions like the principle of screw propulsion instead of paddle wheels, and then twin screws so that one could fail without disabling the ship. Speeds increased so that journeys which at the beginning of the century could last a month or more, were steadily brought down to under a week.

By 1880 there were many fine liners on the Atlantic fitted out more luxuriously than all but a handful of hotels, and ferrying passengers quickly and safely. In 1875 the Inman Line's *City of Berlin* took the Blue Riband for the fastest crossing of the Atlantic in seven days, eighteen hours and two minutes and together with the White Star Line and Cunard Steamship, the three companies dominated the market.

The ships still carried sail in case anything went wrong, and indeed the first two Cunard ships to jettison this safeguard had cause to regret it. Both the *Umbria*, launched in 1884, and the *Etruria*, in 1885, broke down in mid-ocean and floundered about. There were still disasters like the *City of Boston* which sailed in 1870 and was never seen again, and a worse tragedy, in terms of the number of lives lost, would occur when the *Titanic* went down, but once the American Civil War was over and the United States began to play a larger part in economic affairs, the call of Europe drew increasing numbers of American visitors.

It was a two way traffic with Thomas Cook leading tours to the States and British businessmen and holidaymakers surveying the vast continent. The methods of American hoteliers, too, were studied by men like Richard d'Oyly Carte, the creator of the Savoy Hotel, a theatrical impressario deeply involved in the presentation of Gilbert and Sullivan operettas, but with a passion for hotels as well. The American visitors meanwhile brought with them their own standards of taste and hygiene as well as habits of eating and living which differed in small ways from the European. They enjoyed, for instance, their native tomato and eventually this was introduced into England, and they expected the technical achievements of their inventors such as electric light, smoother lifts and better plumbing to be available, so that the hotels which wanted their custom badly enough were prepared to invest in these advances more quickly than might otherwise have been the case. Of course a slump in America would reduce the numbers prepared to spend the considerable sum involved on a trip to Europe, but the trend over the years was steadily upwards.

The Americans did not restrict themselves to London and they could be found in the hydropathic institutions, tramping the Scottish Highlands and visiting relatives from whom they or their parents would often have been separated for only a small span of years.

Those who reached Edinburgh were among the first to see the effects of over-optimistic and unplanned hotel development, as the demand for accommodation created in the 1840s had long since been fully met by the extra bedrooms built. Any form of state control to prevent over capacity would have been anathema to an age where *laissez faire* was the economic religion, but many hoteliers must have wished the situation was different, and in Edinburgh the expansion of hotels was not always a simple question of whether they would pay or not.

As the North British Railway Company was in competition with the Caledonian Railway Company, the North British Hotel was a weapon to get more business for the the former's trains, but when the remodelling and reconstruction of the hotel was mooted in 1885, a number of shareholders opposed it vigorously and even went to court to try to stop it. They pointed out in a manifesto that the city's hotels were nearly empty for much of the year, and even at the peak of the season only a few filled all their rooms.

In 1885 a number of stockholders tried to stop the rebuilding of the North British in Princes Street, Edinburgh, because they said there was more than enough accommodation in the city already. They were right, but they were outvoted.

Hadn't the Douglas Hotel, which was even patronised by the Prince and Princess of Wales, recently been converted into offices? Hadn't the Cafe Royal Hotel, which had been valued at £16,000, been sold in desperation for £9,500 and wasn't the Rainbow Hotel now business premises as well? Within 200 yards of the North British, they said, there were no less than sixteen hotels including the Royal British, Waverley, Cockburn, Star and Imperial while another five minute journey would take the visitor to a further fourteen.

Of these the Caledonian, Roxburghe and George can still be found but there were a number of others at the time which failed to survive. The court listened, but held quite naturally that the railway company had a perfect right to take whatever action it felt fit if a majority of the shareholders approved. There can be no question, however, that the dissenting shareholders were right and that the overall wastage of capital invested in Edinburgh hotels continued to be considerable.

The lessons of Edinburgh, predictably, had no effect on the investors in London, and the 1880s saw the beginning of that flood of new hotels which was eventually to create exactly the same result in the English capital. As early as 1880 the *Caterer* was warning of the dangers of rank amateurs entering the industry. The occasion was the establishment of an ex-Army and Navy cooperative to run a hotel, and the *Caterer* warned the prospective investors that no matter how glowing the prospectus, bankruptcy was bound to follow the operation of a hotel by people who understood nothing about the business. The journal also went as far as it dared by saying of the prospectus that "the art of puffery has been used to the maximum." *Caterer* was proved right and the hotel which opened in 1883 swiftly failed, and was sold in 1886 to a group headed this time by a professional, J. R. Cleave, who renamed it the Windsor and did very well with it. Cleave had worked for seven years as a cashier at the Langham and this training together with

Eastbourne was a backwater for the first half of the 19th century and then expanded very rapidly. The pinnacle of its hotel building was the Cavendish which opened in 1872.

CAVENDISH HOTEL, EASTBOURNE, SUSSEX.——Mr. KNIGHTLEY, ARCHITECT.

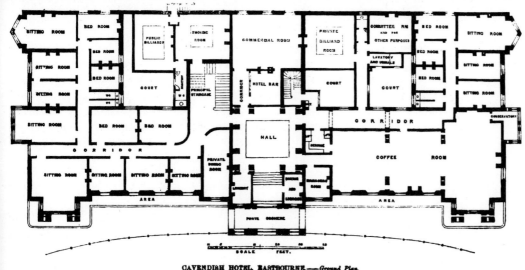

CAVENDISH HOTEL, EASTBOURNE.—*Ground Plan.*

There were bedrooms on the ground floor of the Cavendish because it was a seaside hotel. Notice the public billiards room and the private one. Even as late as 1872 the restaurant was still called the Coffee Room.

the fact that his backers were able to buy the hotel for a fraction of its cost, gave him a good start. The hotel was also freehold unlike many of the other newcomers and within four years Cleave was the joint owner.

Disaster also befell Hatchetts, a hotel in Piccadilly opened in 1886 by a company headed by Frederick Gordon's highly successful relative, Horatio Davies, but which turned out to be one of his few defeats. Together with the land, the initial cost of Hatchetts was no less than £120,000, but in 1887 it went for £65,000.

Even worse befell the Northumberland Avenue Hotel which had first been announced to a gullible public in the summer of 1882. The prospectus modestly suggested that a nineteen-and-a-half per cent dividend would be nothing untoward and a mere £200,000 would be needed to build a 500 bedroom goldmine from which the directors would only take £2,500 a year plus five per cent of any dividends over fifteen per cent. Isaacs and Florence who had been responsible for the Holborn Viaduct Hotel and were to design the Coburg Hotel in 1896 (now the Connaught), were the architects in charge, and Viscount Pollington headed an imposing list of directors. By the spring of 1884 the nine pound shares had nevertheless fallen to two pounds, seventeen shillings and sixpence (£2.87½) and when Judge Chitty put in the liquidator in November there was precious little to salvage. The hotel was taken over by a Croydon contractor called J. W. Hobbs and a new company was formed under the chairmanship of Jabez Balfour, a prominent figure in politics and the city. Even so the hotel was not opened until 1887 at a final cost of £520,000.

Failures were, in fact, quite commonplace like the conversion of the Cannon Street Hotel in Manchester, into a vegetarian restaurant, and the fate of the Royal Hotel, Birmingham, which at one time was the best in the city, but by 1881 was "now regularly going bankrupt". Building and investing in hotels was becoming a fashion giving numerous municipalities status, architects a method of advancing their theories, investors a stake in the equivalent of a stately home, and directors a business which combined glamour with luxury. It was a heady mixture but if "where there's muck there's money" then alternatively where there was glamour there might only be dross as far as profits were concerned.

Around 300 receiving orders a year were made against publicans and hotelkeepers throughout the country, but the hotels which failed were, of course, only part of the story. More bedrooms were genuinely needed for the increase in business in many towns, so long as the hotels were constructed and run on a sensible basis. If the cost of servicing the capital was too great, if they were poorly situated or extravagantly managed, then there was trouble ahead, Many were well run and could offer the new guests higher standards than ever before.

The Metropole at the corner of Northumberland Avenue next to the ill-fated Northumberland Avenue Hotel, was one of the newcomers in 1885 and set out in its 88-page brochure—of which forty-five were paid advertising—to bang the drum. "Particularly recommend it to ladies and families visiting the West End during the Season; to travellers from Paris and the Continent, arriving from Dover and Folkestone at the Charing Cross Terminus; to Officers and others attending the levées at St. James; to Ladies going to the Drawing Rooms, State Balls, and Concerts at Buckingham Palace; and to Colonial and American visitors unused to the great world of London." The Metropole wisely chose not to echo the complaint of the chairman of the Charing Cross Hotel that business had fallen off because of the "dynamite outrages in Trafalgar Square"; the lunatic fringe has been in existence a very long time.

It was the summer when trade was at its brightest, but there would be plenty of businessmen at other times of the year, as well as the revenue from banqueting. At the height of the season accommodation would be hard to find and it was those brief periods which encouraged others to believe that London and the other cities could carry more hotels. So they built them; the Central in Glasgow in 1883 with wine cellars sufficient for 60,000 bottles, the St. Ermins in Westminster in 1887, the Hyde Park Hotel in 1888 full of glorious period furniture, the Park Hotel, Cardiff, in 1884 and many others.

The hansom cabs line up outside the Metropole in London on a grey summer day. There was obviously a fair wind blowing as well.

So much building, so much capital invested provided a goldmine at least for the fortunate companies granted the contracts for furnishing and fitting out the new establishments, and foremost among those which benefited was Maple and Co, with its two guiding lights, John Maple and his son, John Blundell Maple. John Maple (1815–1900) opened his shop at 145, Tottenham Court Road in 1841, and by the time his sons, John Blundell and Harry, joined him in 1862 the store had grown and was well known as a draper, furnisher and carpet supplier. Such a combination was particularly useful to companies putting up hotels, for the alternative was to deal with a number of suppliers, which was costly in terms of time and made it more difficult to get the best wholesale prices. Comparatively few organizations were equipped to handle large orders, but John Maple had the resources and could see what a wonderful opportunity this was to expand his business. The company already had a reputation for quality and though Harry had died by the 1880s, John Blundell had developed many firm friendships with developers like Frederick Gordon.

The contract for the Grand in Trafalgar Square went to Maples and after the press had acclaimed the results, Gordon also gave the firm a £70,000 contract for the First Avenue Hotel, where "In the sleeping apartments and sitting rooms, the upholsterings are of a superb richness and exquisite delicacy." In 1882 Maples handled contracts as far apart as the County Hotel, Newcastle, the New Hotel, Preston, the Queen's, Birmingham, and the Royal Spithead, Isle of Wight. It seems likely that Maples were prepared to wait on occasions for their money, as there was a widespread habit during the period of hiring furniture very much like the system we now call hire purchase. If a hotelkeeper fell into arrears, the company could apply to repossess the furniture though this was a desperation measure as guests seldom took any more care with their bedrooms then than they do today, and there was the usual amount of wear and tear. Maples, of course, did not have the field to themselves by any means, but they were the most popular and had the added cachet that they were also engaged for hotels overseas and thus had an international aura.

Although the public watched eagerly for the opening of new hotels many of the older hotels continued to maintain their special place as long as they filled a particular niche; such a hotel was Andertons in Fleet Street which looked after generations of newsmen at very reasonable charges and produced sufficiently good results to try to go public in 1884, though without success. One hundred bedrooms, a coffee room where lunch cost two shillings (10p), a Masonic temple, and a thriving bar produced a turnover in 1883 of nearly £24,000 for a nine per cent profit after depreciation, and although it wasn't glamorous enough, it was really a sounder proposition than many which did float successfully.

Richard d'Oyly Carte had the vision to hire Cesar Ritz and found the money to build the Savoy in London largely on his reputation as an impresario presenting Gilbert and Sullivan.

The best hotel in London was reputed to be the Bristol which was small and very select, but the Clarendon ran it close. When Lord Chesterfield retired as Master of the Buckhounds in 1880 the banquet in his honour featured a menu for which the hotel charged six guineas (£6.30), a sum which would have kept one of the chefs and his family for a month.

Most of the new hotels in London followed the same pattern of architecture and management that had been pioneered by the Grosvenor and the Great Western twenty to thirty years before, but one was different, and that was the Savoy.

It is difficult today to see the Savoy through eyes clear of the smoke put up by generations of their excellent professional publicists. From the very beginning the Savoy was in show business, a hotel built by Richard d'Oyly Carte in the heart of the theatre district where he had made his fortune. The building was started in 1884 and finished in 1889; it was very different from the type of building put up by Barry and Sir Gilbert Scott. d'Oyly Carte had been influenced by the quality of American hotels and tried to incorporate the best of the two transatlantic traditions; the Savoy was the first hotel to have a really substantial proportion of its rooms equipped with private bathrooms adjacent to the bedrooms, an eccentricity which compelled the builder to enquire whether it was anticipated that the guests would be amphibious. There were eighty private bathrooms originally and the whole building was constructed of concrete encasing steel joists to make it entirely fireproof. Apart from the doors and window frames there was very little wood used and d'Oyly Carte had no less than six lifts installed, though it was still necessary to point out that they were "perfectly safe, their movement smooth, rapid and pleasant." The building was "faced in Doulton Carrara Ware, that is a white, matt, glazed terracotta" and it was far simpler in appearance than the Gothic or Italian Renaissance designs which were fashionable before.

Overleaf:
The interest in luxury hotels led the "Illustrated London News" to produce a detailed cross-section drawing of the Savoy. Notice the artesian well 500 feet deep.

As was natural with a showman, d'Oyly Carte set out to attract his friends in the arts and through them the high society who enjoyed their company. His board included Michael Gunn, the manager of the Gaiety Hotel, Dublin, the Earl of Lathom who was Lord Chamberlain, Hwfa Williams, a sportsman friend of the Prince of Wales, well known in fashionable circles, and two financiers, R. B. Fenwick and A. H. Weguelin. It was a powerful board financially and socially, but it had little knowledge of running hotels.

There is a major difference between constructing a hotel with the most modern facilities and trying to run it to a high standard. It was a good gimmick to have a restaurant committee composed of swinging gourmets like Reuben Sassoon and Arthur Sullivan and a nice piece of stage dressing to have a "seneschal wearing a silver chain" usher you into the dining room, but this did not mean that the food would be cooked well, the waiting immaculate or the wines well selected.

The hotel was designed with great care; there was electricity throughout and you could turn the lights off when you were in bed without having to cross the room. Twenty-four-hour service was the proud boast, with no extra charges for attendance and the rooms on the upper floors were just as large as those on the lower ones. So there were plenty of attractive features for the brochure, but the hotel had taken five years to build, the lavish outlay on the seven storeys, the artesian well 500 feet down, the Genoese lounge and all the other exotic public rooms built up a large capital outlay, and the type of knowledgeable guests who d'Oyly Carte wanted to use the Savoy were not going to come more than once if the hotel was run less than perfectly.

D'Oyly Carte had already tried to get one of the great professionals on the continent to manage the Savoy; this was Cesar Ritz who had built a reputation on the Riviera and in Switzerland and Germany which gave him a fan club of important guests second to none. He was a perfectionist and a true expert but he was also deeply involved in many other undertakings and was not to be persuaded to join d'Oyly Carte. Only after a lot of cajoling and the promise of a massive fee did he agree to even visit the Savoy so that d'Oyly Carte could proclaim his connection with the undertaking. When he first arrived

ENTRANCE DRIVE   COURTYARD   ENTRANCE HALL

STORES

LUGGAGE ROOM   STORES   KITCHEN FOR MALSIA CAFE
                    LUGGAGE LIFT

COLD STORAGE ROOMS   COLD STORAGE ROOM   ENGINE ROOM

MAKING PLANT   SWITCH BOARD   ENGINE ROOM AND BOILER HOUSE
                    BRINE COOLER   DYNAMOS BEHIND YIELDING
                    BEHIND ICE LIFT   1,000,000 UNITS PER ANNUM

DOTTED LINE shows EXTENT of WINE CELLARS BEYOND

                    THE WINE VAULTS EXTEND
                    FROM THIS WALL
                    TO THE MAIN WALL
                    OF SOUTH FRONT FACING RIVER
                    PASSING UNDER BALL ROOM ETC. ETC.

ARTESIAN WELL   STAIRS LEADING TO
500 FEET DEEP   VIENNA BAKERY
YIELDING 240,000 GALLONS of WATER PER DAY

                    ARTESIA
                    EACH

it was announced discreetly that he would be the restaurant manager, but within a few months he had agreed to run the hotel completely.

At the time the hotel was not doing well; in the language of the day "Directors and management are by no means in perfect accord," and the story of Ritz's arrival and the prosperity he brought has been one of the best known happy endings in the industry's folklore. It was not quite that simple though, and it was not to end happily after all. To start with it was necessary to get rid of the incumbent manager, Mr. Hardwicke, and he had a perfectly valid three-year contract. Dismissed by d'Oyly Carte with a lordly wave of his magic wand, Mr. Hardwicke refused to vanish like the demon king, and instead issued a writ for £3,125 which the Savoy, according to the *Caterer*, had to settle out of court for the full amount. Even so the career of a man who had risen slowly and painfully to a high position in his profession suffered a setback from which it was practically impossible to recover, and Hardwicke sank to managing a relatively insignificant seaside hotel on the south coast.

With the Hardwicke problem out of the way, Ritz could settle down with his established and memorable team of departmental heads, starring Auguste Escoffier, his great chef, and including Autour, his Number One, Agostini to look after the accounts and Echenard, a *maître d'hôtel* steeped in experience as a connoisseur of wine. The clients could now be guaranteed to come, but as the expenses involved in opening the hotel had been great and Ritz did not like to economize, it was difficult to make substantial profits from the investment.

The Savoy not only spearheaded the changes to come in constructing and running a luxury hotel, but also symptomised the beginning of the victory of the hedonists over the forces of restraint. The Victorian ideals of self-help, hard work, the Christian virtues, and the rather wide definition of sin had been fundamental in building the nation to its pre-eminent position by the 1880s, but now there was a growing desire to enjoy the fruits of father's labour and instead of building companies by leading from the factory floor, there appeared a numerous class of shareholders only interested in collecting dividends and letting hired managers get on with the job of keeping the wheels in motion.

The restraints were under fire and some of those attacked affected the hotel industry; d'Oyly Carte, for instance, wanted to encourage people to dine out by choice rather than eat in a hotel only if they were staying there, and he also wanted them to be able to dine later, for his restaurant, like all others, was most heavily patronized between 6 and 8.30 in the evening. Others felt the same, for at this time banquets would start with a reception at 5 o'clock in the afternoon and would usually have finished by 11 at the latest. This was understandable in terms of the early days of the century when to be out late at night in ill-lit streets was to invite trouble, but there were no highwaymen left at Hyde Park Corner even if mugging with a sandbag was a risk the unwary pedestrians were warned about. Street lighting had improved and being home early started to seem dull and prudish to many perfectly respectable people. It was a long road to the 20th century but the hotels, for totally selfish reasons, were eager to support any liberalisation of laws or customs affecting dining out.

As business prospered, the seaside hotels did well unless they had to face some luxurious newcomer across the road. The Brighton Grand, for instance, having got over the inefficiency of the original board was able to pay a nine per cent dividend in 1886 and 1887 only to find its good work undermined by the arrival of Frederick Gordon's new Metropole Hotel. Any idea that lavish expenditure was confined to the capital could be instantly dissipated by looking at this new wonder, for the Metropole was designed by no less than the president of the Royal Institute of British Architects, Alfred Waterhouse, who had a passion for red brick and terra cotta, and a great deal of whose work can still be seen around the country.

As this was a Gordon Hotel, Maples were responsible for the furnishings and one of

The hotel brochure for the Metropole in London contained 45 pages of paid advertising including this one for a local dentist.

THE HÔTEL MÉTROPOLE.

THE reputation earned by the HÔTEL MÉTRO-POLE in the past three years justifies the Proprietors in commending it to the notice of visitors as one of the most desirable, convenient, and popular of the great modern hotels of West-end London,

Before colour photography, hotel brochures relied on artist's impressions which seldom failed to flatter. The lobby at the Metropole did, however, look exactly like this in 1888.

Frederick's Riviera friends was also involved; "the fine statuary marble place is from the chisel of Prince Victor of Hohenlohe." There were 700 rooms and "the decorations are in a warm rich golden brown graduating to ivory white." The Metropole had three dining rooms which could be divided by glass walls or seat 500 guests at a time. There was a grand staircase of finely polished marble, a library, smoking room, lounge, billiard rooms, iron wine bins "sufficient for 20,000 dozen apart from wines in the wood" and many different varieties of bath: Turkish baths, Russian baths, plunge baths, Apodyterum and Moorish divans. It was suitably exotic for a town which could boast the flamboyant Royal Pavilion, and from the back windows you could see "the beautifully terraced Italian garden which is one of the beauties of the hotel."

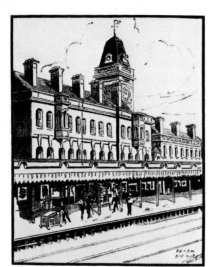

To fill the weekends at railway hotels, bargain rates were offered, and among the first in 1881 was a 35s.— (£1.75) package at the Great Eastern in Harwich, which included a first-class return ticket from Liverpool Street.

The grounds adjoining hotels all over the country were a greater part of the attraction for visitors at this time than they can be today when land is so very expensive. There were tennis courts adjoining the Midland Hotel, Derby, gardens in many of the London hotels, and at the seaside winter gardens were often constructed as well. The winter gardens were a determined effort to avoid the vagaries of the English climate. Roofed in with glass and heated with pipes, they were apparently impervious to the weather and it was hoped that guests would be content to wander through the floral displays, write letters at the tables provided, read, knit, crochet, embroider, smoke cigars, sip wine or just quietly snooze. The idea was sound enough but the upkeep of the buildings was an added overhead to hotels with only a short high season.

The railways tried hard to get visitors during the quieter months and by 1880 they were already running weekend-bargain packaged holidays. The purchaser could depart first class from Liverpool Street on Saturday after lunch and be met at Harwich by a porter from the town's Great Eastern Hotel. Then, his luggage having been carried to the hotel, tea would be served and until Monday morning he would have all his meals and accommodation provided, leaving again for London after breakfast Monday and paying a total of thirty-five shillings (£1.75) for the weekend. Many seaside hotels offered special weekend terms and twelve shillings and sixpence (62½p) was a popular tariff for full board from Saturday till Monday morning at smaller places like the Grosvenor Hotel, New Brighton, in 1884.

In spite of seasonal difficulties and greater competition, hotels in the 1880s fared pretty well because there was an increase in the size of the middle class prepared to use them, and in tourists and businessmen, but at the same time expenses remained very stable. The chairman of the Langham announced in 1881 that "the undertaking has now arrived at a point when its progress would be most marked, and money would be literally coined by the company." Birmingham was so short of hotel accommodation that shops were converted into bedrooms!

An examination of the dividend performance around the country during the decade helps to explain the ready support for new ventures; the Midland Hotel in Birmingham paid twelve-and-a-half per cent from 1882 onwards, the Queens in Harrogate twelve per cent in 1884 when the £5 shares stood at £8, the Alexandra in London nine per cent from 1884, the Queens in Hastings over ten per cent, while with Frederick Gordon's hotels, as one shareholder ruefully recalled in less palmy days in 1912, "ordinary shares went to a fifty per cent premium. They originally paid twelve-and-a-half per cent and could have paid twenty per cent."

Gordon was aiming at a new market with the Grand, believing that there should be hotels offering luxury surroundings at prices which would attract the middle classes, and this proved extremely sound. Hotels, as we have seen, did seek out particular sections of the market, as they had done in the earlier part of the century, for the class barriers of Victorian society made mixing a problem. At the Metropole, London, for example, porters would deliver letters to guests staying in suites, but if you only had a bedroom you would have to collect your post from the porter's desk.

Life in a good hotel at this point was getting steadily more opulent. Your three shillings and sixpenny (17½p) breakfast at the Metropole now included "*Beefsteak au beurre d'Anchois*, Grilled devilled legs of chicken, and fried soles." You could also have grilled ham, porridge, cold meats and various other snacks with your tea, cocoa or chocolate. The basic price of your bedroom changed very little over the course of the decade. At the Grand it was three shillings and sixpence (17½p) throughout the period for a single room. On the other hand the Grand was one of the few hotels which would tell the guest from the start what he was letting himself in for, as there seemed to be some polite reluctance to tackle the hotel manager on this score and tariffs used the word 'from' when listing room prices. Baedeker's famous guide pointed out to its readers that the cost varied according to the floor, and advised them to ask about the exact amount soon after arrival.

It appears likely, however, that prices also varied in many establishments according to how much the client appeared to be able to pay, and how busy the hotel was at the time. The tariff for bedrooms was usually raised if the guest did not accept *demi-pension* but this was an accepted practice. At the Grand "The policy was to get a lump sum. A man likes to know when he enters what he has to pay."

To modern eyes it seems strange that the cost of a meal was often as much or even more than the cost of accommodation. At the Empire Hotel, Bath, for example, the cost of a single bedroom was 'from' four shillings and sixpence (22½p), a double bedroom 'from' six shillings and sixpence (32½p), but dinner was definitely five shillings and sixpence (27½p). In fairness it was quite a dinner "The Empire dinner is served at separate tables in the Dining Room from 7 to 8.30 and consists of Hors d'oeuvres, Soup, Fish, Entrée, Joint, Poultry or Game, Sweets and Dessert, also Coffee served in Lounge." Portions were smaller than today, but not by that much and the diners lived in blissful ignorance of the penalties of excessive over-eating. Luncheon was another heavy meal usually served between one and two-thirty and breakfast was really equally substantial. The Empire Hotel's breakfast was three shillings (15p) but an additional shilling (5p) was charged for guests who wanted poultry—and they didn't mean eggs!

Apart from eating and presumably resting after eating, the guest at a good hotel also expected a considerable amount more help with his entertainment than he receives now. The best tickets for theatrical performances were available, and sightseeing tours would start from the hotel. Carriages and horses would take visitors to the races and in the spas. you could, of course, hire invalid chairs. Frederick Gordon, always one to try to offer that little bit more, had the idea that visitors might like to spend time not only in a central hotel but also in a country mansion, and to that end he purchased Bentley Priory, a splendid mansion in Stanmore, which had for years been the home of William IV's widow. As communications were difficult he also built a railway from Harrow to Stanmore for his prospective guests and until recently the pretty little station still stood in Gordon Avenue. This experiment did not work out though; Gordon swiftly sold the railway and moved into the Priory, with his wife, eleven children and the usual brigade of servants for all of whom he certainly needed a small hotel.

In the 1880s hotel bills recalled the saying that big trees from little acorns grow. Wherever you turned there seemed to be more money to pay. A fire in the bedroom in the evening cost a shilling (5p) and if you were extravagant enough to have one for the whole day in the winter, it would cost as much as two shillings and sixpence (12½p). A sponge hip bath would be sixpence (2½p) and up to two shillings (10p) if you took one in the public bathroom. When you took a hip bath, the chambermaid would come groaning along the passage humping a large jug of hot water and another of cold so that a tip would be almost obligatory; the bath itself would be under the bed. When this habit finally ceased many years later, one wonders what happened to the vast numbers of surplus hip baths dotted about the country. It was not unusual for guests to bring their own baths with them and, in addition to trunks, the porters might have to man-handle metal bath-chairs or rubber tubs into the bedroom. It was not surprising that porters needed wheelbarrows to transport the guests' baggage from entrance to bedroom.

The battle between staff and guests for tips to add to the attendance charge took place on many fronts. It had been the custom for years that guests eating in the dining room would pay their bill to the waiter rather than sign the account and have it placed with the rest of the charges but "paying at the time gives the waiters a too favourable opportunity for exacting fees" and Gordon at least introduced signing. The guest was definitely at a disadvantage otherwise, trying to argue with a waiter in a room filled with other diners, all of whom were in full evening dress. In the better hotels it was *de rigeur* to dress for dinner.

Even in the 1880s the visitors had little choice, but to eat in the hotel. "In those days there were very few respectable restaurants in which to dine out. Lord and Lady Randolph Churchill when they first married, could only find the St. James Hotel (where the Bristol now stands) where according to her memoirs, there was a dingy dining room

In the smallest watering places hotels would spring up, sporting their new Gothic turrets and pedimented windows. Cruden Bay is 30 miles north east of Aberdeen by rail.

lighted with gas and an apology of a dinner." At the hotels there would be an ample choice, but the small touches that one expects as a matter of course now, were almost completely unknown. "If cooks could only be induced to garnish their dishes and serve them up daintily" complained the *Caterer* "they would be far more appetising. For example a few sprigs of parsley around a dish, a little chopped-up and sprinkled over fried potatoes or a beefsteak, makes all the difference in the world to their appearance . . . a few fried onions helps out a beefsteak immensely . . . a handful of watercress greatly helps the look of a roast of beef."

The major complaints against the large new hotels were not, however, in the realms of cuisine or charges for the small extras; the main complaint was the way in which guests had become items on a conveyor belt. Well within the memory of the experienced hotel user were the days when the guest would be greeted by the manager on arriving at the hotel. He was now shown to his room by a receptionist. Guests missed the word of welcome, the personal touch which could still be found on the continent. It was bad enough being away from home in a strange town without losing that personal reassurance that the manager knew you were there and was anxious to see that you were well looked after.

Many of the wealthy guests were much more accustomed to personal attention in their own homes than we are now. It rankled that ringing the bell for service in the bedroom did not result in the almost immediate response from the chambermaid that would be forthcoming from their own servants. A wife who selected her own staff from the countless applicants available did not take kindly to a waiter who was less impressive, and consequently complained that "The down-at-heel shabby-genteel, grey whiskered grandfatherly personage who reeks of gin and invariably says 'comin' sur' as he goes away, still survives in the hotel world."

In hotels in the 20th century the guest does many things for himself without thinking; turning on the tap, pushing lift buttons, switching on the light, and therefore needs help from hotel staff less frequently, but if you had to wait for hot water to wash, for instance, the speed of service became a matter of greater urgency. In a small hotel where there were fewer guests to look after, the problem was not so acute, but in the large units it was a constant source of irritation.

Many guests had by now decided to make the hotel their permanent home; the residents might include well-to-do young men, middle aged bachelors who couldn't be bothered to keep a home, childless couples and wealthy widows, but these regular guests soon learned how to cope.

The danger for the hotels in the future could be seen in the ingenuous comments of one contented commentator in 1887. "And yet with all this luxury and splendour—we refer particularly, of course, to gastronomy—it is pleasant to note that the prices for procuring the same have not increased in anything like the same proportion. A good dinner can now be procured served in a magnificently upholstered and otherwise fitted-up dining hall, resplendent with gilt carving, statuary, mirrors, stained glass, and first class pictures, accompanied by high-class vocal and instrumental music, for from three shillings and sixpence (17½p) upwards, and courses in the menu numerous, and the whole well-cooked and well-served."

All of which was splendid except that the prices had not risen in keeping with the quality of the product. When they had to, it was going to come as an unpleasant shock to the clientele who would react by looking elsewhere.

A pause for the poor—the lodging houses 9

THERE were hotels for the very rich and there were hotels for the very poor; dreadfully poor hotels they were too, but desperately needed by the people who sheltered in them. Without the lodging houses to provide a roof over their heads there could have been thousands totally homeless in the Victorian cities. From the fact that there were literally hundreds of these doss houses in London and a large number outside, it can be imagined how numerous were the circumstances which could reduce a man or woman to such a low ebb, for without doubt the lodging houses were as miserable an existence as it was possible to find outside a workhouse.

With few exceptions they were filthy, bug ridden, bare and squalid and although the Public House Committee in 1853 had talked about legislation to force inspectors to be appointed, very little was done until the end of the century.

What sort of people finished up in lodging houses? Displaced workers from the land, forced into the cities to find work, and trying to live as cheaply as possible in order to send money home to the wives and children they had to leave behind. Itinerant labourers like the building workers who moved from job to job and, in the early days, the railway navvies constructing the termini. Orphans and apprentices, thieves and vagabonds, drunkards, misfits and prostitutes grown old. The lodging house *habitués* did their own cooking, and in the kitchen which was also their lounge "you can watch the pavement artist doing 'all my own work' by deputy, the begging letter writer studying his private directory and drafting a condensed tragedy on the back of a music-hall handbill, the broken-down journalist racking his brains for ideas that obstinately refuse to come at his bidding, the old soldier . . . coaching a comrade in the art of cadging from officers of his former regiment". The street pedlars with their paper flowers, sand bags, toasting forks, miraculous corn cures, 'sweet scented lavender', and buskers.

The lodging houses were as varied as their occupants; there were small houses which could accommodate half a dozen people and there were others that, like barracks, could take over 500. There were general houses, houses for men only, others for women and still more for couples, but most followed the same rules. They opened their doors at four in the morning to let out the market porters and cleaning women and closed their doors about one in the morning when the last inhabitant staggered in. The guest paid his fee when he arrived and was given a metal tag as a receipt with a bed number on it. The door to the bedroom was locked until the 'deputy', as the manager was called, opened it when sufficient people were waiting to go upstairs. This was done in an attempt to reduce theft and noise but was rarely completely successful.

Bedrooms were either cubicles or open dormitories, the sheets might not be changed for a month, and the blankets could breed fleas indefinitely. It was usual for the visitor to go to bed fully clothed because this was the safest way of avoiding anything being stolen while sleeping, and even the remains of whatever food they had cooked for supper would be found close at hand under their beds. The number of beds in a room was always settled by law, but until the legislation was reinforced there were not sufficiently effective fines to make the 'deputy' carry out the law.

The kitchen was the social centre of the lodging house and the smell which permeated the ground floor came from the staple diet, the bloater, the cheapest food which could make a nourishing meal. With its companion kipper it kept many a hard-working labourer alive but there were many for whom even the herring family was too expensive. Such wretches had to live on the scraps they could cadge from other inmates, re-using the dead leaves of the teapots and huddling round the open fireplace for warmth. It would seem melodramatic if there were not such ample pictorial as well as written material to back up every miserable description.

A few people cared sufficiently to try to make the condition of the lodging house dwellers a little better. A Catholic Father Jay in Shoreditch opened a lodging house which was at least clean and bright, and the Salvation Army converted a warehouse in 1891 in Southwark Street on the south bank of the Thames for £2,000 which they called the Ark. The Ark had five floors and there were partitions on the top three floors which divided the area into rooms with only three or four beds in them. These sold for fourpence ($1\frac{1}{2}$p) each and if a separate 'stall' was taken the cost went up to sixpence ($2\frac{1}{2}$p). The partitions were ten feet tall and made of salmon-coloured deal match boarding. On the ground floor there was a dining room where the residents could buy food and there was also a large kitchen in the basement where people could cook their own meals. In the basement also was a general lavatory and instead of living in the kitchen there was a reading room for 150.

The warmest place in the lodging house was likely to be the communal kitchen which acted as Residents Lounge as well. This one was at the Farm House in Southwark, South London.

The kitchen of a lodging house for single women in Spitalfields.

The kitchen of a mixed lodging house in the same area. Tens of thousands of displaced country dwellers had nowhere else to call home.

The Ark was a welcome innovation and the Salvation Army opened another in Bradford soon after. Soup could be bought for a halfpenny (1/5p) or soup and bread for one penny ($\frac{1}{2}$p) and there were even small portions for a child who could have it for a farthing. Boiled jam pudding was a halfpenny, corned beef two pence and coffee, tea or cocoa one penny a mug.

There were also attempts to create hotels for the better off workmen, notably the Kiosk Company which was launched in 1880 under the chairmanship of the Duke of Westminster. The beds they provided were one shilling (5p) or one shilling and sixpence

To improve the standard of lodging houses was a monumental task. A start was made by Montagu Cory, the creator of Rowton Houses who was elevated to Lord Rowton.

(7½p) a night, so they were out of the question for most of the lodging house patrons, but at least they offered an alternative for those who still could not afford the higher priced commercial hotel. There was also a substantial group called the coffee house movement some of whose houses provided beds; both organisations were completely teetotal.

The man who gave his name to a new type of lodging house was Montague William Lowry-Cory, the first and last Lord Rowton. The first Rowton House, in Vauxhall, was built in 1892 at Lord Rowton's own expense, but Rowton Houses were never meant to be charitable institutions; they were to make a small return on the initial investment. The motto of the company which was formed two years later to run them was 'philanthropy at five per cent'. Five per cent in 1894 was little enough, though in bad times it was quite satisfactory for much larger companies at the better end of the market, and plenty of these did not manage it. The Rowton Houses were very large indeed with hundreds of beds and were fit to be inspected by the County Council at any time; Lord Rowton built five enormous lodging houses or Hotels for Working Men as they were called. The odium attaching to the words 'lodging houses' was replaced and so was the whole concept that a man who could not afford more than a few coppers for a bed was entitled only to a doss house.

Lord Rowton's ideal was imitated in many other cities, producing hotels where there was the strong smell of disinfectant instead of bloaters, where there was heat throughout the building, and where food was plentiful at rock bottom prices. At the Bevington House Hotel in Liverpool, sixpence (2½p) was charged for a cubicle and the building which had 350 on offer cost only £27,000 to erect. With money cheap to borrow a profit was not unreasonably difficult to achieve.

Of course, the efforts of Lord Rowton and the Salvation Army were not sufficient to drive the old lodging house out of business; it was just that the higher standards of the philanthropists ensured that their better 'lodging houses' were always full and that they flourished. Elsewhere there was little improvement over the years and yet people would stay not just for days, but for months and years before such innovations as council housing and the dole.

There are few more depressing aspects of Victorian life than the treatment of the poor, and the lodging houses were only one aspect of a malaise which affected wide sections of society.

The washing and cooking facilities at the poorer lodging houses were side-by-side and as primitive as one would expect.

The nine day wonders— 10
1890–1899

"THE GAY NINETIES" is so familiar a soubriquet that it comes as something of a shock to discover that the gaiety was not so apparent to the Victorians who were alive at the time; the decade ended with the Boer War and started with a particularly nasty financial scare as Barings, one of the most solid pillars of the banking establishment, came within an ace of crashing due to South American loans of the utmost recklessness. As a result, confidence in the City was badly shaken, Bank Rate went temporarily to the then crisis level of six per cent and the middle classes pulled in their ample belts in just such areas as spending in hotels. Frederick Gordon was lucky enough to see his enormous flotation of over £2 million successfully completed just before the trouble broke and "within two or three weeks of the issue, the debenture stock was quoted at four-and-a-half to five-and-a-half premium and the ordinary to one and a quarter". Part of the reason lay in the restricted market in hotel shares, and punters wanting a ticket for this glamorous expanding industry could best participate by purchasing some Gordons. And it *was* expanding still. Madame Ritz recalled that it was a time when London couldn't get enough new hotels, and the *Caterer* reported that "in regard to London hotels, the cry is, still they come."

Each new hotel was hailed as the most wonderful ever, but there was no question of which would be the largest, for Jabez Balfour, the owner of the Victoria Hotel, had purchased from the Cecil family a site on the Embankment which was going to be sufficient for the construction of a 1,000 room hotel, and work was progressing on this immense development. Frederick Gordon saw both this venture and the Victoria, which was situated next to his Metropole in Northumberland Avenue, as serious local competitors and indeed Balfour was as important in the City and as respectable as Gordon himself.

Since 1868 when Balfour's Liberator Building Society had first been launched, the public had flocked to place their savings in an organization promoted in many instances by non-conformist ministers endeavouring to augment their stipends. The Liberator offered the splendid return of eight per cent per annum and successive stock issues of new Balfour companies were always over-subscribed. With buildings like the Victoria as tangible evidence of the prestigious uses to which the investors' money was being allocated, Balfour's reputation flourished, and he was elected Mayor of Croydon and a Member of Parliament.

Although Balfour was almost a dwarf in stature, he had a tremendous personality and radiated confidence. He was also one of the cleverest and most heartless crooks of his age and had built his empire on the purest sand; it was the old trick of paying the eight per cent dividends out of the new capital the public subscribed, for the only profits his companies made were diverted into his own pockets and those of his cronies. In Sep-

The Mayor of Croydon, an MP, founder of the Liberator Building Society, and one of the most heartless embezzlers in the annals of Victorian crime—Jabez Balfour.

tember 1893 the bank he had founded to handle the flood of money he was lent, suspended payment and as he was fleeing to Chile, a yawning abyss of £12 million opened up under his unfortunate supporters. Unluckily for Balfour he was recognized by a visitor to South America, extradited and sentenced to fourteen years in prison. The liquidator of the wildly complicated mess he left behind found a partially completed monster hotel to deal with as well as the Victoria. Frederick Gordon stepped in to buy the Victoria and "Gordon Hotels have got rid of a formidable rival by swallowing it whole."

The price was £417,433, a snip compared to the cost of building it in the first place, and the price included not only the lease, the four bathrooms, the furnishings and the stock, but also such trifles as the dinner contracts for the 9th Norfolk Regiment, the Buffs, the Grand Masters Chapter and the Institute of Civil Engineers. There was also an income of £1,500 a year from the sales of showcases to no less than thirty-two companies; Liberty's had a year for £50, Cadbury's for £10, the U.K. Tea Company for £83 10s. (£83.50), and Grierson Oldham, the wine company, three years for £25 a year. Many of the Victorians were extremely able at selling advertising space in their hotels and it is doubtful whether any British hotel today has a comparable income from showcases in real money terms.

The Victoria Hotel was not by any means the only new venture for Gordons during the decade. The Cliftonville Hotel, Margate came in the same year, the Burlington, Eastbourne was enlarged in 1895, the Lord Warden in Dover in 1896, the Metropole, Folkestone, opened in 1898 and finally the Grosvenor at Victoria was leased from the Brighton and South Coast Railway. To pay for all these acquisitions and improvements

more ordinary and debenture stock was issued until the company had to service a capital of approximately £3 million. Raising money in the market to finance expansion was and remains a perfectly normal method of expansion, but having to raise money to keep the existing assets in good shape *was* dangerous. Efforts could successfully be made to disguise the truth by suggesting that the new cash would help to produce greater profits by improving the hotels, but this was only the case when tariffs could be increased accordingly, and often they could not.

Frederick had every incentive to pay high dividends for any distribution above eight per cent meant that an additional payment had to be made to the holders of a class of stock called Founders Shares. There were 100 of these Founders Shares and a one per cent distribution over eight per cent cost the company between £5,000 and £10,000 distributed to the lucky holders. To give an indication of what this was worth to Frederick, the split in 1893 would have brought him £2,560 personally, apart from the ordinary dividend on the ordinary and preference shares he owned. It was not surprising that the *Statist*, a highly regarded commentator on economic affairs, reported to its readers "there is nothing for depreciation from the enormous £2,841,000 at which purchase price the properties and business and capital expenditure stands in the balance sheet. The transfer of only £17,500 to general reserve gives an idea of the disposition to divide profits up to the hilt, which is referred to in the Board of Trade Committee's report, as usually characteristic of founder's shares companies." The criticism had no effect on the price of the Gordon shares which continued to rise to the general satisfaction of all the shareholders.

Gordon Hotels were by no means alone in arriving at the situation where most of the profits had to be distributed. The investors wanted high dividends, the founders benefited even more from the same policy, the hotels when new needed little spending on them, and tomorrow's problems could be taken care of by hoping that they would not materialise. But tomorrow's problems could only be minimised if there were two favourable factors, stable prices and a lack of meaningful competition. The Victorian business community at the time was cocooned by the pre-eminence of the belief that nothing would ever change, and for a number of years there *was* deflation and all was well, but it really could not last as far as the hotel business was concerned, if only because of the expense of repairing dilapidation and fighting the envious competition which did spring up.

Gordon Hotels were only one of the incipient chain operations; another was the group of Midland Railway Hotels which from 1885 had been the day-to-day responsibility of William Towle. The Midland had decided to develop the hotel operation in order to strengthen its position in the major provincial cities along its routes, and as a consequence together with the Midland Grand in London, the Midland, Derby, and the Queens in Leeds, William Towle found himself involved in the building of the Midland, Bradford, which was needed to compete with the hotel of the London and North Eastern, and in controlling hotels in Morcombe Bay and Normanton. By 1890 he was supposed to be taking home the largest salary of any hotel manager in Europe, and in the same year the company purchased the Adelphi, Liverpool, to further increase his responsibilities. The Adelphi went for £105,000 so that the original shareholders got their money back with a five per cent bonus, but in view of Radley's initial achievements the outcome says little for the efforts of his successors.

Towle was a great champion of the industry and a prolific writer on the unfair treatment he felt it received from successive governments and official bodies. In the jubilee edition of the *Railway News* he wrote "the nation owes a debt of gratitude to the Railway companies for the provision of many good hotels which would certainly never have been built by other capital." In retrospect, another writer in the same magazine in 1925 might have been nearer the mark when he pointed out that "In more recent years the Midland Railway developed its hotel building plans to an abnormal degree, erecting big hotels at great expense at Manchester and Liverpool, catering mainly for relatively wealthy travellers. It had over £2,366,000 sunk in hotel ventures." It wasn't, in fact, a lot of money

Facing page:
The Victoria Hotel had 500 bedrooms and four public bathrooms when it was opened in 1887. The elegance of its clientele's dress was obviously not matched by the demands they made on the plumbing.

The roof garden at the Midland Hotel in 1903 was the epitome of Edwardian elegance in Manchester. The bass player's cap might have been particularly practical in a high wind.

by comparison with the total capital involved in running the railway, but the investment could be much more easily justified on political or egotistical grounds than in terms of the intelligent use of the public's funds.

While Gordon Hotels made most of their money from their London operations, Midland had to pay much more attention to the provincial hotels, and Towle was in the odd position of having two head offices. The one in Derby was alongside the company's main railway headquarters and looked after accounts and the wine cellars, while the one in London looked after everything else. It couldn't have been satisfactory, and much of the control of the hotels was the result of an endless stream of memoranda from Towle setting down in great detail every minute policy he wished to have followed. The memoranda were mounted in special reference books and at the end of each missive was the command to 'Acknowledge receipt.'

In each hotel there was usually both a superintendent and a secretary. While the secretary dealt with business matters, the superintendent was responsible for discipline, staff management, the reception of visitors and the maintenance of standards. The supplies the hotels needed were purchased in the open market and the superintendent could personally select them without reference to his head office. The hotels blended their own tea and coffee, bottled their own wine, and supplied refreshment rooms and dining cars in their area. Mrs. Towle, apart from having two sons, Frank and Arthur, also took responsibility for 600–700 female staff and was undoubtedly a very strong personality.

Compared to their father's humble upbringing, Frank and Arthur had the best, both being educated at Marlborough with Frank going on to Trinity College, Cambridge, while Arthur worked in hotels overseas until in 1896 both joined their father in the company. From 1898 onwards they were joint assistant managers under the paternal eye and continued in this role until 1911 when all three became joint managers prior to William Towle's retirement. The Towle's can lay fair claim to being the most distinguished family of British hoteliers as William and Frank were eventually knighted and Arthur came to run the largest hotel company in Europe when all the Midland Railway Hotels were put together under his command after the First World War. Nevertheless, as hoteliers, they had much of the outlook of a major domo in the service of a king, upholding the standards of the court but letting the peasants pay for its upkeep.

There were about 1,500 people engaged in running the seven hotels during the decade, with the chief clerk in London supervising twenty-five staff and the accounts department mustering thirty, but this was not overstaffing at a time when so much of the work had to be done by laborious longhand. William Towle certainly did run fine hotels and he did not skimp on the quality of his employees; chefs like M. Mestivier at Liverpool or M. Briais at the Midland Grand could turn out work comparable with any other luxury restaurant.

The standard of British cuisine rose steadily and the leader of the crusade was Auguste Escoffier, the single most famous hotel name to come out of the whole century. Escoffier was married to a French poetess named Delphine Daffis, but the lady played about twelfth fiddle to his beloved kitchen and when she decided that the London climate was not to her liking and returned to her native land, Escoffier only felt it necessary to visit her on very rare occasions. Otherwise he was left to devote himself entirely to the creation of a cuisine which enshrined not only *his* good ideas but those of many of his less literary colleagues, and also the evolution of a new method of running a kitchen.

Escoffier came to the Savoy in 1890 at Ritz's request and soon realised that British methods of cooking could use a little refining. The tradition of Carême had been primarily a search for ever better displays of food; to serve forty people a meal with the Prince Regent, Carême once produced well over 100 dishes. The food looked magnificent, but it would be tepid when you were finally allowed to eat it, and you could only take what you wanted from the platters within your reach as etiquette would not permit a guest to ask for a dish to be passed along the table. The manner of service changed during the intervening seventy years and in the dining room for instance the guest could now order from a lengthy *table d'hôte* menu in many hotels.

Escoffier, however, improved on the prevailing system in three ways. To begin with he improved the speed of service by producing an assembly line; previously when a chef received an order, he would be responsible for putting together all its ingredients—for an *oeuf poché florentine*, for example, one chef would prepare the spinach, the cheese sauce and the poached egg. In Escoffier's system the vegetable chef would prepare the spinach and the egg and then the saucier would provide the cheese sauce. The dish could thus be prepared more quickly and the finished product would be checked by Escoffier, himself, before it left the kitchen to ensure that it was correct.

When he moved with Ritz to open the Carlton Hotel later in the decade, the kitchen operation had been made so smooth that it was possible to offer the guests a new style of menu; *à la carte*. Instead of the food being cooked in advance, the guest could now pick and choose from a much wider selection of dishes which would be cooked to order, though he might well advise the hotel of his guests' selection earlier in the day. Escoffier also simplified the number of dishes for banquets still further so that, by comparison with Carême's 100 dishes, he might only have forty for a menu for Edward VII.

To Escoffier and indeed to many of the great chefs, the kitchen was more a temple than a factory. He spent much of his life within its walls, and there grew up a meticulous ritual with Escoffier as high priest. Working for the high priest was not only a great honour but a terrifying experience for the new chef until he had settled in. Unlike many

The great Auguste Escoffier, the greatest craftsman in the kitchen of his day. Unhappily his efforts did not produce adequate profits at the Savoy and he was dismissed. This in no way marred his subsequent career at the Ritz in Paris and the Carlton in London. He was often called in to prepare state banquets for Edward VII.

chefs, Escoffier was not a bully; he did not lose his temper and when angry would retire to his cubby-hole until he had cooled off. He allowed no drinking in his kitchen except for an unlimited quantity of a barley drink which was always available. The heat in the Victorian kitchen was fierce for although gas cooking had been patented by Robert Hicks as early as 1831, most hotel chefs still preferred to work with wood and coal. Consequently most managements allowed their chefs large quantities of beer, just like steelworkers, in order to replace the liquid they lost. Beer was safer than water anyway until a better drainage system was available, but the plumbing was much improved by Escoffier's time and the Savoy did have its own well.

Escoffier is, of course, famous for his *Guide Culinaire*, a comprehensive recipe book which has been the 'bible' of chefs since he wrote it. If there are any arguments about the correct preparation of a dish, the last word on the subject is Escoffier's decision in the *Guide* and the great man spent hours not only in setting down the recipes, but also in inventing new dishes. To a public which had been accustomed to a limited cuisine for most of their lives, this new world of exotic tastes had unlimited fascination, and

Escoffier was constantly called upon to create something new and even more exciting. This was his great joy and delight though he grumbled with a good deal of justification that he was the only type of artist who could neither patent nor copyright his inventions, for though the new dishes might take him many hours to create, any chef could then copy them down to the last detail.

The influence of Escoffier was not only in the *Guide Culinaire* but also in his great reputation among his fellow chefs and in the number of men he trained during his long period in London; his disciples looked on him with awe and affection and like any first-class leader he earned their respect, both by being able to do anything in the kitchen better than they could, and by being prepared to work longer and harder than anybody else. Long after he retired to Monaco, where he died in 1935 at the age of 85, he would occasionally accept invitations to visit the kitchens of great hotels where he would be received as a venerable sage by his admirers.

It was Ritz's belief that a great restaurant was vital to the success of a great hotel and this Escoffier provided without either of them apparently being too concerned with the cost as the years went by. Both the maestros wanted to go further by creating the all embracing perfect hotel and any restrictions which came from the board of directors proved increasingly irksome, as they realised how much the clients came to the Savoy specifically because of their professional ability. In Ritz's garden in the country at Golders Green they would talk for hours about new ideas, but the directors could still have the last say. Yet there were plenty of very rich men prepared to back Ritz if he wanted to break away and form his own company and this eventually he agreed to do. His wife, Marie Ritz, in her biography of Ritz blames his departure on the impossible behaviour of a housekeeper to whom she mysteriously refers as Mrs. W. and she suggests that the lady was allowed to ignore Ritz's instructions because of the protection of a member of the board. Stanley Jackson in his book on the Savoy states that this is untrue, but nobody has ever identified Mrs. W. and if the parting was amicable, then it is strange that Ritz's belongings were turfed out of his apartment in the hotel so that he found it necessary to accept an offer of accommodation at the Charing Cross Hotel.

Certainly it would be nothing unusual in the hotel industry for power to be acquired by sexual as against managerial prowess and Marie Ritz obviously didn't invent Mrs. W., but, in fact, the authors of the many books on both the Savoy and Cesar Ritz seem to have been unaware that there was a short paragraph in the *Caterer* in April 1898 which stated quite simply and quite categorically "Actions are pending against the Savoy at the instance of Ritz, Echenard and Escoffier for 'wrongful dismissal and breach of contract'". The resignations, reported the *Caterer*, had occurred in mysterious circumstances, but, in fact, the cause of the trouble was well known at the time. Sir Henry Burdett, the vice-chairman of Gordon Hotels might well have had it in mind when he said in July 1898 "I am impressed, as you must have been impressed with what has appeared in the newspapers about other hotels, and I have asked myself how is it, and why is it, that the Gordon Hotels have escaped these scandals."

The Savoy directors themselves had issued a statement in March 1898 which set out their position. "A matter, however, of greater importance became apparent to the Directors in the autumn (1897) and that was, that there was a much less percentage of profit on the sale of food and wine than in previous years. Upon this, of course, the diminution of the gross receipts has no bearing. The Directors accordingly considered it necessary to institute a searching enquiry into the causes of this diminution of profit, an enquiry which conducted practically day by day, by and under the direction of a committee of investigation, has been a very laborious task and has occupied many months. The Directors have ascertained the principal causes of the deficiencies. They further have ascertained that other abuses have sprung up prejudicial to the business in many ways, and calculated to alienate customers." The Savoy directors had not taken action lightly. "Acting under the advice of eminent counsel, the Directors have found it their imperative duty to dismiss the two managers and the chef from the service of the company . . . the shareholders may rely that the earnest and continuous efforts of the

Directors are being devoted, and will continue to be devoted, to the extirpation of the abuses they have discovered; and the Directors are confident that, though the effects of the past may be felt for some time to come, the result of their effort will be to ultimately put the business upon a sound and satisfactory basis." The situation was that serious, and the *Statist* commented "The investigations which have been going on during a long time past have been made with skill and secrecy. The case it is understood, was made complete in every particular before the Directors took action."

Mr. Jackson who acknowledges that he had a great deal of cooperation from the Savoy and access to a wide range of material, which we have not, suggests that Ritz and the directors had a number of frank and friendly talks and it was amicably decided that he should leave. In that case it is difficult to understand the need for the advice of an eminent counsel, the accusations of wrongful dismissal and breach of contract, and the fact that these friendly talks were proceeding at presumably the same time as a searching enquiry under a committee of investigation which uncovered abuses calculated to alienate customers, and of such seriousness that it became the imperative duty of the directors to dismiss the three men. Like the Hardwicke affair the courts do not appear to have been troubled with the row in the end, but talk of amicable partings or conniving house-keepers are obviously equally wide of the mark. The *Caterer* would not have dared to print a piece about actions for wrongful dismissal unless it was sure of its ground, as a libel suit must have followed and there is no subsequent retraction.

The effect of a day-by-day investigation of Ritz's methods of management on an ego like his would have been devastating; it would have been like asking Graham Hill to take a driving test. Every budding hotelier has been brought up on the glorious achievements of Escoffier and it is mind boggling that he should have been dismissed in the first place and for, of all things, not making sufficient kitchen profit. The industry might swallow the Rolls Royce crash without difficulty, but Escoffier was the Rolls Royce, Lloyds and the Bank of England of the industry put together. Yet the accusation against both Ritz and Escoffier was at the very least extravagance on a serious scale and the language of the directors would be appropriate to dishonest conduct on the part of the employees.

Only a hotelier with the fanatical following of Ritz could have survived such damning criticism from his previous company. The fact that the reputations of both Ritz and Escoffier were unaffected over the years by that directors' report can only be attributed to a subsequent desire on both sides to hush the whole thing up. It would not have helped Ritz to have a lot of dirty linen washed in public when he was trying to raise money for the Ritz in Paris. For their part the Carlton and the Savoy directors could not have relished an unsavoury court case with Ritz defending his honour. Hadn't the Prince of Wales said that where Ritz went, he would go? Who wanted to tackle a man with that sort of support, for it would now appear that the Prince was not just talking of his taste in hoteliers, but was supporting his friend against the accusations which had been levelled against him. Madame Ritz recalled, however, that there had been difficulty in raising money for the Ritz in Paris which eventually, she said, came from the manufacturer of Grand Marnier, and she attributed this to economic conditions. It could well have been instead that some of Ritz's financial support was at least temporarily put off by the criticism.

Resignations were also in the air at Gordon Hotels. Business had been good for some years and the shares had more than doubled so that the £10 ordinary reached £24 while the dividend remained a steady and luxurious ten per cent, but then in April 1897 Sir Blundell Maple decided that he wanted to go into the hotel business and approached Frederick Gordon to chair the board of a new hotel company to be called, confusingly for us, Frederick Hotels. From Sir Blundell's point of view this move made sound sense for if, as his own publicity trumpeted, "whenever one finds an exceptionally well appointed hotel, it may safely be premised that Maples have been concerned in its development" then why not collect the resulting profits as well?

Frederick was not averse to the idea of joining Sir Blundell, for they were good friends and he had cheerfully accepted a seat on the Maples board, but there had been a certain amount of friction because Sir Blundell had not invited any other Gordon Hotels directors to join Maples, and they for their part had insisted on going out for competitive tenders for furnishings and fittings rather than automatically give the new business to Maples. From Sir Blundell's point of view two tenders were no different from two hotel companies, but Frederick Gordon did not want more competition if he could avoid it. His view was not accepted, however, and when Sir Blundell launched Frederick Hotels, the board of directors refused to deal with Maples any more and a war of conflicting statements quickly broke out within the Gordon's board. One faction held that Frederick Gordon could not adequately serve two masters, a view which might seem antiquated in these days of multiple directorships. Gordon, himself, said that his action was in the best interests of the company. His opponents then called an extraordinary general meeting to ask him to resign from the board of Maples though there was no effort to get him to resign from Gordon Hotels. By the day of the meeting on October 14th 1897 the shares had plummeted to £18 10s. (£18.50) and Frederick had a lot of explaining to do.

The main attack came from one of his oldest friends, Alfred Holland, a first class professional hotelier who was to be a director of the Ritz Hotel in London for thirty years and who took over the chairmanship of Holborn and Frascati, a restaurant company of Frederick Gordon's after his death. Frederick Gordon had a great name in the hotel business, but much of the day-to-day work was Alfred Holland's and he complained that "Mr. Gordon in one of his circulars, has belittled the part I and my colleagues have played in bringing the business of the company to its present successful position." He tried to excuse Frederick by making Sir Blundell into a sort of Svengali "inviting Mr. Gordon to join Maple's board was the start of an attempt to unload their untried ventures on this prosperous company."

Unfortunately for Alfred Holland the Gordon magic was much too strong, and Frederick had a unique ace in the hole because his brother-in-law, Horatio, was being installed as Lord Mayor of London in one month's time. The City was not going to back a little known hotelier against a combination of that strength. Gordon won easily enough, but three of his six directors resigned leaving him with a pyrrhic victory. It was pyrrhic because he replaced the defectors with influential city friends who knew nothing of the business, and then himself became involved with other companies as chairman of Ashanti Goldfields and of Apolinnaris and Johannis, the principal mineral water company and as a director of Pears and of Bovril.

From this time onwards Gordon Hotels started to decline. "Experts have been replaced by non-experts, and instead of three hotel specialists, we have an ex-secretary, a brewer, a beef juice manufacturer and a statistician." The retiring directors were missed and their previous performance was highlighted by the comparisons people were drawing with the Hotel Cecil's figures.

Now the Hotel Cecil was the name given by the liquidator of Jabez Balfour's companies to the monster hotel he had been constructing on the Embankment. It had been six years in the building and was opened in the spring of 1896 with 800 bedrooms and great fanfares. It was a very splendid hotel indeed, and the liquidator had done an excellent job in getting the original shareholders to put up the necessary additional money to finish it off, but making it profitable was another matter again. Inevitably the overheads were enormous with Mr. Bertini, the new manager, controlling in the catering department alone a staff of 200 in three separate kitchens. The facilities were exceptional and there was no more imposing room in London than the Grand Ballroom which was over 100 feet long, 66 feet wide and a vast 46 feet high. It says much for the skill of the architect that there were no pillars at all in the room, and it afforded an uninterrupted view for over 600 guests.

When the first set of accounts were produced they showed a handsome turnover of nearly a quarter of a million pounds which can be compared with, say, the Langham's figure of about £100,000; unfortunately the operating costs were very high at the Cecil

which meant that less profit was made out of each pound received. As the financial analysts were not slow to point out, where Gordon Hotels spent £70 of every £100 they took, the Cecil spent £90, and consequently Bertini, the accepted ideal choice of 1896 became the great mistake of 1897 and disappeared from the scene. It might have been the largest hotel in Europe, but as with so many of the new hotels "each was a nine days' wonder and then fell back to become an accepted part of London life." The managers who were dismissed usually fell back to become an accepted part of the life of small country or seaside towns far from the scenes of their former glory in the capital, and it is sad that so many careers which were painstakingly built over twenty or thirty years could be destroyed in such a short space of time.

The overbuilding in London was taking its toll even in the '90s. Berners Hotel was only one to go into receivership in 1895 and the year was a bad one for the industry everywhere. "The depression in general business of the country and the hotel trade in particular, is emphasised by the reports of hotel companies which have reached us since the beginning of the year. Never were the number of non-dividend and shrinking dividend concerns greater. For the first time in twenty-eight years even the White Hart, Salisbury, is paying no final dividend."

Amid all this gloom there was still a growing desire to live it up. Banqueting and eating out grew more popular, and clubs of every description were formed and flourished. There was even a London 13 club with many members from Lloyds, courageously dedicated to ignoring every form of superstition. One hundred and sixty nine guests was the quorum which gathered for drinks, and dinner was announced by the head waiter who gained everybody's attention by the simple expedient of smashing a large mirror on the floor. The guests then went under two ladders into the dining room where all were seated at thirteen tables of thirteen and continued solemnly to disobey every superstition they could. After the meal came speeches, with the chairman inviting the members to spill salt with him and then to break their own little mirrors which were thoughtfully provided.

There were less eccentric groups than the 13 club and overall for those who could afford it, there were more opportunities for entertainment. One minor obstacle remained which was the habit throughout the country of early nights, and the major problem here was the law which closed restaurants at eleven o'clock. Ritz was particularly keen to get this amended and with a good deal of lobbying in the right quarters from Edward's Marlborough House set, Parliament relented and allowed restaurants to remain open until half-past midnight. Many restaurants, notably the Savoy, benefited and it became extremely fashionable to take after-theatre suppers.

Because it is still one of the finest hotels in London, the opening of the rebuilt Coburg Hotel in December 1896 deserves to be recognized. The Coburg was loyally named after the Royal house to which Prince Albert had belonged and its position just off Grosvenor Square could not have been better. During the First World War when German names were very unpopular, the Coburg became the Connaught, but the high standards did not falter; the first manager of a hotel can usually set the tone for good or ill for years to come and the Connaught was fortunate to have Kossuth Hudson whose previous experience had been on the Riviera with one of the top Gordon managers, and who was able to translate that excellent training into London terms. To be saddled with the name Kossuth can be likened to a child today being christened Castro but Mr. Hudson survived without noticeable ill effects.

In the countryside there were a number of developments. The invention of the bicycle had provided the first sign that the wheel of fortune was at last turning in favour of those hotels which had survived the passing of the stage coach. The bicycle provided a cheap means of transport compared to a horse and trap and fitted in well with the new emphasis on exercise and sport of which the growth in leisure activities like football, cricket, and rugby were other manifestations. In 1878 the Bicycle Touring Club first made a register of approved hotels for the benefit of its members, long before the R.A.C. undertook the same task for motorists in 1897. By the 1890's there were sufficient cyclists to make a substantial market for the country hotels, and the cyclists were not only likely to need overnight accommodation but were customers for packed lunches as well as for drinks. While the motor-car remained a luxury until well after the First World War, the cyclists were able to discover the beauties of the British countryside peacefully and economically. The road system was more than adequate for the amount of traffic, and the dangers of long ago had passed into folk lore.

Golf was another sport which had grown in popularity and among the first of the hotels built, specifically to cater for this type of visitor was the Golf View Hotel in Nairn, which

Though it was very desirable and prestigious to have a large hotel at your terminus, the Great Central Railway could not afford the cost of construction at Marylebone. The site was therefore leased to Frederick Hotels who built the Hotel Great Central. It is now the headquarters of British Rail.

The advertisements in Baedeker and the other guides were shouting in a crowded market place. The description of the Hotel Great Central as "a temple of luxury" was almost restrained.

was opened in 1897. It was a brave venture but the Lord Provost in wishing the proprietress good luck drove well into the verbal rough when he pontificated "getting well away from the tee, might find an easy course, and loft off to the green of prosperity and there land on the tee of success." Perhaps the Scotch had flowed a trifle freely before he started his speech.

By the end of the century the seaside towns had their characters fully formed. The small villages had developed into thriving towns though this was not always beneficial to the hotels. Some towns had been adopted by the factory workers so that when the Wakes Weeks were created in the north, the inhabitants through the medium of saving with holiday clubs, were able to go to stay at boarding houses in nearby resorts. Young resorts like Blackpool which had only five hotels in 1856, and old ones like Scarborough, boomed, but the upper crust looked for fresh horizons. A town like Brighton could uniquely mix the two types of clientele, but a number of other resorts lost the carriage trade to an increasing extent. The wealthy turned to those seaside towns which emphasised the quieter life; Bournemouth began to publicise more intensely its convalescent qualities and the town council discouraged the more plebeian attractions. It was a question of parks versus amusement machines or, in Folkestone, a question of whether the Metropole Hotel could block the access for the general public to the Lees in order to make their hotel more exclusive; the answer was that they could not. The big spenders started to search further afield for their holiday homes and more twin towns like St. Annes for Blackpool emerged. The Isle of Wight was very popular because of Queen Victoria's love of her palace at Osborne and of course, the journey across the water helped to keep the island remote.

There was now a much larger tourist industry at the seaside towns and a proliferation of boarding houses and private homes as well as hotels, so that the old picture of a quiet fishing village trying to become a small town was quite out of date. It is important, however, to notice the power structure in these towns as it had a major effect on the influence of the industry nationally. In most seaside towns there were a small coterie of influential families, mostly landowners, who had a vested interest in the expansion of the resort, like Jervis in Bournemouth. To expand meant using more land for housing and this was more valuable to the owner than for farming or grazing. It was inevitable, therefore, that these families were in the forefront of the effort to get investors to put up money for those big hotels which would give additional status to their towns, and indeed the families contributed themselves and often occupied seats on the board of directors.

These men were never professional hoteliers and yet they came to represent the hotel industry in their locality because of their financial stake and local prestige. Most other industries retained a strong leavening of professionals in places of power but hotels were controlled when it came to the crunch, by part time amateurs. The local M.P. who would be unlikely to be adopted by the constituency if he were *persona non grata* with the great families, would certainly understand *their* interests but did not represent hotels as the Labour men represented the workers in the next decade. Occasionally, as we have seen, a hotelier broke into the charmed circle, but the industry was shackled right across the country from the beginning in terms of political influence. The professionals had neither the education nor the grievances to spur them on; they were spread thinly across the country, composed of many nationalities, and being nomads by nature they could not take a long term view. Only a threat of the utmost severity would unite the two sides and that was not forthcoming in the '90s.

As the decade drew to a close the rumblings of war rang ominously in the hoteliers' ears. Lord Kitchener's handling of the Fashoda incident in 1898 had inflicted a humiliating defeat on the French and it became unpatriotic for them to holiday in Britain. The outbreak of the Spanish American War had reduced the number of American visitors and the Boer War was to have an even worse effect on trade. Nevertheless for the three months season which London enjoyed there was still a great demand for accommodation as there was for the even shorter seaside peak.

Sir Blundell Maple had managed to float his Frederick Hotels with the aid of Frederick

Not all the Victorian hotels were exotic buildings. The Sandringham Hotel, in Hunstanton, was almost cosy in aspect. Note the large sun lounge on the far right of the entrance.

Gordon as chairman and totally without the assistance in his prospectus of any details of the past trading of the operations involved; the issue was oversubscribed and raised nearly £1½ million from the public. It said much for the reputation of both Sir Blundell and Frederick that this was possible, but once the public has faith in a section of the stock market and in entrepreneurs with good records, it tends to support them unquestioningly. Frederick Hotels did have some nice properties including the new Majestic Hotel, Harrogate, the Royal Pavilion, Folkestone and the Great Central Hotel at Marylebone Station, which the Great Central Railway had been unable to afford to run itself. The Great Central Hotel managed to find one new attraction for its visitors by offering a cycle track on its roof for guests in need of exercise, but this hardly compared to the improvements first provided by earlier hotels at termini.

The Carlton had been opened by Ritz in the last year of the century without too much in the way of publicity, firstly because a new hotel was no longer news and also because there was some question of whether a management so recently in serious disagreement with the Savoy would be effective on its own. (The Savoy company, for their part, had expanded by rebuilding Claridges.) Ritz soon proved himself anew by producing a really lovely hotel whose frontage was an exact duplicate of the present Her Majesty's Theatre, and which contained many special Ritz touches. The walls were painted because Ritz considered wall paper unhygienic and there was a system of double windows to reduce traffic noise. Every room had a bathroom and the selection of fixtures and fittings showed Ritz at his best. It was in the restaurant, however, that Ritz and Escoffier triumphantly achieved their finest results with the new *à la carte* menu and the promotion of after-theatre dining. The restaurant became one of the favourite rendezvous of London's society and as the ladies swept down the staircase which Ritz had thoughtfully provided for the purpose, the scene was set as surely as on the stage next door.

What a long way the hotel industry had come from those early days at Euston, Derby and York, from the candles and the jugs of water, the tin baths under the bed and the rough cooking in the dining room. A lot of money had been sunk in the business, some lost without trace, some cast like bread upon the waters and making fortunes for the faithful, but it isn't just because of economic success that we think of the period as the Golden Age of British Hotels; it was the contribution they made to the standard of living of the people and the development of a more civilized way of life.

Every manufacturer knows that the fastest way to make his product popular—if it is any good—is for people to try it, whether it is test driving a new car or switching to a new washing powder. The Victorians had to experience gracious living to want it and the hotels were one of the shop windows. It certainly was not just a question of new recipes or fashionable decor; it was far more the opportunity many guests had of using a bathroom for the first time, switching on an electric light or turning on a tap. Better systems of drainage could be devised for a hotel so that the domestic market benefited from the improvements which started with hotel construction. The Prince of Wales once moved house because he could not stand the stench of the drains. Hotel management had to demand a far higher standard of hygiene than existed in many a wealthy private home, and these standards had to be good enough for foreign visitors as well as British. Consequently the home country was influenced, as it had been in its cuisine by French chefs a hundred years earlier, by American inventions, by Italian grace, Swiss organisation, and that same old German efficiency. Though Britain was the most powerful country, it still learnt from its foreign visitors and its foreign staff, and these lessons were disseminated throughout the land through the agency of the hotel industry.

This was the contribution that hotels made and although they continue to do so, the opportunities were never greater than in the period covered by the reigns of Queen Victoria and Edward VII.

Unfortunately for the hoteliers themselves, the cost to an old hotel of continually modernising its plant was exorbitant and the public's demand for new inventions made life difficult for the older established companies. If the cost of living had continued on an even keel it would have been easier, but at long last the situation changed and the reason was the Boer War. The significance of this conflict to the British economy has been overshadowed by the far worse effects of the Great War, but this comparatively minor action in South Africa dealt two severe blows to the hotel industry; it created inflation and it cut down the amount of business the hotels enjoyed. From the time of the war onwards, British hotels operated under much greater strain than before and after the vast expansion which had been seen between 1860 and 1900 the size of the industry first levelled off and then started to decline.

The Great Central Railway did own some hotels and tried hard to encourage visitors.

A pause for Cesar Ritz— I I
the inspiration

Facing page:
Cesar and Marie Ritz. He
drove himself mad seeking a
superhuman degree of
perfection.

CESAR RITZ has undoubtedly been the greatest influence in hotel management in the history of the industry and the ultimate accolade—the conversion of his surname into an adjective—only emphasises his importance. The ambition of tens of thousands of budding hoteliers during his heyday and since, has been to equal the standards of the great man while any thoughts of emulating his achievements have been considered out of the question. Today, throughout the world, there are hundreds of managers of fine hotels who continue to copy his methods faithfully, imitation here being without doubt the sincerest form of flattery, and many of the catering colleges who train the hoteliers of the future are still teaching the ways of the master.

In spite of the overwhelming legend and the universal praise, there remains a real question of whether Ritz was either a brilliant businessman or a good influence on the industry. After all the primary aim of a businessman in a public company is to make the maximum profit for his shareholders just as this is the task of any manager of other people's money, and the evidence seems to be that by that criterion Ritz was only a limited success and unnecessarily extravagant during his London period.

The record at the Savoy speaks for itself even without the final uproar. When Ritz took over control in 1889 the hotel was not paying its way and there was a considerable burden of debt from the opening and construction expenses. At the end of five years of Ritz's management both ordinary and preference shares were still below par and the hotel was only paying a five per cent dividend, which was less than both new companies, like Gordon Hotels, and the old established firms like the Langham and the Westminster Palace. Ritz certainly made better profits in 1895 and 1896 and he paid off the debts he inherited, but with his following and the brilliant team he had carefully nurtured, he should have produced a much healthier balance sheet.

It is very doubtful, however, whether this was ever his sole aim from 1890 onwards. In his early days on the continent he had to submit to the disciplines of owners who wanted the best possible returns on their investments, and during that time the combination of that restraint and his own creative intelligence achieved very good results. As his reputation grew, though, he was subject to less control and his backers at the Carlton were wealthy enough to want the prestige first and the profits later, even if the small shareholders expected the interests of the investors to receive priority. The Savoy board were also extremely wealthy. D'Oyly Carte was a rich man because of his presentation of Gilbert and Sullivan, and had no real need for the Savoy to be more than a hobby, even if the directors did finally investigate the low profit margins as we have seen. It is, of course, difficult at this distance in time to know for certain whether the major financial decisions were those of Ritz or the Savoy board, but for all his grumbling Ritz would appear in reality to have had a pretty free hand for a number of years.

Supper at the Savoy became very fashionable, particularly as opening hours were extended until half-past midnight.

Ritz, himself, had an obsession which finally destroyed his reason; like the dancer in the *Tales of Hoffman* whose red shoes would not stop, Ritz's search for the ideal hotel operation eventually overwhelmed him. With single-minded total application over a long period of years, Ritz sought to refine and refine again his concept of how the perfect hotel should be furnished, staffed and managed. Nothing was too small to ponder for hours, to experiment with over and over again. For example, instead of the glare of naked electric bulbs, Ritz devised concealed lighting and the more flattering lampshades, trying tint after tint until he could settle on a delicate apricot pink he felt was exactly right. His whole life was hotels just as Escoffier's whole life was the kitchen, and it was of course this mutual striving for perfection which united the two men so closely.

Of course it is unromantic and materialistic to suggest that the search for the ultimate in a product is not the prime aim of a business concern. Nevertheless it is realistic to appreciate that development costs have to be related to some yardstick of profitability if a firm is not to founder, and this was not Ritz's outlook. As a manager his ability to delegate was limited by his quest for that same perfection, in this case a superb standard of service. We arc left with a sad picture of a man at the very limit of his strength, with no financial worries, advised by his doctor to take things easily, and yet still dictating letter after letter from whichever of his hotels he was visiting, tellings managers round Europe of the numerous quirks of his clientele. That this one liked cherry jam for breakfast, that another liked his beef well done, and a third needed an extra pillow. Naturally Ritz was placed on a pinnacle by his clients but at what cost to the man and to his family.

Ritz came from a poor Swiss home and during his early career he not only survived on a pittance as a waiter, but also lived through the difficult days of the Franco–Prussian War seeing the ephemeral nature of possessions and so-called security in such conditions. During the siege of Paris even the richest inhabitants were reduced to eating dogs if they could find them. All his working life Ritz was a wanderer, the seaside in the summer, the mountains in the winter, or in his great years rushing from city to city, supervising and creating, trying to cram a week's activity into every single day. He settled down only when he collapsed and by then it was too late. In contrast, Frederick Gordon, who had equally difficult problems to overcome in his early years, managed to make half a million pounds, control far more hotels than Ritz, sit in addition on the boards of companies as diverse as Guest, Keen and Nettlefolds, Maples, Apolinnaris, Pears and Bovril, dominate the West African gold market and still live at home. Although not an innovator on the scale of Ritz, there were many original items attributable to the Englishman who was a far better businessman.

Ritz deserves and would only have wished to be judged by the highest standards and like many great craftsmen he possessed the necessary egotistical streak which alone can provide the determination to move forward in spite of the leaden weight of tradition and apathy which so often hampers progress. His egotism was fed by his supporters, many of whom contributed to his mental decline by involving him in wild projects; the Ritz Hotel Development Company in 1897 had plans for hotels in Johannesburg, Cairo, Madrid and New York, and at least a dozen other cities. The only reason why such extravagant and unrealistic plans ever saw the light of day was because of the South African members of his board, and the international outlook all the directors possessed. Ritz might well have been able to achieve near miracles by getting from Paris to London in eighteen hours, but how was he to supervise the hotels in Johannesburg and New York? Was it expected that he would allow his name to be associated with a hotel he could *not* supervise? All the evidence shows that this was not in his nature. Of course he was away from any one of his enterprises for long periods of the year, and this was true even when he was being paid to manage the Savoy, but he was there when the season was on, whether it was Switzerland, England, France or Italy, and even that schedule was to prove beyond him in the end.

An extravagant, near megalomaniac with an obsession for perfection is, however, only one side of the coin. As a craftsman Ritz set the standards by which the finest hotels can still be judged. No matter how large his hotels, the guest always had to remain an individual, entitled to enjoy his stay without conforming to rules that would have made life easier for a man who actually had to run a large hotel; it was the manager's problem that he had a lot of guests to cope with, and not the customers'. Furthermore Ritz was a stickler for cleanliness in an age when hygiene was still a comparatively novel idea. The provision of additional bathrooms which resulted in the Carlton being the first hotel in London to have all its rooms equipped in this way, was far sighted, an excellent sales point to his visitors, but also in keeping with his views on cleanliness. He hated heavy drapes and other dust traps, probably remembering in the gloom of a 'London Particular' three-day fog, the sparkling air of his native Switzerland.

Ritz was a great showman, with Johann Strauss and his Orchestra brought to play in the dining room and a glittering record of glamorous banqueting, which included flooding the courtyard at the Savoy for a Venetian evening, mammoth floral displays, fountains flowing with champagne, and the most exotic menus. He gave every encouragement to Escoffier to produce special dishes linked with his publicity-worthy clients, and he planned every detail of a function meticulously. He knew his business intimately and one can believe his wife's story of Ritz looking at a bedspread and announcing that the bottom sheet which was apparently completely invisible, was nevertheless obviously incorrectly folded.

The Carlton Hotel which Ritz built in the Haymarket after he had been dismissed by the Savoy directors. The Carlton even had the Prince of Wales as a guest in the public restaurant, an unprecedented honour. It was damaged by bombing during the Second World War and eventually demolished, to be replaced by New Zealand House.

Economically Ritz was not a good influence on the industry of his time and for this he must accept responsibility. As an influence for the future he has been a heavy cross to bear, but naturally cannot be blamed for that. In 1914 *The Economist* wrote "the necessity for perpetually bringing luxury up to date and making ostentation more ostentatious results in heavy expenditure, which adds to the value of the property for only a very short time. Such expenditure very soon loses its profit-earning capacity, and companies thus tend to pile up large capitals without adding to profits in proportion."

Admittedly every new hotel tries to outdo its competitors and this is inevitable; what Ritz did was to intensify the necessity for heavy expenditure on extravagance by placing his ideal ahead of his profits. Any company can be profligate in its expenditure if the shareholders are not the first concern. We have seen Cotes in Bournemouth spending £100,000 on his hotel even though it could never be economically justified, but Cotes was using his own money. In our own time when the Danziger brothers took over Gordon

The Savoy and the Cecil stood side by side in the Strand.

Hotels, there was a sound case for ploughing back the profits to improve the value of the properties rather than fritter the money away on trying to pay preference shareholders part of their twenty years arrears. But Ritz with his highest of all standards was making the biggest rod for the industry's back and it was materially responsible for breaking many hotels. The client was not given value for money, but excessive value for money and this was one reason why so many of the investing public eventually lost their capital in hotel shares. Perhaps Ritz could not have foreseen this situation, but if he had—and there was precedent in the condition of the hotel industry in many British cities—he would not have allowed the fact to distract him from his life's ambition, to create a perfect hotel; yet the evidence was there for those who chose to look.

Many hoteliers tried to copy Ritz in every detail, but the majority were chiefly influenced by the new quality that Ritz and Escoffier brought to the cooking and presentation of food, and by the little extra touches. As a consequence the school of thought which Frederick Gordon represented that the business was all about filling beds lost ground. It was more and more believed that if the hotel was good enough, the public would find their way to it, but this was not, in fact, Ritz's entire viewpoint. It ignored his ability to sell potential customers on the idea of using his hotels, the letters he sent, the encyclopaedic knowledge he possessed of his clients' tastes and preferences. Ritz believed that a large hotel could still remain a private home to hundreds of people when a man prepared to work as hard as he would was in charge. With anyone less committed, the hotel industry had to move away from that standard because it could not be sustained.

The large Victorian hotel unit gave the clients a wider and better variety of public rooms, and the hotel company an economic base for more highly paid senior management, the ability to purchase more cheaply, and to provide more ancillary services. What it had to mean in addition, however, was a loss of contact between the manager and his guests because he became a 'factory' manager and could not be the sales manager at the same time. Ritz with his demoniacal energy was able to stem the tide and cover both tasks for a number of years, but his legacy that this was possible proved harmful. As the public continued to expect the same degree of personal attention they could receive in small hotels, the reputation of larger establishments suffered. The complaints grew that people were treated like numbers, like units on a production line, like cattle. The arguments that were used in other industries to justify everything from mass production to, in later years, supermarkets were ignored by the hotels; instead they denied the accusations which were often justified, and refused to accept that Ritz was exceptional in this respect and lesser mortals could not hope to follow.

In America, where the reputation of Ritz was smaller, solutions to the problems of large hotels were easier to find; in particular salesmen and advertising played a bigger part, with the salesman taking over from the manager much of the personal contact which he now no longer had time to cover. Advertising was used to create a greater appreciation among the public that the hotel management wished their guests to receive every attention, so that the management's inability to say it personally was not such a source of discontent. The concentration on the publicity value of individual guests, which was the Ritz tradition—Pêche Melba, Poire Belle Hélène—was not to blinker the view of the American hoteliers who sought to fill their numerous rooms with groups of people travelling for the same purpose.

The British hoteliers could have seen very early the possibilities inherent in all types of mass travel, for the railways had moved large numbers from the earliest days of Thomas Cook, and what is more they *had* stayed overnight on occasions. The first weekend holidays packages were to be found, as we have seen, as early as 1881 but again the ideas were allowed to fall into disuse, and it was the influence of the Ritz school of thought which flourished. The argument may be advanced that there were not sufficient people in the country who could afford to stay in a hotel of any description, but this fails to explain how so many were able to save up to come to London for the two great Victorian exhibitions. If the general public are offered something they want badly enough, they will try very hard to obtain it, but the hotels ignored this and concentrated on the small number of rich people. If they had not, it might have been possible to extend the season, the brief nature of which was so disastrous for many seaside hotels among others. If a hotel was open for only a few months and the weather was poor, there was no hope of a profit, and therefore an extra month at either end aimed at a completely different clientele might have saved many from making an overall loss.

Even where the hoteliers tried to copy Ritz's cooking and presentation of dishes, they missed one major point completely. From a marketing viewpoint, *haute cuisine* became bogged down in Escoffier's recipes which have continued in fashion to the present day. Escoffier was, however, not simply trying to write his version of the culinary ten commandments, but had produced new dishes specifically to attract the leaders of fashionable society to his hotel; the dishes were brilliant sales promotion, for which lady could resist going to a restaurant which featured a dish named after her?

One of the only restaurants which subsequently elaborated on the basic idea was Isows in Soho, where the names of celebrities were written on the chairs to encourage people in show business to come to take their own personal seat, and other guests to have the vicarious pleasure of sitting where somebody famous had been before. Few people could now name more than a very few Victorian celebrities who Escoffier flattered, Nellie Melba being, of course, the most memorable.

Where today is the standard Pêche Tutin, Toast Thorndike or Steak Glenda? The art died with the men who invented it, but their expensive legacy of large kitchen staffs, a very wide selection of *à la carte* dishes, and an equally elaborate formation of restaurant waiters, marched on. For all who have suffered from the gap between the promise of the dish on the menu and the disappointment of the reality on the plate, it is only possible to blame the delusions of grandeur of hoteliers who were incapable of living up to the standards of a luxury hotel in Victorian London when running a more modest operation.

To take just one example: while Escoffier would have prepared the *à la carte* dishes to order, his successors developed short cuts which made the final product inferior; the fact that poached eggs, for instance, can be kept for days in cold water without losing their soft yolk, resulted in them often being cooked beforehand to save time and labour, and then simply reheated when required for an *à la carte* dish. While the appearance under, say, a cheese sauce, might not suffer, the flavour, colour and texture inevitably would. *À la carte* in the main is no longer what Ritz and Escoffier conceived.

Cesar Ritz had a favourite saying "*Le client a toujours raison, mais il paie toujours*" the customer is always right, but (make sure that) he always pays. For the market he sought, money was really not a consideration and this only emphasises that Ritz either got his sums wrong or was not primarily interested in profit as a businessman has to be. Whether Ritz would have done as well in Edwardian times when the pressure of competition and the deteriorating economic conditions made hotelkeeping far less remunerative is difficult to say. The first year's operation at the Carlton produced a seven per cent dividend, but Ritz had the advantage that this was the first hotel in London to be completely under his own control, and he had a ready-made clientele headed by the man who would soon be King. Probably he would have thrived in later years because he was always imaginative and would have found the solutions to the new problems. Those who thought they could beat him at his own game were less fortunate not only in his time but for years afterwards.

The law and hotels 12

THROUGHOUT the golden age, the position of hotels at law was in many ways obscure. Mr. Dixon Kimber, writing a memorandum for the Incorporated Association of Hotels and Restaurants in 1914 said "the legal position of an Innkeeper today is complicated and uncertain. It is founded on unwritten law of the realm, and can only be ascertained by a lengthy reference to decided cases dating back to the reign of Queen Elizabeth".

The root of the problem was that a modern hotel was not really an inn. A classic example of this was the law regarding the billeting of troops where there was not an adequate barracks. In such cases the hotelier in 1890 had to accommodate them for twopence-halfpenny (1p) a night, and provide stabling for the horses. If he didn't possess his own stabling, he had to hire it elsewhere and then give it free of charge to the military. He also had to provide each man with one and a quarter pounds of bread, one pound of meat, one pound of vegetables and two pints of small beer for tenpence (4p). It wasn't just small country hotels which were affected; the hoteliers of even fashionable Hastings had to accept a hundred soldiers in the summer of 1890, and in 1914 billeting was still on the statute book.

Another nonsense was the law on gaming which was designed to keep the pubs from deteriorating into gambling dens, but nevertheless resulted in a hotel manager being liable to a fine if he played cards with his own guests in his own apartment. The licensee of the Coffee House Hotel in Carlisle was fined £2 for this in 1879, yet at Beverley in 1890 only costs were awarded in a similar case and the Bench said it was "a very harsh and abominable law". The definition of gambling was wide, and though the Victorians loved the turf, played cards for high stakes at their country house parties, and were very welcome visitors to casinos all over Europe, the official policy was to pretend that gambling was frowned upon by all intelligent and law abiding people, particularly when the poor were involved, as they were in the pubs.

The Gaming Act also prohibited the playing of billiards out of licensing hours in a hotel, even by resident guests, although it was alright to play in a licensed billiards hall! Also, the billiards room could not be opened in the hotel "on Sundays, Christmas Day, Good Friday and public act of thanksgiving days", and again there was a case in 1876 when a fine was imposed for this offence.

Much of the law was decided by precedent rather than by statute, for by 1914, there had still been no attempt to define by statute the rights or liabilities of either an inn-keeper, and hence a hotelier, or of his customers. Such legislation as had been passed dealt with subjects like the enforcement of the common law right of lien, the limit of liability under certain circumstances and the sale of drink.

The right of lien is the right to hold on to the luggage or valuables of a guest until the

THE
PICCADILLY
HOTEL & RESTAURANT
Regent Street & Piccadilly LONDON.

The Terrace Restaurant

The Terrace Restaurant

Afternoon Tea

The Louis XIV Lounge

Tariff & Full Particulars
Sent Free on application to Town & Country Offices
389 FIFTH AVENUE, NEW YORK.

bill he owes has been paid, and this a hotelier was entitled to do. The only way the law had changed over the years was on the question of whether the hotelier could sell the goods to settle the debt: this had been illegal until it was permitted by the 1878 Inn Keepers Act. The property was required to have been left with the hotelier for six weeks and an advertisement to the effect that he was going to sell it had to be put into the local newspaper a month before he did so. After all that the goods could finally be disposed of without the owner's approval.

Before 1863 the hotelier, under common law, was responsible for the full cost of any loss or injury to property in the hotel belonging to his guests. It was not necessary for the property to be put in a hotel safe, nor for the guest to tell the hotel manager what valuables he had brought with him. As a consequence the liability was extremely onerous and there were ample opportunities for unscrupulous guests to indulge in sharp practices. Indeed, many hotels made it easy for thieves as well. Keys to bedrooms were either on a board in the lobby or hanging up in the service area on each floor. A thief could wait until the coast was clear and pick up the key or even walk into unlocked bedrooms. It was only after the Grosvenor Hotel guests had been robbed of more than £500 worth of valuables that simple security procedures were introduced and the concept of master keys and doors with safety locks came to be adopted. After 1863 the law was changed so that the hotelier was only liable for up to £30 as long as certain conditions were complied with, and these included the exhibition of a notice consisting of the appropriate section of the Act, so that the guest was aware of the law. It was also necessary that neither the hotelier nor his staff were guilty of neglect. Even so one hotelkeeper complained that some guests "seemed to stay in hotels to lose valuable jewellery". If the valuables were expressly deposited with the hotelier the liability was for their value. The Act further altered the law by releasing the hotelier from responsibility for the guests' carriages or animals.

Facing page:
The importance of American visitors at the turn of the century is shown by this advertisement which refers prospective clients to the New·York office.

The part of the Act which caused the judiciary the most headaches was the question of neglect, and, unfortunately for the hotels, different magistrates and juries gave different decisions on very similar evidence. When Mr. Jones, for instance, went to bed at the Norfolk Square Hotel in London in 1878, he put his watch and chain on the chest of drawers. It was not there in the morning. The manager said that the hotel had not been guilty of any form of neglect but the guest sued and got £27 damages; other cases however, were dismissed. Guests who left umbrellas on the appropriate stand outside the hotel restaurant might get damages if they were then stolen or might not, and as we saw at the Grand Pump Room Hotel, Bath, a lost case could be very expensive indeed.

Damage to property was only one aspect of the results of neglect. Sometimes the argument concerned damage to life and limb, and particularly as new inventions created dangers to which the general public were unaccustomed. Mr. Jones only lost his watch, but Mr. Smith lost his life when he wandered into a service area near his bedroom in the middle of the night, looking presumably for a toilet, and went straight down the lift shaft. The Midland Grand Hotel in 1883 could well have done without the subsequent publicity, but when a lower court awarded damages of £3,500 they decided that they must appeal, and they won in the higher court by two to one.

Any guest who asked for accommodation was entitled to receive it, so long as there was a room empty and that he paid a reasonable deposit if required. Up to 1914 the hotelier was not entitled either to ask the name of the guest if he wished to remain incognito nor for any other personal details, and the manager had to accept the guest even if he believed him to be bankrupt. What is more he had to accept not only a man but his wife and family and within reason his companions and servants. Admittedly if you had a large and unwholesome dog you could be turned away (R. *vs* Rymer 1877). It was in 1899 that a case occurred which established that dress could be a factor in providing service or not. Viscountess Harburton was in cycling clothes and the proprietress of the Hautboy Hotel, Ockham, Surrey, refused to serve her in the coffee room. The bar, yes, but the coffee room, no. The Cycling Touring Club financed the prosecution but the jury found for the defendant. This was in spite of an impassioned plea by the prosecuting counsel, who told the jury that such a verdict would result in future generations considering them purblind and perverted. Viscountess Harburton had felt that it was improper for her to be asked to take refreshments in a room where gentlemen were smoking and where there were even one or two members of the 'working class' but to no avail. (R. *vs* Sprague 1899).

Failure to provide goods and services or to cut corners could, however, be dangerous as there so often seemed to be solicitors or their clerks on the receiving end, In 1891, for example, Mr. Philpott, a solicitor's clerk, took a room for his wife and himself, together with his three children in a Bournemouth hotel and contracted rheumatic fever from, he alleged, damp beds; that cost the hotelier £150 damages. A solicitor in Birmingham in the same year stayed in a hotel and was charged for five breakfasts he had not eaten. He sued and got his money back.

The case, however, which epitomised the difficulties between admitting guests and also accepting liability, concerned two electoral workers who returned to their hotel at two o'clock in the morning and were refused admission by the landlord because of the lateness of the hour. This case was eventually decided by the Lord Chief Justice who held that the licence given to a hotelier was in the nature of a monopoly, and that therefore he had to receive guests at any time. Now there was obviously a danger in opening a locked hotel at dead of night when you were responsible for the belongings of everybody in it, but that was just unfortunate.

Cases came to court on the most unlikely points of law; that a hotelier was responsible for damage to his guest's property occasioned by a fire which didn't start on the premises, but had no liability if the fire broke out in the hotel. That if you signed on behalf of a guest for a registered letter, you were responsible for its contents (Whalley *vs* the Washington Hotel, Liverpool 1885). That if you leave your trendy bicycle with an ostler who has subcontracted the yard from the hotelier, the hotelier remains responsible for your machine if it is damaged, (Briggs *vs* the Angel Hotel, Leamington 1886). The vast majority of the cases and most of the law didn't really worry many hoteliers during their careers but there was one area where they were constantly concerned and that was licensing.

If a hotelier lost his licence, he lost an important source of his profits and invariably it would put him out of business, yet the Licensing Laws were also interpreted differently and there were many new Licensing Acts during the Victorian and Edwardian periods, and agitation for changes all the time.

We have seen how the temperance movement began in the 1830s and it grew and flourished for well over seventy years. There were many different societies representing slight variations of viewpoint, but as far as hoteliers were concerned the battle was over local option. The idea behind local option was that the inhabitants of an area should be able to vote on the question of whether they wanted licensed premises in their district or not. If a sufficient proportion voted that they did not, the justices would be able to withdraw the licences that existed and make the area 'dry'. The supporters of local option had decided that the path to total prohibition in the country led along this winding subsidiary road, rather than down the main highway of outright prohibition which they realised would never be passed by Parliament.

In 1864 a Bill was moved "to enable owners and occupiers of property in certain districts to prevent the common sale of intoxicating liquors" if there was a two-thirds majority in favour. The voting in the Commons was 292–35 against, and although the Bill was introduced annually in slightly modified form for some years afterwards, it never looked like being passed. Indeed it even failed to obtain support from some areas where one might have expected the most enthusiastic reception; many churchmen were against it and Dr. Magee, the Bishop of Peterborough, provided the rallying call for its opponents in the debate in 1872 when he said "it would be better that England should be free than that England should be compulsorily sober".

"Better free than sober" had a splendid ring to it, and the battle might have seemed to be over until the leader of the local option lobby, Sir Wilfred Lawson, changed his tactics and in 1879 brought in a resolution rather than a Bill. While the Commons would not pass a Bill, a resolution in favour of a temperance measure was not an immediate attempt to create a law, and could be supported by many members whose constituencies had large numbers of temperance voters, and who wished to curry favour with them. The resolution was at first defeated by 252–164 but passed 229–203 in 1880. Although a witness before a select committee, who was himself a prominent teetotaller, said in 1878 "the hotel system is one by itself and it may be fairly conceded that while a traveller is residing at a hotel, it is as though he were in his own house" the hoteliers were convinced that once the pubs had been destroyed, they would be next on the list. Certainly Sir Wilfred kept his eye on hotels as well; in 1879 he told the House that the magistrates at Aberystwyth had been attending a function at the Lion Hotel, and as they did not want to go home, they granted an extension of the licence on the spot. The Home Secretary gravely agreed that this was very wrong though it is doubtful whether Sir Wilfred was mollified or the magistrates unduly perturbed.

Ladies were increasingly well catered for in the new hotels This is the drawing room of the Hotel Cecil.

With the resolution passed, the local optionists waited for a Bill, but the government under Gladstone did nothing. In 1883 the resolution was carried by a larger majority, 228–141, and still the government did nothing. The political climate was now right, however, for licensing justices to refuse new applications and on occasions to refuse to renew licences. The most famous case of the time was Sharp and Wakefield (1887) where Miss Sharp, the licensee, was refused a renewal because her public house, said Mr. Wakefield and the Mendal, Westmorland magistrates, was surplus to the requirements of the locality and, as it was remote, too difficult to supervise. Four years' litigation later the House of Lords held that licences were only given at the discretion of magistrates and nobody had an inalienable right to renewal just because they had obeyed all the rules and their livelihoods depended on it. The way in which this decision affected a locality depended entirely on the views of the local justices, but in one year in Birmingham fifty licences had to be surrendered, and the local brewers arranged compensation for the dispossessed licensees among themselves.

The Winter Garden at the Midland in Manchester where wind and cold were kept out, but the sun could still shine in.

The hotel industry watched with disquiet the whole question of compensation, as it was agreed from the beginning that any compensation fund for dispossessed landlords would have to be provided by all the remaining licensees and these included hotels. Because of the compensation clause, the 1888 Local Government Bill had to be dropped, and Bills failed to pass the Commons in 1893 and 1895. In 1899 an opponent of the Veto Bill stood at a by-election at Osgoldcross, Yorkshire, specifically on this issue against a veto supporter and won by a margin of two to one, but still the agitation continued and, although Lawson died in 1906, the rout of the Conservative Party in 1908 enabled Asquith, the new Home Secretary, to bring in a Bill to get rid of no less than a third of the 100,000 public houses in the country. We shall see the galvanising effect this finally had on the efforts to form a body to speak for the hotel industry, a project which had been sunk without trace through almost total apathy in spite of regular attempts to get it to float. The compensation which Asquith's Act required from the hotel industry was very large indeed, and there seemed no hope that the Bill could be stopped because the Liberals had a large majority in the House of Commons. In spite of frenzied efforts by the whole catering world, the Bill passed all its stages in the Commons, the third reading by the great margin of 350–113. But then at the last gasp the legislation was overwhelmingly rejected by the Tory-dominated House of Lords, 272–96. It was the final piece of major legislation that the Lords were ever to block completely, for the constitutional crisis concerning reform of the House of Lords followed immediately and when the dust had died down, the Lords were never the same again.

Sir Wilfred Lawson introduced his first Local Option Bill in 1864 and Asquith introduced his Licensing Act in 1908; forty-four years during which the hotel industry was constantly aware of the growing power of its enemies, and their determined efforts materially to alter the industry's balance. Of course hotels would have survived even if Britain, like the United States, had agreed to prohibition, but just as today the industry is aware of the tourist's unfavourable comparison between our licensing laws and those on the continent, so the effect of prohibition was a serious worry. Hotelkeepers had seen already that the Victorian Sunday, compared with the continental freedom to enjoy more pastimes at least on Sunday afternoon, irritated their visitors from abroad as well. Undoubtedly for many people in the hotel industry it was simply a question of their not being allowed to make as much profit as they would like, but for others it was a question of principle that people should be allowed to make up their own minds about their religious observances; even so the wish of the majority of Victorians in power was for strict observance of Sunday and they got their way.

Prominent hoteliers did their best to get successive governments to treat the hotel industry separately from pubs but Sir William Towle, writing in 1914 with a lifetime of experience behind him of all the problems of running the Midland Railway hotels, summed up his own feelings with resignation "The genius of the English people is not in the direction of hotel keeping. In addition to this, the extraordinary want of sympathy displayed by so many of the justices in connection with these enterprises, and their persistent endeavours on every opportunity to treat large hotels and their representatives as common public house keepers in their dealings with them seriously militate against private enterprise being directed to hotel keeping in England".

The existing licensing laws were, in fact, less onerous than they are today; it was only after 1872 that children under sixteen were forbidden to drink alcohol in hotels and the Licensing Act of that year made opening hours five in the morning to midnight! A Leamington case had established that guests staying in hotels could entertain their friends outside licensing hours and, indeed, the country depended heavily for its tax revenue on drink. As the *Caterer* commented in 1885 "Not only are we, as a trade, under greater legislative control than any other country in the world, and our intoxicants are also more heavily taxed than those of any foreign nation, but we pay more than one fourth of the whole national revenue".

The Victorian problem was to stop excessive drinking without reducing the revenue to the Exchequer, just as today there is a positively schizophrenic attitude towards

The French restaurant at the Midland Hotel in Manchester. The head chefs in the best Midland Railway hotels were very often Frenchmen, and the standard of the cuisine has been very high for 100 years.

smoking as the government tries to balance the dangers from cancer against its immense income from cigarette sales. Legislation was passed in the '70s to prevent short measures and to provide inspectors, but hoteliers really had little to complain about except being lumped together with the meanest drinking house.

The value of a licence was well illustrated by Rudd and Blackford in 1886. The owner of a Bournemouth hotel offered £1,000 to the plaintiff if he could get the hotel a licence, but when the plaintiff did so the owner refused to pay. He was taken to court and judgement was found against him in full. If a licence was worth such a vast sum of money, it is no wonder that hoteliers were frightened of the local option lobby.

At the height of its fame as a spa there was practically no acceptable hotel accommodation in Bath. In the 19th century when its heyday had long vanished, new hotels like the Empire were built.

THE EMPIRE HOTEL, BATH.

After the ball was over 13

"Profits have been adversely affected by the high price of provisions and supplies and by the ever increasing public demand for the maximum of convenience and luxury. The wave of temperance and the tendency of customers to economise have helped to sap a one time profitable source of revenue—wine consumption. The burden of taxation increased by the Compensation Act which came into operation with the year, is now exceedingly onerous". To make the best of a poor situation the *Caterer* told its readers that what was needed was "enterprise in advertising, close buying, stopping leakages, adopting improvements, keen personal supervision, and a quick appreciation of ever developing public requirements".

This was in 1906 and neatly sums up the difficulties which had arisen or worsened since the old Queen died. It had not been a happy five years; where the hotel industry had been accustomed to dropping food prices, stable fuel costs and deflation, the Boer War had changed the picture. Now prices were beginning to rise and interest rates were climbing too. This had a serious effect not only on the cost of overdrafts, but also on the reserve funds of a number of existing hotel companies.

What happened was this. When times were good every company put a small part of its profits aside to be there in case of emergencies, and there was often another reserve fund for future refurbishing of a major kind—new boilers, major roof repairs and similar items. These reserve funds had to be invested safely, and indeed, when Frederick Gordon put money into more speculative securities, like New Zealand Loan and Mercantile, the shareholders complained, and not without cause as Frederick had not chosen wisely. Consequently Gordons, like most of the other companies put the bulk of the money into Consols, that great British government security which gave you a fixed three per cent on your money with total safety, and which had the strength of the whole British Empire behind it. After the war, though, you could get more than three per cent equally securely from other investments, and therefore Consols fell in price. Although you still got your three per cent the value of the reserve funds diminished if your business needed the money for the purpose for which it was originally intended. The company balance sheet might show a reserve fund of £100,000, but its realisable value might be much less.

As these funds were also usually much smaller than the more prudent management of today would demand, the effect was greater, and shareholders who had welcomed the distribution of large dividends in the past, now found their companies short of reserves. If it became necessary to raise more capital as a consequence, the interest charges were up as well, and life for the directors grew even more difficult.

During the war it had been necessary to levy additional taxation, and when the conflict ended the government was not able to return to the pre-war levels. Instead income tax at one shilling (5p) in the £ remained at an all-time peak, and prices rose as a consequence.

Almost all the goods needed for refurbishing and running the hotels became more expensive, whether it was carpets and curtains or plates and cutlery. Wages went up as well; a chef who had been earning £1 a week in 1880 was by 1914 earning £2 a week, and a kitchen porter £1 a week instead of £2 a month. The new salaries were, of course, still very low, and the inflation looks puny by modern day standards, but where we are accustomed to rising prices the Edwardians were shocked by them.

Hoteliers were further troubled by extra charges: David Lloyd George introduced his Insurance Bill which went towards providing a very necessary dole and a pension, and Asquith introduced the new Compensation Act. When a licence was revoked and a publican forced out of business, it was necessary to compensate him and the funds came from those who still held licences, and who paid a levy each year towards its upkeep. With staff costs doubled, food costs up fifty per cent and additional taxation, the result should have been a higher tariff for the hotels, but in many cities there was now much too much competition for this to be possible. The Midland Grand which charged fourteen shillings (70p) for dinner, bed and breakfast in 1873 was only charging twelve shillings (60p) in 1912. Prices simply could not rise with so much spare capacity in the industry, and with still more hotels being built. In London alone the decade saw the opening among others of the Piccadilly, Ritz, Waldorf, Imperial and Strand Palace Hotels, the latter charging only six shillings (30p) for bed and breakfast and attracting large numbers of guests as a result.

Norman Shaw built the Piccadilly when going through his "imperial period". The cost was vast, the result impressive, and within 18 months the company was bankrupt.

When hotels ran into difficulties the arguments raged fiercely about who was to blame, and all too often these arguments eventually finished up as inquests. Was it the fault of the manager accused of taking commission from suppliers, stealing the food and wine in conspiracies with his heads of departments, overcharging customers and turning a blind eye to the visits of prostitutes so long as he was well paid to do so? Or was it the directors forcing the managers to buy uneconomically from friends of the board, thus cheating the shareholders but feathering their own nests? Directors who invested the reserve funds unwisely, insisted on unprofitable capital expenditure, on retaining inefficient staff because of their personal friendships, and persisting in interfering where they should have left the control in professional hands?

The truth depended on which company you were studying, but the best generalisation is that it depended on the strength of both directors and management for good or evil whether a hotel prospered and not so much on the excuses which economic conditions provided. Certainly there were abuses on both sides, but then hotels were close to the sources of Edwardian sin and there were many who would take advantage of the situation.

Of the new London hotels both the Piccadilly and the Ritz added poignant footnotes to great traditions. The Piccadilly was the brainchild of the nephew of Sir Polydore de Keyser, who was also called Polydore, and who had taken over the de Keyser Royal after his uncle's death. Young Polydore was determined to write a new and even greater chapter in the family annals and sunk his personal fortune as well as that of many of his friends in creating "the most unashamedly Baroque piece of stage design, a thickly rusticated ground floor, and above, colossal columns". The architect, R. Norman Shaw, had reached a period in his work when he wished his buildings to epitomise the grandeur which was Imperial Britain, and in Polydore he found a nincompoop who would agree to foot the bill. Although the Piccadilly was superbly situated almost on top of the Circus, the initial outlay was far too great and the company crashed.

It had taken the de Keysers fifty years to build up their business and it took young Polydore less than ten to lose it all again. He died in Montreal and the de Keyser Hotel passed into the hands of Lever Brothers after the First World War and became their headquarters. The accounts department moved into the grand ballroom, the executives into the bedrooms and the precursor of many other take-overs had reduced the competition by one. Meanwhile the Piccadilly, with its fine masonic temples, the dining-room panelled exquisitely in Australian oak of a quality unobtainable today, and its labyrinth of public and private rooms was taken over by a new company who installed Fritz Heim, a hard working German manager, and he quickly made the operation profitable. The ingredient which made all the difference was, of course, the fact that the company no longer had to service the original capital, but only the money involved in buying a failed enterprise.

Quite different in concept was the Ritz which was built some years after the successful creation of the Ritz Hotel in Paris, and which incorporated the same ideas which had made the Carlton so popular. There was one major change and that was the absence from command of Ritz himself. In 1901 he had been working like a beaver to ensure that the Carlton would outshine every other hotel in celebrating the coronation of his greatest client and most cherished patron, Edward VII. Indeed Ritz owed a very great deal to the man who had among other favours broken the conventions by actually coming and dining in public at the Carlton. The hotel, of course, benefited enormously from this open expression of his approval. The Carlton was to be host to a shining array of famous guests, and Ritz might well have seen the great day as the absolute peak of his career. On June 24th, however, just a few weeks before the event, Edward developed appendicitis and much to his disgust, he had to postpone a coronation for which in all conscience he had waited an almost record number of years. The departure of the offending, if useless, organ and the majority of the capital's visitors could have been synchronised, so rapidly did the one follow the other. As Frederick Gordon told his sorrowing shareholders "Well, I won't say that all the visitors in the hotels, but a very large proportion of them, immediately the announcement was made, left bodily". While Frederick was no doubt

Norman Shaw

cursing his luck which had been turning sour of late, poor Cesar Ritz collapsed. He had a complete nervous breakdown brought on by driving himself far too hard for years and culminating in endless hours of labour towards a royal anticlimax. Though he rallied after a while for a couple of years, he had a relapse in 1903 and thereafter sank slowly into both public and mental oblivion. Today he would probably have been brought back to near normal with electrical treatment and modern drugs, but such progress lay many years in the future, and there was no cure for the finest hotel craftsman of his time. "Do what you like" became the stock answer of the man who had taken such delight in helping and supervising, and by 1908 he had resigned from all his companies and was an invalid. He died in 1918 in a Swiss sanatorium at the age of sixty-eight.

The hotel which was named after him was built on the sites of the old Bath and Walsingham hotels and it had a steel frame, the first of its kind in London, though the Waldorf soon followed. Since the Ritz is also faced with Norwegian granite it must be one of the most solid structures in Mayfair and with its covered colonnade it rightly merits its present position as a protected building. Though Ritz never managed the Ritz, its grace and charm, its light and spaciousness and its thoroughly elegant taste all bear witness to the man it helps to immortalize. True to his teaching, the hotel had no dust traps like the tops of wardrobes or heavy drapes, and was painted rather than wall-papered. The board had been fortunate enough to persuade Alfred Holland to join them after his resignation which was exactly what was needed after Ritz succumbed. To the end of his life in 1937 Holland served the Ritz and the Carlton watching the fortunes of his old love decline as Gordons reaped the whirlwind of amateur controllers.

Extract from a presentation book for the Midland Hotel, Manchester, dated September 5, 1903.

Frederick Gordon had still found the going rough after the Boer War was over. The ten per cent dividend, which shareholders had been told after the Holland fracas they might expect to improve, had in fact declined to eight per cent, and the shares had slumped near to par. In the last full year, however, of Frederick's chairmanship he had

LEEDS ORCHESTRA
WILL PLAY IN THE LADIES' FOYER.

INSTRUMENTALISTS:

SIGNOR L. RATTI (from Milan).
SIGNOR FORTONI
SIGNOR ZANABONI } from Florence.
Mr. SMART (from London).

March	"Stars and Stripes"	…	Sousa
Waltz	"Blue Danube"	…	Strauss
	"Forget-me-not"	…	Mackenzie
Selection	"Faust"	…	Gounod
	"Idylle Passionelle"	…	Razigade
	"Smoky Moky"	…	Mill
Selection	"Belle of New York"	…	Kerker
	"Rose Mousse"	…	Bosc
Selection	"Three Little Maids"	…	Rubens
Waltz	"Serenade"	…	Metra
Polka	"Tapageuse"	…	Blanc
INTERVAL			
March	"A Sciantosa"	…	Gambardella
Waltz	"Dans le Fleur"	…	Berger
	"Musica Proibita"	…	Gastaldon
Selection	"The Casino Girl"	…	Englander
	"La Paloma"	…	Yradier
	"Salome"	…	Lorraine
Selection	"Merry England"	…	German
Waltz	"Souviens Toi"	…	Waldteufel
Selection	"Toreador"	…	Caryll
	"Slumber Song"	…	Squire
March	"Chicago"	…	Salabert

ST. PANCRAS ORCHESTRA
WILL PLAY IN THE CONCERT HALL.

INSTRUMENTALISTS:

SIGNOR BENOTTI, Leader } from Milan.
SIGNOR BIGI, 2nd Violin
SIGNOR VANNUCCINI, Pianoforte }
SIGNOR RUTINI, Double Bass } from Florence.
SIGNOR ROSSI, 'Cello

March	"Viennese"	…	Trepka
Waltz	"Espana"	…	Waldteufel
Mazurka	"Naturaliste"	…	Ganne
Selection	"Martha"	…	Flotow
	"The Venetian Serenade"	…	Beeby
	"Frou frou"	…	Petit
Selection	"La Poupée"	…	Audran
	"Sunny, Sunny Flower"		
Selection	"Kitty Grey"	…	Shaw
Waltz	"Feishe Geister"	…	Strauss
March	"Honeymoon"	…	Rosey
INTERVAL			
March	"Petits Pierrots"	…	Bosc
Waltz	"Aus dem Hochwald"	…	Kaulisch
Reverie	"Volpatti"		
Selection	"Country Girl"	…	Monckton
Waltz	"Bleu"	…	Margis
	"The Rose of Riviera"		
Selection	"The Girl from Kay's"	…	Caryll
	"Down South"	…	Myddleton
Dance	"Nell Gwyn"	…	German
Waltz	"Toreador"	…	Royle
March	"El Capitan"	…	Sousa

been able to report "the improvement is a very satisfactory and substantial one but it is not as great as the Directors would have liked to put before you". It is very likely that Gordon could have pulled the company round if he had been in his prime, but now he was an old man, and in the autumn of 1903 he fell ill and was advised by the doctors to go to his hotel in Cannes to recuperate. On March 22nd 1904 he went to the opera at Monte Carlo and suffered a heart attack late at night which proved fatal. The man who had earned the title 'Hotel Napoleon' as surely as Ritz was called "Hotelkeeper to Kings and King of Hotelkeepers" left the scene at almost the same time as his rival, but unlike Ritz, Frederick Gordon had never seriously been under attack. The business he had founded was still sound and his own reputation still intact. The disappointing results of the last few years were almost universally regarded by the public as a regrettable but temporary pause after the twenty years of unbroken prosperity he had given his supporters. Many of the hotels were freehold, the Gordon Hotel wine stocks alone were worth £180,000, and 1903 had been a better year. Frederick probably felt that the economic conditions in the '70s when he started were much more difficult than the post-Boer War, and we shall never know whether he would have triumphantly overcome the industry's malaise or whether, like Henry V for instance, he died at the right time for his fame to be untarnished. There were, however, even in his lifetime, two significant and disturbing factors: in the ten years since 1893 the number of nights when Gordon beds were occupied had declined by eleven per cent and this was a direct result of the new competition. Secondly the sale of wine had dropped ten per cent in 1902 alone and this was because money was so much tighter.

The *Caterer* had suggested that advertising could help, and Gordons were well to the fore and even employed their own advertising manager. Mr. Robert Donald gave an interview in 1902 to the *Advertising World* and they were able to elicit full details of his carefully worked-out strategy. "We use the society papers regularly" explained Mr. Donald "as well as the Ladies' Weeklies and some of the dailies. We want to get to the travelling public. The quantity of circulation is not everything. We advertise in the half-penny dailies to keep on the right side of the newspapermen".

ADELPHI ORCHESTRA
WILL PLAY IN THE ROOF GARDEN.

INSTRUMENTALISTS :

SIGNOR G. CINGANELLI, Leader
SIGNOR BELLESI, 2nd Violin
SIGNOR C. CINGANELLI, 'Cello   from Florence.
SIGNOR BILLI, Pianoforte
SIGNOR BOSI, Double Bass

March	...	...	"Nuit folichonne"	Porinelly
Waltz	...	...	"Sourir d'Avril"	Deprét
Mazurka	...	...	"Mousmé"	Ganne
Selection	...	"Florodora"	...	Stuart
Waltz	...	"Lettre d'Amour"	...	Stewart
		"At Georgia Camp Meeting"		Mill
Selection		"The Girl from Kay's"	...	Caryll
		"The Rose of Riviera"		
Selection		"The Messenger Boy"		Caryll
Waltz		"Jolie Viennoise"	...	Ziehrer
March	...	"Manhattan"		Sousa
		INTERVAL.		
March	...	"Toreador"		Damaré
Waltz	...	"Parfum"	...	Ziehrer
		"Whistling Rufus"	...	Mill
Selection		"Country Girl"		Monckton
		"The Mosquito Parade"		Penn
		"Simple Aveu"		Thomé
Selection		"Toreador"		Caryll
March		"El Capitan"	...	Sousa
Selection		"The Silver Slipper"	...	Stuart
Waltz		"Aimer boir chanter"	...	Strauss
March	...	"Edward VII."	...	Sousa

ROMAN ORCHESTRA (Specially engaged for the Manchester Hotel Season)
WILL PLAY IN THE GARDEN.

SIGNOR MORI, Musical Director and Conductor.

INSTRUMENTALISTS :

SIGNOR AVANZI, 1st Violin
SIGNOR AVANZI, 2nd Violin   from Milan.
SIGNOR PECORINI, 2nd Violin
SIGNOR FACCINI, Viola
SIGNOR MARCUCCI, 'Cello   from Florence.
SIGNOR DEL PERUGIA, Clarionette
SIGNOR ROVELLI, Flute
SIGNOR TARTARINI, Pianoforte   from Bologna.
Mr. FRAUDY, Double Bass   London Academy.
Mr. FLYNN, Cornet

March		"Liberty Bell"	...	Sousa
Waltz	...	"Mon Rêve"		Waldteufel
Mazurka		"Czarine"	...	Ganne
Selection		"Country Girl"	...	Monckton
		"The Rose of Riviera"		
Waltz	...	"Bleu"	...	Margis
Selection		"Toreador"		Caryll
		"The Coon Band Contest"		Prior
Waltz		"Amour et la Vie a Vienne"		Komzak
Selection		"Merry England"	...	German
March	...	"High School Cadets"		Sousa
		INTERVAL.		
March		"Kaiser. Frederic"		Friedelmann
Waltz		"Wiener Burger"		Ziehrer
		"Down South"	...	Myddleton
Selection		"Three Little Maids"	...	Rubens
		"Manajada Cake Walk"		Mori
		"Amoureuse Valse lente"		Berger
Selection		"The Girl from Kay's"	...	Caryll
Waltz	...	"Sobre las olas"		Rosas
Selection		"My Lady Molly"	...	Jones
		"The Swanee River"	...	Myddleton
March		"Stars and Stripes"	...	Sousa

It was easier to obtain favourable editorial coverage in Edwardian times than it is now, but Mr. Donald also knew how to provide the right stories. "Look at the large number of dinners, dances and other gatherings held at our hotels; they each mean a certain amount of publicity for us if managed properly". The use of public relations operated side by side with heavy media purchases. "It is nothing out of the ordinary for us to run a dozen pages in *Bradshaw*, and we are large advertisers in the other guides as well. We supply all the leading steamship companies with literature as well as producing tariffs and souvenir books". All of which was potentially very sound, but how did Mr. Donald measure the effectiveness of his advertising? "We are not like the proprietor of an ordinary article" parried Mr. Donald, "for us to the present it has been found impossible to systematically check the returns afforded. Until this is overcome we are totally dependent on our judgement. We have found that advertising as a whole pays very well".

So the classic defence of the advertising manager wandering around in a fog of unsubstantiated judgement had been formulated as early as this. It wasn't possible to say that advertising paid very well; a good season usually turned out to be good for

The motor car and the earlier bicycle brought new life to the hotels in the countryside. Here in 1912 a rally was held to the New Bath Hotel in Matlock.

everyone and a bad one hurt the people who advertised as much as those who didn't. Advertising was expensive and the occupancy had dropped by that eleven per cent.

In the countryside it was different. The revival of the country hotel left to rot by the departure of the stagecoach was now a greater possibility than had ever seemed likely during the past seventy years. We have seen how the bicycle and later the motor car brought new traffic onto the roads, but the provision of a new market did not automatically produce the necessary capital to revive the near derelict hotels. Many were in the ownership of the local gentry, but leased to the brewers, and there were a lot of complaints that the only item of any quality obtainable was the drink. Food was either of a poor standard or unobtainable, and the bedroom areas had not seen a lick of paint for years, far less any refurnishing.

Where was the money and the drive to come from to alter the situation? The answer in part was Albert Henry George, 4th Earl Grey, a former Governor-General of Canada and yet another from that apparently endless supply of Victorian humanitarians. Grey wished to bridge the gap between the out and out prohibitionists on the one hand, and the brewers on the other. He proposed that each English county should set up a trust to run country hotels. The original name chosen was The Public House Trust and the principle advocated was that the gentry should not renew the brewers' leases on suitable properties, but instead put them in good order and reopen them as decent hotels. It was a very ambitious scheme but Grey was a powerful and determined fighter, and with the help of a number of the Lord-Lieutenants the idea slowly got off the ground.

The first hotel was at Ridge Hill, sixteen miles from London on what had been the mail road to Holyhead. It was called The Wagon and Horses and had exactly three bedrooms. The county trust found an ex-policeman to run it and this worthy was paid a salary, and commission on whatever he sold, except for alcoholic drinks. The basic wage was a slim thirty shillings (£1.50) a week which had to cover not only the manager and his wife, but also one servant to help them run the hotel. Admittedly they had a coal allowance, but the normal drink commission would have been more rewarding financially and there was a deduction for living in the hotel. Perhaps a policeman was chosen because no hotelier worth the name would look at the job.

The experiment, nevertheless, was a success as far as the move in emphasis from drink sales was concerned, and the Barnet brewer who had been sending the hotel its beer, soon found that he was supplying it with an equal amount of fresh water so that the demand for tea could be satisfied. The Wagon and Horses was run by the Trust from 1903, and in 1904 it was joined by the Rose and Crown at Tring, another Rose and Crown at Tewin, also in Hertfordshire, and the Red Lion at Radlett. Although the efforts of other Trusts were also important, it was Hertfordshire which made the most progress and when it was decided to amalgamate the Trusts, it was the emblem of Hertfordshire, the hart couchant, which was adopted as the symbol of the new company. It was not until after the First World War, however, that the name Trust Houses was finalised.

There was plenty of opposition to Earl Grey because almost uniquely, he managed to antagonise both the brewers and the temperance supporters. The brewers didn't like the way the managers were turned to any kind of sale except drink, and the temperance lobby objected to the fact that drink was sold at all. The magistrates did on occasions turn down the applications of the Trusts for licences, and progress was slow in many parts of the country. Indeed Trust Houses was entirely confined to southern England and the Midlands until after 1918.

But if there was opposition, there was also very powerful support. Lord Rothschild built the Rose and Crown at Tring for the Trust and then leased it to them at a moderate rent. The Countess of Caledon owned The Wagon and Horses and was also generous in her terms. Many people bought shares in the Trusts even though the dividend was not allowed to be in excess of five per cent and was likely to be much lower, like the two-and-a-half per cent paid in 1910. The limit was raised to seven per cent in 1914, but the supporters of Trust Houses were not investing for the sake of the return on capital. They were anxious that the supporters of moderation should win the drink war, and they also wanted to save as much fine architecture as they could. They took pleasure in rescuing such historic inns as the 15th century Roebuck at Broadwater which was reopened in 1911, the 15th century Red Lion at Colchester which was acquired in 1913, and many other buildings which were hundreds of years old.

The founders of Trust Houses sank their capital into an ideal, and if they had known that their company might eventually strengthen the asset position of a take-over bidder like Allied Breweries one can only imagine their indignation. Through their charitable efforts, by 1914 there were thirty-two hotels with accommodation, five more without and Trust Houses were becoming a permanent part of the hotel scene.

The temperance issue reached a climax, as we have seen, after the Liberals swept into power in 1906 and Herbert Asquith, the Chancellor of the Exchequer made it clear in his first budget that he was going to honour the election pledges and take steps against the licensed trade. He could count on the support of the official Labour party was well, for Keir Hardie, their leader, was a strong temperance supporter, believing as so many of his colleagues did, that drink held back the working man from overcoming his disabilities. The Conservative M.P.s were reduced to a small rump just making up the numbers in the Commons and the hotel trade could see that they needed a voice, as they never had before. One commentator compared their lot with the Israelites in Egypt and decided that the Israelites "were really in a happy position compared with the licensed trades under the partisan control of Campbell-Bannerman, Asquith and Co".

Frank Bourne Newton, the publisher of the *Caterer*, seized the opportunity to try yet again to gather the hoteliers together into one body. Newton had become a partner of the *Caterer's* founder, Frederick Barrett, in 1879 and took over from the Editor within a year. In 1893 he bought the magazine for very little and launched it as a public company. He died during the Second World War when he was over ninety. The stumbling block in the 1880's, when Newton had tried before, was the £5 annual fee but there was now the Compensation Fund to be contended with, and £5 was the least of the hotelier's problems. After canvassing for support, the *Caterer* was able to publish a manifesto in April calling for the formation of a national organization, though the support came almost entirely from the provinces.

Why the London hotels thought they could stay out of the Association and still gain the ear of the government is obscure, though they might well have considered themselves superior to their country cousins, and decided to place their trust in the time honoured 'word in the ear' of their influential clients. There was one exception, Dudley James, the manager of Morleys in Trafalgar Square, and he was made chairman at the Association's inaugural meeting. By the end of the year, the Incorporated Hotel Keepers' Association had been registered, and it had three declared objects:

"*a*. To encourage and promote the interests of hotel-keepers and hydropathic proprietors in general, and particularly of those carrying on business in the United Kingdom. *b*. To collect and disseminate statistical and other information relating to hotel and kindred interests. *c*. To consider all questions affecting the interests of hotel-keepers and hydropathic proprieters, and, if necessary, to petition Parliament to promote deputations in relation to Public and private legislation affecting the same".

To the modern eye there are many interesting points about these aims. They specifically apply to hydropathic institutions so that these operations which had originally a medical *raison d'être*, were now accepted completely as a form of hotel. It was ironic that a body devoted to fighting licensing laws should also represent operations originally devoted to teetotallism, but the hydropaths had themselves often given up abstemious principles. The Association did not represent restaurants in the beginning and there was a lot to be said for this. Hotels are basically in competition with restaurants for the patronage of the public and the fact that people nowadays primarily think of eating in restaurants and sleeping in hotels is, as we have seen, a considerable change from the early days of the 19th century when the hotel flourished on the revenue from eating and drinking, and the bedrooms were less important.

It is desirable that hotels should be known equally for sleeping and eating, but the connection of hotels and restaurants in one Association has made it impossible to have a hotel industry campaign along the lines of "next time you eat out, eat in a hotel". The original members of the Association did, however, object to one type of restaurant, and that was the late-night club which was able to serve food and drink after the hotel restaurant had had to close, and the hoteliers protested against these supper clubs, though with little success.

The Association would have been unsuccessful in fighting many of the provisions of the new Licensing Act, but the House of Lords threw it out anyway. What the Association was able to deal with successfully were more minor items concerning the price of champagne, a questionnaire on wages, and insurance rates. In 1909 when swingeing increases in licensing duties were introduced, the larger London hotels were forced to

In 1905 the Viscount Duncannon, left, succeeded his father as the Earl of Bessborough. He was chairman of the London, Brighton and South Coast Railway and took over Gordon Hotels after the death of the founder.

By 1920 when he died (right) the hair was whiter but the noble Earl seemed to have been relatively unaffected by the disasters which had struck his country, his hotel company and his railway. Bessborough was the first president of the Incorporated Association of Hotels and Restaurants, the predecessor of today's British Hotels, Restaurants and Caterers Association.

close ranks with the Association, and in 1910 the restaurants joined with the hotels in a renamed Association of Hotels and Restaurants.

Before the War, Lord Bessborough, who had taken over from Frederick Gordon as chairman of Gordon Hotels, agreed to act as president of the Association which gave it the right aristocratic cachet but was hardly a dynamic choice. Bessborough also took the credit, which was rightly Newton's, for the formation of the Association and passed it to the major London hotels who didn't deserve it. In writing to new members Lord Bessborough said "Unfortunately, there was at that time no duly authorised society in connection with hotels and restaurants, with the result that a committee had to be, and was, hurriedly formed by the Directors of the principal London Hotel companies and the position of hotels in relation to licences and taxation was put before the government."

It is quite possible that the original Association carried little weight without the London companies, but ignoring the 1908 Association was very petty. Bessborough's task was to unite the hotels throughout the country, and he might have looked at his own performance when he said at the annual general meeting in 1914 "A publicist (for hotels and restaurants) cannot expect support from men which until a few years ago they declined to give to their own representative body, and which, as this report shows, they even now only render half heartedly." *The World* which was an influential magazine put it all down to a rampant jealousy. "Jealousy is the blight of their industry—for hotels and restaurants are in truth today a great and growing industry. The industry is honeycombed by jealousies. There is jealousy of rival concerns, jealousy of personal ties, jealousy of administration and management, jealousy of caste, jealousy of race between British born and foreigner and between nationalities."

This was the murky undercurrent which seldom broke surface but which prevented the industry from fighting together, from sustaining its development as a "great and growing industry". It was a paradise for snobs in a narcissistic age and few hoteliers could cope when supply exceeded demand. What excuses could they give for the practice which grew of writing to visitors in other hotels and asking them to cut short their stay and move to the writer's place? It was hardly saving a guest from a fate worse than death, and not unnaturally the average hotel manager started to look warily at letters addressed on plain envelopes which arrived at about the same time as the newcomer. Yet the hotels continued to publicize lists of their expected guests in order to see their hotel's name in print, and if the competition got valuable information, the manager at least had his ego inflated.

Amid these increasingly difficult economic rapids, the Midland Railway hotels steamed on, and at the beginning of the decade they had started to build a hotel in Manchester. Cottonopolis, as the Victorians had nicknamed it, had not been noted as a good city in which to build hotels. In 1886 the 350 room Victoria had opened at an initial cost exceeding £100,000. It had a dome on each corner of the building and an enormous one in the middle so that it looked more like a child's sand castle than a hotel. No effort had been spared to make its decorations as elegant as possible. The designers had used Burmantofts Faience, a type of porcelain, Minton Ware, Lincrusta Walton, which was a mural covering, marbles, cathedral glass and Tyneside tapestry. There was a steam laundry at the top of the building, a ten-table billiards room which was much admired, and within two years a large overdraft and bankruptcy for the original company. The Manchester Corporation who were the landlords, found the hotel back on their hands and were bailed out by a London brewer, Sir Alfred Kirby, who got a number of prominent men to form a syndicate.

But where there were very successful hotels in other provincial centres like Birmingham and Liverpool, there was no comparable operation in Manchester. William Towle intended to put this right by building the Midland in the heart of the city. Like the builders of the Westminster Palace in earlier days, Towle and his architect, Charles Trubshawe, travelled round Europe and America looking for the best of the new ideas, and when the hotel finally opened it had more rooms than the Manchester Town Hall. It also had at least one major improvement on its predecessors in the shape of an elaborate ventilating system to keep the air in the hotel fresh. The atmosphere in the big cities was polluted to a considerable degree and the choking yellow fogs descended in the winter and stayed for days. Now at the Midland "a series of filter screens of linen and coke which receive 80,000 cubic feet of air a minute remove impurities." To keep out the street air on the ground floor, revolving doors were introduced. By ducting through grids into the bedrooms the air was kept circulating and the atmosphere must have been a great deal pleasanter than the customers were used to finding.

There were many little touches at the Midland which showed Towle's meticulous and detailed attention to advantage. Every bedroom had a clock on the wall synchronised from a central point in the hotel and electrically illuminated from the bed by the press of a switch. There were, of course, telephones in every room, and Towle built nearly a hundred bathrooms as well. This was an exceptional number for a provincial hotel, but in Canada the Canadian Pacific Railway Hotels were built with a complete set of private bathrooms even though they were often in quite small towns, and Towle might well have taken note of this on his travels.

The hotel opened in 1903 and became extremely popular almost immediately. It was well run and much needed, but the fact remained that the investment was large and the tariff that could be charged comparatively moderate. There was the immediate difficulty that the hotel was half-empty or worse at the weekends, particularly during the winter, and consequently the hotel was not likely to make even a reasonable return on capital. It was the old story all over again. In these last years of Towle's hegemony before handing over to his sons, it would have helped if they had at least appreciated the results of this type of extravagance, but the lesson they actually absorbed was that quality was all that mattered and that the shareholders were rich and their interests way down on the list of priorities. The Adelphi was pulled down again in Liverpool and a fine new building was opened just before the war broke out, but it was to be the last new city hotel the railways ever built.

As the decade wore on, the hotel industry became steadily less profitable. From 1904–1914 the Cecil, for instance, paid no dividend and yet had to sink fresh capital into keeping the hotel up with the times. They spent £40,000 on the creation of very large palm courts within the hotel where the visitors could enjoy their afternoon tea and bask in the sunshine under great domes of glass. One court was ninety-three feet long, forty-five feet wide and thirty-two feet high, and the other one hundred and ten feet by twenty-eight feet by twenty-eight feet. When they were opened the public flocked to see them, but what profit could be made from such a costly investment?

By 1910 most of the hotel shares were standing below par again. The Savoy £10 shares which had been as high as £20 in 1896 now varied between £4 and £6, and even the Carlton £1 shares sank to ten shillings (50p). At these prices the return was still over eight per cent, but the shareholders were losing capital, pressure was constantly on the hotels and the public continued to be offered a wider and wider choice.

There were exceptions, of course, in the prevailing gloom but they were usually on the periphery. The great success story was the growth of J. Lyons and Co. whose tea shops were all the rage, and who distributed on four successive years to their fortunate shareholders the stupendous dividend of forty-two-and-a-half per cent. Where Gordons had struggled to achieve profits of £250,000 in their heyday, Lyons notched up figures in excess of one and a half million pounds. Meanwhile in Wales the ability of Mr. R. E. Jones who had many catering establishments as well as the Mackworth Hotel, Swansea, and the Carlton Hotel, Cardiff, produced twenty per cent dividends, but these were situations which depended on the genius of the original entrepreneurs. Gordons declined

Not all the large, new provincial hotels were a success. The Victoria Hotel in Manchester was a disaster though the Grosvenor across the street is still operating today.

without Frederick Gordon, Frederick Hotels without Sir Blundell Maple who died young, and after Ritz it was a question of holding onto the existing position rather than making further progress.

At the seaside the public remained fickle and chose whatever was newest and most fashionable. The *entente cordiale* fostered by Edward VII with the French led to a growing tourist traffic from Britain to towns like Dieppe and Deauville and the big hotels on the coast lost a further section of their upper crust clientele. The tourist centres still suffered from a short season and this was well illustrated by the manager of the North British in Edinburgh who protested about the new valuation which had been placed on his hotel by the rating authorities. He opined that the building should be regarded as a monument, but that it certainly shouldn't be rated as a hotel. In the season which only lasted nine or ten weeks he needed 145 staff, but that number could not be too heavily reduced when the hotel was not full, and there were times in the winter when he had "three servants for each guest." He suggested that a rate of £4,000 a year would be far too high, but he had to pay £10,000.

The whole question of what to do with the seaside hotels in the winter was a very vexed question. There were certain towns with mild climates, like Torquay and Bournemouth, which attracted permanent residents during the period, but these were exceptional. In most coastal towns there was little business, but to close was often as costly as to stay open. The position was complicated where the railways owned hotels and wanted them to stay open in order to get more travellers on the train. For the small numbers involved it looked an unnecessary expense, but if one railway did it, the competition often stayed in line. Gordon Hotels on the south coast stayed open until the First World War in spite of vigorous protests by many shareholders, and Bessborough's dual role as chairman of the railway which served the towns and chairman of the hotel company as well, was bound to be considered an important factor in this decision. If Gordons had shut the seaside hotels in the winter it would have saved money, but made the railway journey less attractive by removing the best hotel at several destinations.

There were still hoteliers who would place principle above the crying need for custom, and in one of the earliest examples of an attempted colour bar, the managing director of the St. Ermins Hotel at Westminster took a firm stand. At the time of the Ecumenical Methodist Conference in 1901 the hotel accommodated "a number of eminent coloured divines" and American guests approached the director, Harry Richardson, to ask that the ministers be told to leave. If the hotel was not prepared to abide by this wish, not only would the Americans leave, but they would also spread the word back in the States. Richardson angrily refused and the general concensus of opinion was that it was thoroughly bad form for the Americans to interfere, they should leave their primitive habits at home, and the British would put up whoever they pleased.

Such sturdy independence did not unhappily survive into the middle of the twentieth century as the case of Leary Constantine during the Second World War illustrated. Indeed in the 1950s and early 1960s the St. Ermins was once again the home of a large number of eminent coloured visitors because the luxury hotels refused to accept them unless they were world famous names in entertainment. At the hotel accommodation desk at BOAC's terminal at Victoria in the '50s every entry on the list was marked either 'C' where coloured guests were accepted, or 'NC' where they were not. This situation does not exist today except surreptitiously in a very few hotels who are still failing to uphold the traditions of the industry as a whole.

By the time George V came to the throne, the great Victorian hoteliers had all but vanished into eternity. The showbiz arena of the spas had changed into the less romantic, but far more effective medical centres which they are today, or alternatively achieved precarious existence as holiday homes for the genuinely idle rich. The Celtic fringe of the country was still undergoing development which never seemed to produce the hoped-for results. There were no seaside towns to mention in Devon and Cornwall, and Wales as a whole was poorly provided with hotels. Scottish hotels were there in profusion, but many of the follies were still going bankrupt whenever the economic situation took a turn for the worse. Oblivious to all the facts, the Scottish railway companies were again putting up hotels, and the completion of Turnberry was only the signal for the building of Gleneagles, both of which are jewels in the crown of British hotels but can never have justified their cost in terms of profits.

In Ireland the efforts to bolster the country's economy with the benefits of tourism were only partially successful. During the terrible years of the potato famine in the '40s, the population had been decimated and when the massive emigration followed, the country seemed to develop an air of doom. Hotels were built in Ireland by the railway companies as in England and Scotland, the Irish landowners encouraged investment, and there were many scenic views and leisure activities to enjoy, but apart from a few elegant hotels in Dublin, the Irish hotel industry remained rustic in the extreme. The local labour was untrained, there was not the same influx of continental staff that helped the 'mainland' hotel world, and again there was only a very short season. In all the peripheral areas of the country it was more difficult to take advantage of the new inventions because gas, electricity, telephones and good roads took longer to reach them.

The new generation of top management faced a very different situation from their predecessors. Frank and Arthur Towle took over Midland Railway Hotels when the whole railway system began to run into debt, the brilliant George Reeves-Smith at the Savoy had to fight far more competition than Ritz, and Bessborough at Gordons, with infinite *sang froid*, went down with the ship.

It might have been possible for the hotels to have overcome their problems of overproduction if the world had remained at peace. The number of tourists was increasing both from America and the continent, and slowly but surely the habit of staying in hotels was growing and coming within the compass of more and more people. The bicycle and the motor car were helping to make travel easier, and holidays at the seaside were becoming more popular. A realistic hotelier in 1913 might have accepted that there had been mistakes, over enthusiasm, over confidence, but could reasonably have looked forward to a sounder future. Like so much else, however, the dream was shattered by the reverberations of that fusilade in Sarajevo.

Frederick Gordon knew the promotional methods used in Monte Carlo, such as the famous motor rally. His Metropole Hotel in Brighton was soon the finishing point of the London to Brighton RAC rally. The "Old Crocks" run is still held each year.

Sixty less than glorious years—1914–1974 14

THE HOTEL industry thrives on tourists unhindered by wars, revolutions, air raids or submarines, an economy buoyant and booming, with full employment and plenty of confidence in the future, long periods of good weather and no inflation in costs. By and large the British hotel industry has had little to thrive on in the past sixty years.

When the First World War broke out there was immediate trouble for hotels. Everybody went home even though August 4th was the height of the season, and future bookings were cancelled. The Americans soon found that ships were likely to be torpedoed on the Atlantic, and this only reinforced their decision to give Europe a miss until it was over, over there. Due to the vast size of the United States the fact that trouble in one European country has no effect on another 1,500 miles away, never has completely sunk in, but the missing American tourists obviously had a good case between 1914 and 1918. With the tourist traffic cut off, the holiday season ruined, and the staff situation growing more difficult as men enlisted and enemy nationals left, the hotel companies felt in the middle of an unexpected tornado.

It tends to be forgotten that the First World War which broke out as a consequence of the murder of the Archduke, Franz Ferdinand, of Austria began only six weeks after he was shot, and *The Times* originally made his death in June only their second leader. It was a complete shock to most people when war was declared, but the hotels were among the first to feel the pinch. During the next four years they had to cope with shortages, inflation, endless government regulations on the sales of food and drink, and, indeed, many hotels were commandeered.

When the wounded started to arrive back from the battles of attrition, the government quickly realised that the existing hospitals were not going to be able to deal with the huge numbers of casualties, and as the problem grew they took over more and more hotels. In London the running of the war effort also demanded extra space for civil servants and again hotels came to be requisitioned. In Gordon Hotels for instance, the Hotel Metropole, in London, was taken by the Ministry of Munitions in January 1916 and the Grand and Victoria within another year. The Metropole, Folkestone, the Grand, Broadstairs and The Lord Warden, Dover followed before the war ended. Even before they were commandeered, air raids on the south coast in 1915 had caused panic among holidaymakers, the port of Dover was taken over completely by the military to use for the embarkation of troops, and the accommodation in London was needed a piece at a time.

As Lord Bessborough reminded Gordon shareholders in 1919 "All this entailed an immense deal of work, and very anxious work too, clearing out and finding store room for an immense amount of furniture, linen, and a great variety of other things, besides the making of inventories and agreements. During this time a great many orders

The Royal Station Hotel in Newcastle upon Tyne was in marked contrast to the city's famous coaching inn, The Turks Head.

restricting the sale of food, wines, and other things were ordained by the government." In 1916 he had reported with regret that "profits have also been seriously affected by factors of which you are all probably aware. The considerable rise in costs of all sorts of foodstuffs as well as of all necessary commodities such as linen, glass, china, cutlery, cloth etc, and all round increase of wages and the restrictions of wines and spirits, placed on practically all the English hotels in the system by the Liquor Control Board."

The experience of Gordons was, of course, that of every other hotel playing its part in the war effort, but it was ironic that a war should have enabled so many of the objectives of the high minded temperance movement to be finally achieved; shortages made it necessary to limit opening hours and reduce the strength of spirits and beer with the consequence that cases of drunkenness fell sharply as the reformers had always promised. It was more universally regretted that food rationing had to be introduced during the war and Britain came closer to being starved out than in 1939–1945.

For the hotels which were not requisitioned the war was a mixed blessing. To begin with nobody holidayed abroad and there were eventually large numbers of officers on leave who could reach Brighton or London, but had more difficulty getting home to northern towns if their time was limited. They provided the hotels in the south with a new clientele and they were augmented nationally by the many thousands of people who found the shortage of servants an impossible barrier to running a large house. They, too, moved into hotels until more normal times returned.

By 1914 the supply of hotel accommodation in many cities had been too great for normal demand, and the only solution in the long run was for many of the hotels to go out of business. Requisitioning achieved this during the war and for the lucky hotels who escaped there could be a bonanza; some hotel companies towards the end of the war paid as much as twenty-five per cent dividend, but over the four years they suffered like any other business. When the armistice was finally signed a great spending spree started which helped the hotels already in operation, but came too early for those which had been commandeered, and as the hoteliers settled down to get these properties back into order, their patriotic belief in the generosity of a post-war government was belatedly shattered by the inflation in prices. Compensation for damage which would have covered the costs at pre-war levels were now inadequate, and hotels which wished to raise new money on the market found the costs unbelievably high compared to the low interest days of 1913. If they turned to their reserve funds instead they found all too often that the conflict had turned the surviving pre-war blue chips into so much waste paper, and that consequently their investments showed heavy losses as well.

To build a great new hotel in the 1920s was an act of faith by the board of the struggling Gordon Hotels Company. Sir Francis Towle, the managing director, may well have made the right decision had the slump not occurred, but it did and the company slid even deeper into debt.

THE MAY FAIR HOTEL
BERKELEY SQUARE W.1

Though often burdened with debt, hotels did recover during the early '20s. A flood of visitors starved of Europe for years, returned to their old haunts, and special events like the Wembley Exhibition in 1924 and 1925 helped the tourist season as well. Seaside holidays were still affected by the weather but plenty of people took the children to Blackpool and Bournemouth, Scarborough and Southend. A few new hotels opened, notably the May Fair in London in 1927 which marked a recovery in the fortunes of Gordon Hotels under their new managing director, Sir Francis Towle, and Gleneagles which brother Arthur Towle had completed in his capacity as chief executive of the Midland Hotels. The Dorchester and the Cumberland also opened between the wars in London and the '20s saw the growth of dinner-dancing and cabaret, which were expensive for hotels but fitted in well with the new fashion for staying out later. So, little by little, the situation improved as real wages increased and world trade expanded, but unhappily it was not to last, and the Wall Street crash finally killed off many British hotels for good.

Hotels flourish when people are confident that they can spend money because they can earn more in the future. The slump destroyed confidence and made people apprehensive. If tomorrow might be still worse, then economy had to be the watchword and for hotels, public economy is a disaster. Instead of businessmen staying overnight, they

A new hotel was still an event and King George V and Queen Mary arrived to inspect the May Fair. They were greeted by Sir Francis Towle, and the chairman of the company, Major General Guy Dawnay, seen shaking hands with the King.

make the effort to get back home in a day; instead of entertaining buyers, they conduct their negotiations in offices, and holidaymakers make do with a week when they would in better times take two. Everywhere business dropped off, and in towns where there were too many hotels even for the good times, the effect was calamitous. Of course it was London which suffered most and although voluntary pay cuts in many companies staved off the evil day, eventually it had to dawn. The list of hotels which London lost reads like the 19th century honours list; Sir George Gilbert Scott's Midland Grand became offices, Sir Polydore de Keyser's Royal which had become Lord Leverhulme's headquarters after the first war, was finally knocked down to be replaced by Unilever House. The Cecil was razed and became Shell Mex House, the Metropole and Grand were shut, and the Buckingham Palace Hotel became part of ICI. Others vanished as well; it was all very sad, but it was worse to be one of the two million unemployed.

The Dorchester was built before the slump arrived and Gordons were allowed to manage it in exchange for accepting liability for a second mortgage, but they were unable to hump the burden and the builders, the McAlpines had little alternative but to go into the hotel business. Lyons built the Cumberland, taking a risk on a brighter future and bolstered by their continuing success in popular catering, and the railways kept their hotels going in the same way that the trains kept running, but a reasonable return on investment was out of the question.

Shareholders may grumble, but business goes on. It was, for instance, the age of the great bands, many of which played regularly in hotel restaurants and of whom the name of Carroll Gibbons at the Savoy remains evergreen. The standards of the best British hotels remained very high as the finest French wines, the pick of the hand made Havana cigars, and many great chefs still worked in Britain.

Left:
An economist by profession, Lord Crowther accepted a seat on the board of Trust Houses comparatively early in his career. He eventually became chairman and merged the company with Forte & Co

Right:
Sir Charles Forte built a catering empire from very small beginnings, showing all the energy and determination of the great entrepreneur.

Maxwell Joseph, chairman of Grand Metropolitan Hotels, who by 1973 had built the 12th largest company in Britain from a base of one small hotel in 1948.

It took another world war to put the hotel business in the cities back on its feet. The war which broke out in 1939 was worse for the seaside than the 1914–1918 conflict. This time the beaches were mined and bombing of the south coast was more regular. In London the hotels that survived the blitz were very full, but the Carlton and the Langham suffered direct hits and never opened their doors again. The blitz destroyed large areas of the city, and office accommodation became very valuable and very scarce, so that while as hotels many buildings had been unsuccessful, they could now be purchased lock, stock and barrel for offices, and by the end of the war a lot more had vanished. One article in the *Daily Telegraph* in 1955 suggested that only eleven London hotels survived from the one hundred and ten listed in *Baedeker 1900*.

After the war broke out the price of a meal was limited to five shillings (25p) and remained at that artificial level until well after it was over. As a consequence the British public became used once more to paying a price for a meal which did not represent a reasonable profit for the hotelier, but again accepted overcharging for drinks.

The growth of the tourist market after the war was the result of more efficient air transport and America's new role as the leader of the Western world. The dollar had become far more powerful during the war and would buy more abroad than in the United States. Americans consequently came to Europe on great buying expeditions as well as to see the sights, and during the long summer season British hotels in tourist centres did very well. Indeed the demand now outstripped supply for long periods, but it is important to remember that only hotels going out of business had made this possible. The problems the Victorians gave themselves by overbuilding could not have been solved by the tourist demand until fifty years later, but by that time few of their hotels had survived. Even those which had, were often unsuitable for the demands of the modern traveller.

Clients from overseas during the 1950s complained of the lack of private bathrooms, inadequate heating in the bedrooms, and poorly cooked food. The hoteliers complained that their predecessors had not had the vision to put the bathrooms in when they built originally, that the installation of new heating systems was difficult because of the solidity of the original structure, and that kitchens were badly situated and set out for days when labour was cheap and plentiful. The truth was that the world had moved on, and hotels were not like a child's kaleidoscope to show a new pattern just by a little shaking.

This fact had not escaped the banks and the investing public, many of whom had had their fingers burned in the past and looked for safer securities. The share market's hotel section was dominated by Trust Houses, the Savoy, Lyons and Gordons. Trust Houses had a rule limiting dividends to five per cent and the Savoy while representing all that was good in British hotel craftsmanship, was not using its assets to the best effect, as Lord Samuel and Sir Charles Clore proved by making individual fortunes from an abortive take-over attempt. Lyons was now a sleeping giant with a dull dividend record, and Gordons had become the sick man of hoteldom, saddled with a load of preference share-holders who had not received any payment for many years, and therefore, as set up, with little hope of paying a penny on the ordinary stock.

With a dismal track record as an industry and at a time when the demands on the existing capital in the country were coming from all sides of an economy fighting to recover from a disastrous war, it was very difficult indeed for hotels to raise the cash to improve their properties. As a result there was a good deal of improvisation; terraces of houses were knocked together, decorated with a canopy and called hotels. They didn't even have to be terraces; you could convert a rambling Victorian house into fifteen or twenty bedrooms, and many hotels were just that. Any complaints could be stifled with an appeal to the customer to appreciate the ravages the war had wrought and the resulting austerity, so that standards dropped but remained acceptable because there was little alternative.

Apart from Trust Houses and the amalgamation of all the railway hotels after nationalisation, there was little to be seen of chain operations. While many industries were becoming more and more confined to a few large companies, the hotel world remained totally dominated by the individual unit. Like flint knapping or thatching there was ample room for the little man, and the owner manager would often put more personal effort into making his clients welcome than the employee manager; the spur of the danger of going bankrupt is that much greater than just the loss of a job.

In the provinces and at the seaside, conditions were much the same with standards well below pre-war days. For many years after the war there was no question of building a new hotel, and the Dover Stage and the Leofric in Coventry, the Westbury in London and one or two motels in the countryside were just about all the industry produced in the way of new structures before 1960.

The effects of antiquated machinery after the war lost Britain many markets which had traditionally purchased her goods, but antiquated hotels had little effect on the pleasures of Britain as a tourist centre. Steadily, year by year, the number of visitors rose, attracted by those virtues which really had little to do with the quality of the available accommodation; the shopping, the sightseeing, the entertainment and the lack of violence. The common language between Britain and America had seldom been more useful, and hotels enjoyed a lengthening season and a steady demand which continued to exceed on many days their capacity to satisfy it. The businessman returned to the provincial hotels from his war service, retracing the steps of commercial travellers over the years, or attending meetings in the towns. Currency restrictions made the opportunities for the British to go abroad very limited, and the seaside hotels did not have to face the competition of warmer climates to any extent until the 1960s.

It was still a short season for them, but an increasing number of national conferences could be sought as such meetings came into vogue, usually achieving little in concrete terms but providing an acceptable social gathering, usually not at the delegate's expense.

Harrogate distinguished itself by seeking this type of business more forcibly than anybody else, but as a spa town there was a greater need for urgency because taking the waters had now become almost exclusively a medical decision.

As an industry, hotels remained well outside the influence of government or trade unions, neither of whom really paid much attention to the way the demand for hotels was increasing. The government could understand invisible exports like banking or insurance, but what was tourism? The possibility of seriously competing with the traditionally successful areas like Italy or the Riviera must have seemed remote after the war and government backing was not forthcoming, nor could it be expected when the hotel industry's lobby in Parliament was so ineffectual, and while its representative body, the BHRA, lacked powerful leaders. Approximately fifty M.P.s sit for constituencies where the condition of the hotel industry is of major importance to the economy of their area, but compared to the representatives of, say, the miners or the aircraft industry, they still have very little to show for their efforts. There was, however, a negative advantage to the government's indifference to the industry in that when it did boom, there was no restrictive legislation to stop its progress, but this was too good to last and, as we shall see, the government's eventual awareness of the 'export' possibilities created a scheme which could revive the worst days of Victorian overproduction.

The unions, too, made practically no progress in influencing the development of the industry. A hotel can survive a strike almost indefinitely because there are alternative places for the clients to eat, and therefore the management staff have only to make beds and lightly clean rooms to keep the operation going. On the only occasion when hotel staff attempted a strike, which was at the Savoy soon after the war, the management held the line until the staff capitulated. On the other hand, the workers in hotels after the war found themselves with a weapon not given to all sections of labour; there was a shortage of trained men and this shortage has got worse ever since. Salaries were negotiated on the basis that almost any skilled man could get another job next door and unemployment, unless voluntary, was non-existent.

New hotel accommodation is often built as an annexe to an existing hotel or historic house. The Europa Lodge at Blackwell Grange, near Darlington, was formally the home of the Havelock-Allen family.

Moreover there was no question of craftsmen or management being too old at forty, or fifty or sixty for that matter. Experience and ability made it possible for men to hold jobs into their seventies and eighties if they were fit enough, though this situation also reflected the generally poor state of hotel company pension schemes. Few employees expected hotel companies to have made proper pension arrangements, and the mobility of hotel labour enabled management to ignore this unhappy state of affairs. The lack of craftsmen, of course, enabled rogues to survive so that there was little fear of dismissal ruining a career, but turning a blind eye did not solve the labour problem; as the hotel industry expanded all over Europe there emerged an international shortage of certain grades of staff, such as chefs, and this put up salaries dramatically. As the industry remained one of the few where employees could receive tips from the customers, there were also illegal, tax-free pickings to be earned and although a service charge of ten per cent was common, this did not stop staff from trying to get a little more from the customers direct. Albert Smith must still be turning in his grave at the continuance of this practice which he had so deplored well over a hundred years ago.

The shortage of craftsmen and the absence of great businessmen in the industry reflected the attitude of the British people towards their hotel world. The middle class father, up to the '60s, did not hope that his son would grow up to be a chef or a banqueting manager; hotels were for foreigners to run and hotel managers were likely to be either retired officers, or waiters who had finally made the grade. The board of Gordon Hotels in 1920 with its five barristers reflected the thinking for years afterwards. Such companies as there were in the industry had, with few exceptions, boards where any profession other than hoteliers was represented; the Salmons and Glucksteins of Lyons were the only trained hoteliers really to have much chance of sitting on the board of a major public company.

It was because the industry was fragmented and had little status for the better educated that fortunes were to be made by those who had the ability and were not concerned with face; the hotel industry became the happy hunting ground for entrepreneurs, of whom the two most successful were Maxwell Joseph and Sir Charles Forte, but whose ranks also included Fred Kobler of Grand Metropolitan Hotels, Frederick Muller of De Vere Hotels, the Erskines of Associated Hotels, Henry Edwards of Centre Hotels, and occasional players like the Danzigers, Lord Samuel and Sir Charles Clore. The traditional forces of the establishment were nowhere to be seen while all this was going on. Even the brewers missed the early boat, for apart from a few bedrooms on top of the bar, they were solely concerned with selling drink. The profits came from drink, they manufactured drink, their management was trained in the mystique of brewing, and Frederick Gordon's business of selling bedrooms was no profit-maker in their eyes.

There were a number of major organisations interested in diversifying after the war who could have entered the hotel industry; Unilever and GUS are the two most obvious, and indeed GUS did have a substantial stake in Grand Metropolitan with a seat on the board at one period. The Rank Organisation tried to join the hotel industry and had immense teething problems, but up to 1973 nothing has been heard of such companies as Imperial Tobacco and Unilever who have both diversified widely outside their initial concepts.

Gradually during the 1960s more new hotels started to be built in different parts of the country. At the beginning they were mostly to be found in London and the major provincial cities. The Europa, Britannia, Royal Garden, Royal Lancaster and Hilton arrived in the West End, and the Piccadilly, Manchester, Albany, Birmingham, Grosvenor House, Sheffield, and the Unicorn, Bristol, provided much needed, good quality, new accommodation out-of-town as did a number of other newcomers. Nobody had the confidence to build new hotels at the seaside, but there were a number of town councils who insisted that developers of bombed town centres should include a hotel in their plans. Such investment could often only be justified because of the profits the developer would make from the offices, shops and flats in the rest of the scheme, because the demand for accommodation in a small town was primarily midweek for visiting business-

Facing page:
The airlines, like the railways before them, are investing in hotels. This is the London Penta Hotel, owned by a consortium of airlines, banks and Grand Metropolitan Hotels who manage it.

men, and therefore the hotels ran for seven days on a four or five day income.

After the extravagance of Victorian and Edwardian architecture, the new hotels were less elaborate in appearance, but far more practical. Corridors were reduced in size, public rooms were kept to a minimum and the space used instead for profit-making conference and banqueting facilities, because, as the British economy lurched from crisis to crisis, more and more meetings were held to consider how to avoid going the way of all flesh. There was a strong move towards restaurants with a more limited choice of dishes, but better prepared, and service in hotels became poorer as staff grew more difficult to come by, and more expensive. The new hotels did have the side effect of raising the standards of decor of their older competitors and at least one major luxury hotel redecorated its lobby for the first time in twenty-five years when faced with a newcomer only a short distance away.

The 1960s also saw the growth of motor hotels and chain operations run by the brewers. The motor hotels were partly an attempt to cash in on the increasing number of cars, as the United States had done with motels, but with the drawback that Britain lacked the great distances the Americans could travel. Moreover the British were not a motor oriented society to the same extent, and the profitability of both independent motor hotels and the brewer's chains are difficult to assess. The annual reports of the brewers talked generally of progress, but without ever specifying what financial investment had been made in their hotels, and the specific results. In this the brewers acted very much like the 19th century railways. The correct equivalent of the 19th century railways was, however, the 20th century airlines, but apart from a financial interest in hotels in Belfast and St. Andrews, neither of the British airlines developed hotels at home. The American airlines were represented in London because of their subsidiaries, Hilton and Inter Continental, but they had nothing like the effect of the early railway companies on the development of the hotel industry.

The 1960s was a good decade for hotels in general, but they weren't good enough for a government which belatedly realised the possibilities, in terms of foreign currency, which the industry represented in days when the balance of payments was suddenly critical again. There had been a cry in the Press and among travel agents for years that there was insufficient hotel accommodation, and the Labour government decided to give grants of £1,000 a room towards the cost of hotels completed by the end of March 1973. This measure was enthusiastically greeted by considerable numbers of entrepreneurs who had failed to realise that the cream on the cake had already been eaten.

In fact, the measure had all the attractions of Cleopatra's asp because what it promised was an industry geared to the maximum demand from visitors in the height of the tourist season. If every traveller could get the sort of hotel bed he wanted in the peak months, then there was bound to be a massive over-supply situation during the quieter periods. A price war was bound to develop and only the fittest were likely to survive. The likelihood was that the bad days at the turn of the century were returning again.

Those most fitted to survive were likely to be the hotel companies which had diversified on their own account into other industries, or had a large number of units which helped their purchasing power.

During the '60s two major organisations emerged in the industry, Grand Metropolitan Hotels and Trust Houses Forte. Both became conglomerates, taking in industrial and popular catering and other activities allied to leisure. Both were led by strong chairmen, though the battle for control of Trust Houses Forte between Sir Charles Forte and Lord Crowther, the chairman of Trust Houses before the merger, only ended after a most bitter board room battle and with Lord Crowther's resignation and, later, his death. Lyons supported by their food business, the brewers' hotels buttressed by the pubs, and the railway hotels by the trains, could also view the stormy days ahead for the hotel industry without much alarm.

What finally of the future? There are few tasks as thankless as looking into a crystal ball to see how a hotel will fare in the years to come, which is why there are more historians than clairvoyants. Will the next fifty years be another golden age for hotels or will the industry suffer as it did between 1900 and 1950?

There are grounds for being optimistic because using hotels is part of a higher standard of living. Just as the housewife wants labour-saving machinery and prepared foods, so she wants somebody else to do the housework, the cooking and indeed all the drudgery. Hotels fill that want, and as prosperity gradually increases to cover wider sections of the community, so will there be more customers for the industry. In the same way travel is part of a better life and the opportunity to visit a country with the attractions of Britain will bring additional visitors almost without end.

It is obvious that hotels are part of the leisure industry but less appreciated that people's leisure has got to increase over the years because otherwise, with more efficient machines, there will be massive unemployment. Shorter hours bring the opportunity and the need to develop other interests, and hotels can be used as centres for angling, bird watching or whatever takes the public's fancy.

To solve the labour shortage the industry will have to look again at its ability to stand comparison with other types of work. The hours of work will have to diminish to match other industries, there will have to be better staff conditions and welfare, but the hotels remain a very superior form of factory and infinitely more desirable than, for instance, a tyre plant, steelworks or paint manufacturing unit.

It seems, therefore, that the hotels in towns which are tourist attractions should flourish, but the same unfortunately is unlikely to be true for the seaside. This is because a holiday abroad in the sun is also part of the better life, and good weather is one ingredient that Britain cannot reliably provide. The seaside towns grew up when there was no alternative: today there is. Moreover, few seaside towns can offer the specific attractions needed to lure a major section of the special interest markets, as Stratford attracts the Shakespearian addict or Turnberry the golfer. The decline of the seaside will be a long drawn-out process, and conferences, weekend trips and courses will stave off the inevitable, but the main appeal of the seaside has always been the sea and the sun, and now these can be obtained more certainly and often more cheaply in Spain or Italy.

The salvation of many of the seaside towns would seem to be in their development as havens for the steadily growing numbers of elderly people who need surroundings and amenities which are geared to their particular requirements. In such situations the land on which the hotels stand is often more valuable when the hotel is knocked down and flats or houses can be constructed in its stead.

As competition increases throughout the industry, there will have to be more amalgamations, but the small hotelier prepared to take trouble with his customers can survive better than any small shopkeeper faced with a supermarket. The amount that guests will spend on hotels depends ultimately on the quality rather than the price charged because the money is disposable income, that part of the salary that can be frittered away on luxuries.

There will be plenty of opportunities for the good businessman to make a fortune in hotels because although there have been great improvements in craft areas like steak bars, wear-resistant materials, and labour-saving devices, the marketing side of the industry remains for the most part very amateurish.

History does repeat itself though, and whatever happens in the future is most likely to be no more than a reflection of the original Golden Age of British Hotels, for it was the Victorians who were the pioneers, for all their mistakes, extravagance and difficulties, and within their experience we can find the seeds of everything important we know today and are likely to develop in the foreseeable future.

Bibliography

A.B.C. Hotel Guide 1858 & 1860

A.B.C. Hotel Guide 1886

W. Adam—*The Gem of the Peak—or Matlock Bath & its Vicinity*—Longman 1843

W. Addison—*English Spas*—Batsford 1951

Baedeker Karl—Publishers of Guide Books

B. H. Becker—*Holiday Haunts*—Remington & Co. 1884

Elizabeth Bowen—*The Shelbourne*—George G. Harrap & Co. Ltd. 1951

John Malcolm Brinnis—*The Sway of the Grand Saloon*—Macmillan 1972

P. R. Broemel—*Romance and Realities of Mayfair and Piccadilly*—Mills & Boon, London 1927

Arthur Bryant—*English Saga*—Collins 1940

Buxton Corporation—*Historic Buxton and its Spa Era*

Ethel Carleton—*William's Companion in to Derbyshire*—Methuen's 1947

Henry Carter—*The English Temperance Movement*—Epworth Press 1933

The Caterer, Hotel Keeper and Refreshment Contractor Vols. 1–37

Robert Cecil—*Life in Edwardian England*—Batsford 1969

G. E. Clarke—*Historic Margate*—Margate Public Libraries 1972

Phyllis Deane—*Industrial Revolution in England 1700–1914*—Fontana 1969 3 vol. illus.

Dickens' Dictionary of London 1880.

George Dow—*Great Central*—London Locomotive Publishing Co. (1959–65), Pictorial Supplement Ian Allan 1969

Aytoun Ellis—*The Penny Universities*—Secker 1956

R. C. K. Ensor—*England 1870–1914*—Oxford 1936

Exhibition Guide to London 1851

C. R. Fay—*From Adam Smith to the Present Day*—Longmans Green 1928

D. Feilding—*The Duchess of Jermyn Street*—Eyre & Spottiswoode 1964

M. Gellati—*Mario of the Caprice*—Hutchinson 1960

Hankinson's Guide to Bournemouth and District 1892

Brian Harrison—*Drink and the Victorians*—Faber and Faber 1971

T. Hartley Hennessey—*Healing by Water*—C. W. Daniel Co., Rochford 1950

A. Hern—*The Seaside Holiday*—Cresset Press 1967

Illustrated London News 1838–1914

Incorporated Association of Hotels and Restaurants Monthly Reports 1914

Stanley Jackson—*The Savoy*—Muller 1964

John R. Kellett—*The Impact of Railways on Victorian Cities*—Routledge and Kegan Paul 1969

R. Lennard—*Englishmen at Rest and Play 1558–1714*—Oxford Clarendon Press 1931

Norman Longmate—*The Water Drinkers*—Hamish Hamilton 1968

E. T. MacDermott—*History of the G.W.R.*—Great Western Railway Co. London, 1927

(*Continued on page 170*)

Compton Mackenzie—*The Savoy*—(Edward Montague) Harrap 1953)

Philip Magnus—*Gladstone*—John Murray 1963

Philip Magnus—*Edward VII*—John Murray 1964

Stella Margetson—*Leisure and Pleasure in the 19th Century*—Cassell 1969

S. Medlik—*British Hotel and Catering Industry*—Pitman 1961

Arthur Mee—*Derbyshire—The Peak Country*—Hodder 1949; revised by F. R. Banks 1969

continued on page 170

Index

NOTE: Hotels mentioned in the text appear in the Index under the entry for the nearest town — Bath, Empire Hotel.

Bibliography *continued from page 166*

Moncrieff and Gardner—*The Peak Country*—Adam & Charles Black 1908

Page and Kingsford—*The Master Chefs*—Edward Arnold Ltd. 1971

J. A. Pattmore—*An Atlas of Harrogate*

L. du Garde Peach—*John Smedley of Matlock and his Hydro*—Bemrose Publicity 1956

N. Pevsner—*The Buildings of England*—Penguin books—1968

J. A. R. Pimlott—*The Englishman's Holiday*—Faber & Faber, London 1947

W. MacQueen Pope—*Twenty Shillings in the Pound*—Hutchinson 1948

John Pudney—*The Thomas Cook Story*—Michael Joseph 1953

V. Fraser Rae—*The Business of Travel*—Thomas Cook & Son 1891

Marie Ritz—*Cesar Ritz*—Paris 1948

John Roberts—*Europe 1880–1945*—Longman 1967

Royal Hotel Guide 1856

Ruffs Hotel Guide 1850

Jack Simmons—*St. Pancras Station*—Allen & Unwin 1968

George Sims—*Living London*—Cassell 1903

John Smedley—*Practical Hydropathy*—London 1877, 15th edition

Albert Smith—*The English Hotel Nuisance*—David Byce 1855

Gerald Sparrow—*The Great Swindlers*—John Long 1959

Joan Tarbuck—*Southport as it Was*—Hendon Publishing Co. 1972.

The Times

Edmund Vale—*The Trust House Story*—Trust House 1949

Stephen Watts—*The Ritz*—Bodley Head 1963

Arthur White—*Palaces of the People*—Rapp and Whiting 1968